RECLAIMING THE
AMERICAN REVOLUTION

RECLAIMING THE AMERICAN REVOLUTION

THE KENTUCKY AND VIRGINIA RESOLUTIONS AND THEIR LEGACY

By
WILLIAM J. WATKINS, JR.

FOREWORD BY RICHARD N. ROSENFELD

AN INDEPENDENT INSTITUTE BOOK

RECLAIMING THE AMERICAN REVOLUTION
© The Independent Institute, 2004

First published 2004 by
PALGRAVE MACMILLAN™
175 Fifth Avenue, New York, N.Y. 10010 and
Houndmills, Basingstoke, Hampshire, England RG21 6XS
Companies and representatives throughout the world

PALGRAVE MACMILLAN is the global academic imprint of
the Palgrave Macmillan division of St. Martin's Press, LLC and of
Palgrave Macmillan Ltd. Macmillan® is a registered trademark in the
United States, United Kingdom and other countries. Palgrave is
a registered trademark in the European Union and other countries.

ISBN 1–4039–6303–7 hardback

Library of Congress Cataloging-in-Publication Data
Watkins, William J. Jr.
    Reclaiming the American Revolution : the Kentucky and Virginia
    Resolutions and their legacy / William J. Watkins, Jr.
        p. cm.
    Includes bibliographical references.
    ISBN 1–4039–6303–7 (he)
        1. Kentucky and Virginia resolutions of 1798. 2. State
    rights—History—Sources. 3. United States—Politics and
    government—1797–1801. I. Title.

KF4621.W38 2003
320.973'09'033—dc21   2003049835

A catalogue record for this book is available from the British Library.

Design by Newgen Imaging Systems (P) Ltd., Chennai, India.

First edition: January, 2004
10 9 8 7 6 5 4 3 2 1

Printed in the United States of America.

To My Mother

CONTENTS

IMAGES

The Kentucky and Virginia Resolutions and The Threat of an American Monarchy

A Foreword

What would happen if the U.S. Constitution failed to protect our basic rights? What would happen if, in the name of national security or some other perceived good, the federal government—indeed the U.S. Supreme Court—countenanced an abuse of liberty so great that we felt our fundamental principles of government were at risk? What would "the father of the constitution," James Madison, have done? What would our most famous democratic founder, Thomas Jefferson, have advised? In this first book-length treatment of Jefferson's and Madison's Kentucky and Virginia Resolutions in more than one hundred years, William J. Watkins, Jr. provides these founders' answers and shows how their answers have contoured American thinking ever since. In so doing, Watkins offers fundamental insights into the issues of American federalism and a poignant reminder that, to protect American liberty, sometimes Americans have to rise up, and, in the worst case, they may even have to strike down.

At the birth of this nation, those who fought in the American Revolution were not concerned with constructing a new national constitution. They wanted to shatter the ties of an old constitution. Americans had "to dissolve the political bonds which have connected them," proclaimed Thomas Jefferson in the Declaration of Independence. "[W]hen a long train of abuses and usurpations, pursuing invariably the same object evinces a design to reduce them under absolute despotism, it is their right, it is their duty, to throw off such government . . . " And so they did.

Just two decades later, Jefferson and his friend James Madison penned similar words in bidding defiance to the new government of the United States of America. In the autumn of 1798, persuaded that President John Adams was leading the country toward monarchy and that Adams and his fellow Federalists were distorting the Constitution's meaning to augment ("monarchize") the power of the federal government, Jefferson and Madison drafted respectively the Kentucky and Virginia Resolutions, which were adopted by those state legislatures at the end of the year. Condemning the repressive Alien and Sedition Acts as unconstitutional, Madison's draft protested a tendency "to transform the present republican system of the United States into an absolute, or at best, a mixed monarchy." Jefferson's draft asked, in view of these acts, "what the Government is if it be not a tyranny." Jefferson warned that, "successive acts of the same character, unless arrested at the threshold, may tend to drive these States into revolution and blood," and he urged other states to declare the repressive federal acts "void and of no force." Finally, he cautioned, "the several States composing the United States of America, are not united on the principles of unlimited submission to their General Government." These were revolutionary ideas. They were not, however, of these men's making.

During the time of the Enlightenment (in which the American Revolution and the U.S. Constitution were born), the most prominent school of political philosophy held that all government was a compact, which—should it degrade into tyranny—could be dissolved or disregarded by the governed. The best-known of these philosophers, the Englishman John Locke, explained this very much as Jefferson did: "But if a long train of abuses, prevarications and artifices, all tending the same way, make the design visible to the people, and they cannot but feel what they lie under, and see whither they are going; it is not to be wondered, that they should then rouse themselves, and endeavour to put the rule into such hands which may secure to them the ends for which government was at first erected."[1]

The idea that one could break the governmental compact if the government became tyrannical came to prominence in the seventeenth century, when—despite the royal claim that a monarch was "accountable to none but God only"[2]—the English people rose up, in a fit of regicide, civil war, and tumult, to end the tyranny of their Stuart kings and to revise their compact so that the king could only act with "the advice and consent of the Lords Spiritual and Temporal and Commons in Parliament."[3] In his famous work *Leviathan* (1651), the English philosopher Thomas Hobbes explained that the purpose of any social compact was to avoid a warlike state of nature (with its "continual fear, and danger of violent death; and the life of man, solitary, poor, nasty, brutish, and short"[4]) and that any social compact could be broken if a government waged war against its people. At the same time, Englishman James Harrington, in his *Commonwealth of Oceana* (1656), explained England's shift of sovereignty from the king (where it resides in a monarchy) to the parliament (where it resides in a commonwealth) as mirroring the shift of property ownership to a burgeoning middle class of commoners whose property ownership entitled them to a stronger voice in government. At century's end, John Locke opined, in his *Second Treatise on Government*, that, "The great and chief end . . . of men's uniting into commonwealths, and putting themselves under government, is the preservation of property" or, as he otherwise stated it, to secure the people their "lives, liberties and estates."[5]

Though England's "Glorious Revolution" moved English sovereignty from the king to the king-in-parliament, Englishmen expected their government to remain a mixture of king, lords, and commons, which found time-honored justification in the writings of Greek and Roman philosophers, most notably in those of Polybius (b. 204 B.C.) who divided the forms of government into rule by one (monarchy), by the few (aristocracy), and by the many (democracy) but warned that each of these forms, in the absence of the other two, would degenerate into tyranny, oligarchy, or mob rule respectively.[6] Thus, the English constitution embraced all three of these forms, with its monarch (the one), an aristocratic House of Lords (the few), and the more representative House of Commons (the many). Most believed, as England's most famous jurist William Blackstone stated in his *Commentaries on the Laws of England*, "if ever it should happen that the independence of any one of the three should be lost, or that it should become subservient to the views of either of the other two, there would soon be an end of our constitution. The legislature would be changed from that, which (upon the supposition of an original contract, either actual or implied) is presumed to have been originally set up by the general consent and fundamental act of the society: and such a change, however effected is, according to Mr. Locke . . . at once an entire dissolution of the bands of government."[7]

In the century that followed England's "Glorious Revolution," philosophers in France, politicians in America, and Whig critics within England itself had much to say about the English constitution and whether its balances secured or threatened liberty. Chief among them was the French philosopher Charles Montesquieu who, in his *De l'Esprit des lois* (1748), affirmed the balance among the one, the few, and the many but saw a more important guarantee of liberty in the separation of executive, legislative, and judicial functions.

As France and America approached the time of their own revolutions, some democrats in each country accepted Montesquieu's theory of separation, but many condemned the British balance among monarchy, aristocracy, and democracy. They argued, as many Whigs in England did, that the monarch's power of appointment (patronage) and expenditure could (and did) corrupt the British Parliament and prevent Parliament from representing the people it was supposed to represent. Looking despondently upon these developments, English Whig James Burgh wrote, in his *Political Disquisitions*, that William Blackstone had "placed the sovereignty wrong, viz. in the government; whereas it should have been in the people."[8] Suffering "intolerable" and "coercive" acts of the British government, many in America agreed.

America fired its opening shot at England's mixed constitution in January of 1776, when the great democrat Thomas Paine published his best-selling pamphlet *Common Sense*, asking Americans "to examine the component parts of the English constitution" and see them as "First.— The remains of monarchical tyranny in the person of the king. Secondly.—The remains of aristocratical tyranny in the persons of the peers. Thirdly.—The new republican materials, in the persons of the commons, on whose virtue depends the freedom of England." "Mankind being originally equals," he wrote, "exalting one man so greatly above the rest cannot be justified on the equal rights of nature." Urging and foreseeing America's independence, Paine proposed that, in future American governments, "assemblies be annual, with a President only. The representation more equal." Relying on Burgh, Paine suggested "a large and equal representation."[9]

Paine's democratic message of January found its echo in July when Jefferson's words became the nation's words in the Declaration of Independence. Proclaiming that, "all men are created equal," Jefferson insisted that governmental power rested on "the consent of the governed" and that the purpose of government is to secure certain inalienable rights, among them "life, liberty and the pursuit of happiness." (Jefferson didn't use John Locke's "lives, liberties and estates," which would have tied political rights to property ownership, as in Britain.) Again, Jefferson warned, "whenever any form of government becomes destructive to these ends, it is the right of the people to alter or to abolish it and to institute new government."

Americans began to "institute new government" in the summer of 1776, writing new state constitutions to replace their royal colonial charters. In September, Thomas Paine and another great democrat Benjamin Franklin superintended the drafting of the nation's most unbalanced and democratic state constitution—that of Pennsylvania— which called for a single-house legislature without wealth or property qualifications for voters or representatives and with a weak plural executive that had no power to initiate or veto legislation.[10] One month later, Franklin carried this new Pennsylvania constitution to France, where it became the darling of Frenchmen like the Duc de la Rochefoucauld, the Marquis de Condorcet, Jacques-Pierre Brissot de Warville, and other supporters of the American Revolution, sometimes called *américanistes*,[11] who saw Franklin's Pennsylvania constitution as the embodiment of America's democratic ideal and, with Jean Jacques Rousseau's *Social Contract* (1762), as a model for the French Revolution to come. Not everyone saw it that way.

In America, the leading opponent to the idea of a very democratic constitution was future American president John Adams, who viewed Paine's *Common Sense* and its plan of government as, "so democratical, without any restraints or even an Attempt at any Equilibrium or Counterpoise . . ."[12] In answer to Paine's pamphlet, Adams published his own pamphlet *Thoughts on Government*, which argued that any American government should have two houses in the legislature and a strong executive branch and that "equal interests among the people should have equal interests in it."[13] As an alternative to Paine's and Franklin's Pennsylvania Constitution of 1776, Adams drafted (in October of 1779) the first constitution for his home state of Massachusetts, including a strong executive, a small senate of the wealthy, and a more democratic house of representatives, each with the power to veto the others and each with special wealth and property qualifications for electors and those who would serve.[14] One month later, Adams carried a copy of his "balanced" Massachusetts constitution to Paris, where it served the vision of French *anglomanes*[15] (such as Pierre Victor de Malouet and Jean Joseph Mounier) who admired the British constitution and wanted future constitutional change in France to be similarly "balanced."

In the minds of Thomas Jefferson and James Madison, John Adams displayed a belief in monarchy in the first volume of his *A Defence of the Constitutions of Government of the United States of America* (1787), which Adams wrote to provide *anglomanes* in France and delegates to the federal constitutional convention in Philadelphia with arguments that Paine and Franklin's Pennsylvania constitution was the wrong model and that constitutions built on his Massachusetts model were better.[16] Yet, in fashioning his arguments, Adams relied heavily on Polybius[17] (among others), concluding that "the English constitution is, in theory, the most stupendous fabrick of human invention"[18] and that "instead of projects to abolish kings and lords, if the house of commons had been attended to . . . there [would not] have remained an imperfection perhaps in the English constitution."[19] Jefferson would later ask "Can any one read Mr. Adams' defence of the American constitutions without seeing he was a monarchist?"[20] Madison wrote Jefferson, "under a mock defence of the Republican Constitutions of this Country, he attacked them with all the force he possessed."[21]

When the French Revolution brought down the French monarch, "balance" was hardly the order of the day, so Adams lost his argument to *américanistes* in France whose influence is found in the French Constitution of 1791 as well as the first constitution of the new Republic of France (the Constitution of 1793), both of which called for a unicameral legislature and a weak executive authority (subservient to the legislature). Jefferson was American minister (ambassador) to France when the French Revolution began. Paine came to Paris in 1792, serving with *américanistes* Brissot and Condorcet (among others) on the committee that drafted that first Constitution for the new French Republic.

In America, Adams's *Defence* found its echo at the federal constitutional convention, so Adams was generally pleased with the Montesquieuian separations and the tripartite balance that the new federal constitution entailed.[22] Adams saw in the U.S. Senate (with only two senators per state, all chosen by state legislatures) a "resemblance of aristocracy" and saw the powerful presidency (with its veto of Congress) as "monarchical."[23] The elderly Franklin, who had argued against a two-chamber legislature and a powerful presidency, had to resign himself to the new constitution's undemocratic structure, though generously conceding on the last day of the convention, "there is no *Form* of Government but what may be a Blessing to the People if well administered."[24] James Madison spoke similar words, at the Virginia ratifying convention: "No theoretical checks, no form of government, can render us secure. To suppose any form of government will secure liberty or happiness without virtue in the people is a chimerical idea."[25] In the final analysis, he argued, "The federal and State governments are in fact but different agents and trustees of the people."[26] In America, revolution had shifted sovereignty to them.[27]

The revolutions that overturned the established governments of England, France, and America were justified by monarchical tyranny. In each case, a new government compact was devised. Yet in each country, apprehensions of monarchy remained, and a final legal buttress against the threat of monarchical tyranny was put in place. In England, the Glorious Revolution produced the English Bill of Rights and the Toleration Act, both of 1689 (a Habeas Corpus Act against arbitrary imprisonment had been passed ten years earlier). In France, Jefferson assisted the Marquis de La Fayette in drafting a Declaration of the Rights of Man and of the Citizen, which was adopted by the new unicameral national assembly in August of 1789. In America, with the encouragement of Jefferson (and the demands of Anti-Federalist critics of the Constitution), James Madison drafted the American Bill of Rights, which were amended to the Constitution in December of 1791. In all three nations, though in varying degrees, these enumerations of rights protected religious freedom, freedom of opinion, speech and the press, and fair trials and punishment from the tyrannies that monarchy had imposed.

As late as two weeks before the start of the federal government, Jefferson wrote Madison, "I know there are some among us who would now establish a monarchy."[28] Both knew that Adams was not alone in what he thought. Madison had recorded Alexander Hamilton's statements at the federal constitutional convention, "that the British Government was the best in the world; and that he doubted whether any thing short of it would do in America."[29] At the start of the federal government, Adams was vice president. Hamilton was secretary of the treasury.

Within weeks after the start of the federal government, Vice President Adams created a stir in the Senate (where he presided as Senate president) with a proposal that the president be addressed as "His Highness, The President of the United States and Protector of the Rights of the Same." Had Adams succeeded with that proposal, Madison wrote Jefferson, it would have "given a deep wound to our infant government."[30] Shortly thereafter, Adams's friend Benjamin Rush warned Adams that monarchical pageantry was unseemly for a republic,[31] to which Adams caustically replied, "You seem determined not to allow a limited monarchy to be a republican system, which it certainly is, and the best that has ever been tried."[32]

Ten months later, Vice President Adams put his pen to a series of newspaper articles, published anonymously under the title "Discourses on Davila,"[33] that defended, among other things, the idea "that hereditary succession was attended with fewer evils than frequent elections."[34] Jefferson recognized Adams as the author and, in letters to Madison, condemned him as a "heretic"[35] and observed that "[s]ince he has been the 2d. Magistrate in the new Republic, his pen has constantly been at work in the same [antirepublican] cause."[36] Jefferson also expressed his reservations to Washington, citing Adams's "views of drawing the present government to the form of the English constitution."[37]

While Adams's *Davila* essays were appearing in the *Gazette of the United States*, the nation's first Treasury Secretary Alexander Hamilton was proposing a plan for the federal government to "engage the monied interest" of the country, including a new national bank that would issue stock to them and float bank notes. Despite Jefferson and Madison's protests that the U.S. Constitution gave no power to the federal government to create such a bank, Washington and Hamilton found this power "implied," and financially interested congressmen supported the program. Seeing congressmen speculating in old government certificates they knew would become valuable if they voted for Hamilton's program, Jefferson wrote Washington,

> That all the capital employed in paper speculation ... has furnished effectual means of corrupting such a portion of the legislature ... That this corrupt squadron, deciding the voice of the legislature, have manifested their dispositions to get rid of the limitations imposed by the constitution on the general legislature, limitations, on the faith of which, the states acceded to that instrument: That the ultimate object of all this is to prepare the way for a change, from the present republican form of government, to that of a monarchy, of which the English constitution is to be the model.[38]

Subsequently, Jefferson wrote Washington that congressional votes for Hamilton's programs were "no longer the votes then of the representatives of the people, but of deserters from the rights & interests of the people."[39]

In the years remaining under Washington's administration, Madison's and Jefferson's rapidly developing "Republican" party became increasingly upset with the government's apparent preference for the British monarchy over the new democratic Republic of France. When—despite America's obligations to France under its alliance of 1778—Washington proclaimed the nation's neutrality in the war between these countries, Madison wrote Jefferson that the president's declaration was "an assumption of prerogatives not clearly found in the Constitution and having the appearance of being copied from a Monarchical model."[40] Jefferson agreed. When the president and the Senate confirmed the Jay Treaty with England, advancing the interests of American merchants trading with Britain again at the expense of the country's treaty obligations to France, Jefferson wrote Madison that the Jay Treaty was a bold act "to undermine the constitution" and an "attempt of a party, which finds they have lost their majority in one branch of the Legislature, to make a law by the aid of the other branch & of the executive, under color of a treaty."[41] The following spring, Jefferson wrote his friend Philip Mazzei that "an Anglican monarchical, & aristocratic party has sprung up, whose avowed object is to draw over us the *substance*, as they have already given us the forms, of the British government" and that this party included "British merchants & Americans trading on British capitals, speculators & holders in the banks & public funds, a contrivance invented for the purposes of corruption, & for assimilating us in all things to the rotten as well as the sound parts of the British model."[42]

When John Adams became president in February of 1797, Jefferson was vice president, and Madison was in retirement. Within two months, the mood of the country turned ugly. On learning that France had refused to accredit a new American ambassador, Adams delivered an angry speech to Congress, which warned Americans against French-sympathizers, such as Jefferson and his fellow Republicans, who held "different affections, principles, and interests from those of their fellow-citizens whom they themselves have chosen to manage their common concerns."[43] After that speech, as Jefferson wrote Edward Rutledge, "Men who have been intimate all their lives cross the street to avoid meeting and turn their heads another way lest they be obliged to touch their hats."[44] Within a year, Jefferson would describe Adams and his governance as a "reign of witches."[45]

In March of 1798, confronted with continuing diplomatic slights from France, Adams delivered a "war message" to Congress but failed to ask for a declaration of war. As Congress and the president went forward to create, equip, and officer a federal army, Jefferson wrote Madison, "We see a new instance of the inefficacy of Constitutional guards. We had relied with great security on that provision which requires two-thirds of the Legislature to declare war. But this is completely eluded by a majority's taking war measures which will be sure to produce war."[46] Yet constitutional abuses, in the eyes of Jefferson, would only get worse.

During the spring and into the early summer of 1798, Adams and Congress enacted the infamous Alien and Sedition Acts, which threatened to suppress all political opposition to the government. Under these laws, noncitizens could be deported, without notice or trial, if Adams "suspected" them of wrongdoing. Citizens faced imprisonment if they voiced or wrote any criticism of the government. As war preparations began, Adams declared federal holidays for prayer and fasting, enlisting the nation's clergy to preach on the government's behalf. Jefferson feared that the Sedition Act's suppression of speech and the press would spread to freedom of religion, later observing that the assault "on the clause of the constitution which, while it secured the freedom of the press, covered also the freedom of religion, had given to the clergy a very favorite hope of obtaining an establishment of a particular form of Christianity thro' the U.S."[47]

By the late spring of 1798, Adams's opponents in Congress began to abandon their posts. Voluntary "committees of surveillance" followed

Jefferson and fellow Republican leaders wherever they went. On the day before Jefferson left for Virginia, the federal government arrested the editor of the nation's leading Republican newspaper (a grandson of Benjamin Franklin) and charged him with sedition for criticizing the government.[48] That summer and fall, it arrested other newspaper editors and a U.S. congressman for doing the same.[49]

Jefferson saw the American compact as unraveling and monarchical government at the nation's door. That autumn, back in his home state of Virginia, he wrote Virginia's U.S. Senator Stevens Thomson Mason that the Alien and Sedition Acts were "merely an experiment on the American mind to see how far it will bear an avowed violation of the constitution. If this goes down, we shall immediately see attempted another act of Congress, declaring that the President shall continue in office during life, reserving to another occasion the transfer of the succession to his heirs, and the establishment of the Senate for life."[50] He then set about, with James Madison, to draft the Kentucky and Virginia Resolutions, with their essential doctrines of federalism that— as William J. Watkins, Jr. so powerfully demonstrates—challenge us even today.

The Kentucky and Virginia Resolutions should remind us that the American Revolution left sovereignty in our hands and that should the federal government exceed its constituted authority, trample on our Bill of Rights, or allow a "monied interest" to corrupt our laws, Thomas Jefferson and James Madison would say that "We the People of the United States" provide the ultimate check against "monarchy."

Richard N. Rosenfeld
Author, *American Aurora: A Democratic-Republican Returns:*
The Suppressed History of Our Nation's Beginnings
and the Heroic Newspaper that Tried to Report it.

Acknowledgments

This book would not have been possible without the support and encouragement of David Theroux, President of The Independent Institute, and Alexander Tabarrok, the Institute's Research Director. Dr. Tabarrok's attention to the manuscript and candor in making suggestions were instrumental in the completion of the book. A special debt of gratitude is owed to Professor William J. Quirk of the University of South Carolina School of Law. Professor Quirk encouraged me to expand my article, "The Kentucky and Virginia Resolutions: Guideposts of Limited Government," that appeared in the *Independent Review* (Winter 1999) into a book-length work. Throughout the process, his input has served to keep me focused on the book's purpose and message. Also deserving the highest encomium for their work and encouragement on this project are Ian Steinberg, Ray Massie, Jonah Straus, Penny Burbank, Priscilla Busch, Brenda Paschal, Mukesh V.S., Armen Alchian, Henry Manne, and Bob Staaf.

Abbreviations and Short Titles
Used in the Notes

Annals	*The Debates and Proceedings in the Congress of the United States*, ed., Joseph Gales (Washington, D.C.: Gales and Seaton, 1834–56) 42 vols.
CAJ	*Correspondence of Andrew Jackson*, ed., John Spencer Bassett (Washington, D.C.: The Carnegie Institution of Washington, 1926–35) 7 vols.
Elliot's Debates	*The Debates in the Several State Conventions on the Adoption of the Federal Constitution*, ed., Jonathan Elliot (Washington, D.C.: J. B. Lippincott & Co., 1888) 5 vols.
NLAA	*New Letters of Abigail Adams, 1788–1801*, ed., Stewart Mitchell (Boston, Mass.: Houghton Mifflin, 1947).
PAH	*The Papers of Alexander Hamilton*, ed., Harold Syrett and Jacob E. Cooke (New York: Columbia University Press, 1961–79) 27 vols.
PJCC	*The Papers of John C. Calhoun*, ed., W. Edwin Hemphill et al. (Columbia, S.C.: University of South Carolina Press, 1963–) 22 vols.
PJM	*The Papers of James Madison*, ed., William T. Hutchinson, William M. E. Rachal, et al. (Charlottesville, Va.: University Press of Virginia, 1962–) 17 vols.
PTJ	*The Papers of Thomas Jefferson*, ed., Julian P. Boyd et al. (Princeton, N.J.: Princeton University Press, 1950–) 26 vols.

The Republic of Letters	*The Republic of Letters: The Correspondence Between Jefferson and Madison*, ed., James Morton Smith (New York: W. W. Norton, 1995) 3 vols.
VCCG	*We the States: An Anthology of Historic Documents and Commentaries thereon, Expounding the State and Federal Relationship*, ed., Virginia Commission on Constitutional Government (Richmond, Va.: The William Byrd Press, Inc., 1964).
WFA	*Works of Fisher Ames: As Published by Seth Ames*, ed., W.B. Allen (Indianapolis, Ind.: Liberty Classics, 1983) 2 vols.
WGW	*The Writings of George Washington*, ed., John C. Fitzpatrick (Washington, D.C.: U.S. Government Printing Office, 1931–44) 39 vols.
WJA	*The Works of John Adams*, ed., Charles Francis Adams (Boston: C.C. Little, J. Brown, 1850–56) 10 vols.
WJM	*The Writings of James Madison*, ed., Gaillard Hunt (New York: G.P. Putnam's Sons, 1904) 9 vols.
WTJ	*The Works of Thomas Jefferson*, ed., Paul Leicester Ford (New York: G.P. Putnam's Sons, 1900–10) 12 vols.

Chapter 1

Monocrats and Jacobins

The Kentucky and Virginia Resolutions, written over two decades after the colonies declared independence from Great Britain, represent a reaffirmation of the spirit of 1776. At the core, the Resolutions are intrepid statements in favor of self-government and limited central authority. A product of the political and constitutional battlegrounds of the 1790s, the Resolutions serve to link the federal union created by the Constitution with aspirations of the patriots of the American Revolution. Indeed, the touch of the author of the Declaration of Independence is unmistakable when one reads the Kentucky Resolutions of 1798.

The Resolutions, however, cannot be understood without delving into the formative years of the Republic and the accompanying political strife. The developments during the Constitution's first decade provide insight into why Thomas Jefferson and James Madison, via the Resolutions, were compelled to remind their countrymen of the first principles of the American Revolution. Jefferson and Madison viewed the disputes of the 1790s not as mere growing pains, but as involving the very survival of republican government. It was in this crucible of discord that the story of the Kentucky and Virginia Resolutions begins.

* * *

As the new national government began to take its first steps, men who once fought shoulder to shoulder against the British found themselves divided over the meaning of the Constitution of 1787 and the course steered by the Washington administration. Alexander Hamilton's financial plan, the French Revolution, and disputes over foreign policy eventually led to the rise of American political parties. The Federalist party[1] of Hamilton championed commercial interests, a pro-British foreign policy, and a liberal interpretation of the Constitution meant to energize the new government. On the other hand, the Republican party of Jefferson and Madison championed agriculture, a pro-French foreign policy, and an interpretation of the Constitution meant to limit national power.[2] To use terms from British political discourse, the Federalists were a "Court" party determined to expand the ambit of the new government, while the Republicans were a "Country" party ever on guard against the slightest hint of corruption or usurpation of power.[3]

Realizing that precedents set in the nascency of the Republic would not be easily overturned, the combatants fervently pressed forward with competing agendas. Unless state power could be circumscribed, the Hamiltonians feared that the Constitution of 1787 would be no better than the enervated Articles of Confederation. Foreign powers would trample on the rights of the new nation while the states fought among themselves. Republicans, however, held the states in higher esteem. Rather than a threat, Republicans viewed the several states as a blessing. The states and their subdivisions were the places where the people exercised their rights of self-government. The many could participate in local government, whereas only the powerful few could hold national office. The states could also serve as a check on the national government, thus preventing it from metamorphosing into a variant of the omnipotent British central government against which the colonies had rebelled.

Jefferson framed the question of the day as follows: "Whether all should be consolidated into a single government or remain independent as to internal matters, and the whole form a single nation as to what was foreign only, and whether that national government should be a monarchy or republic. . . ."[4] Monarchial government is often associated with centralization, but Americans today undoubtedly see Jefferson's fear of monarchy as misplaced. Was not a purpose of the American Revolution to throw off kingly government?[5] How could Washington, his advisors, and the elected members of Congress countenance such a government?

While it is true that Washington had earlier rebuffed attempts by his officers in the Continental Army to make him king, sympathy for monarchy thrived in the upper ranks of the Federalists.[6] For example, Alexander Hamilton, who served as Washington's secretary of the treasury, was a great admirer of the British Constitution. As a delegate to the Constitutional Convention in 1787, Hamilton averred that "the British Govt. was the best in the world" and "doubted much whether any thing short of it would do in America."[7] He also warned of the "vices of democracy," and advised that in designing an executive branch for the new government the hereditary interest under the British model was "the only good one on the subject."[8] John Adams, the vice president of the United States under Washington, had also applauded the British

Constitution in his *Defence of the American Constitutions*. Adams, like Hamilton, believed a monarchy was necessary to preserve the balance between nobles and commoners and asserted that the people could be just as despotic as the privileged classes.[9] Adams raised many eyebrows in 1789 when he suggested that President Washington be addressed as "His Highness, the President of the United States, and Protector of their Liberties."[10]

In light of such Federalist doctrine, Madison maintained that the followers of Hamilton believed the people "should think of nothing but obedience, leaving the care of their liberties to their wiser rulers."[11] Madison saw the Federalists "mak[ing] *power* the primary and central object of the social system, and *Liberty* but its satellite."[12] Of course, in the late 1780s Madison was one of the chief supporters of the Constitution and collaborated with Hamilton in writing *The Federalist Papers*. The Madison of the 1790s, though opposing the Hamiltonians, was still a supporter of the Constitution, but the Constitution as ratified by the several states—not the expansive Constitution Hamilton advocated. With common ground disappearing daily, the rival parties would eventually bring the United States to the brink of a constitutional crisis.

Hamilton's Financial Plan

The conflicting views of the Constitution and national destiny fully emerged as Secretary of the Treasury Hamilton crafted a plan to put the nation's financial house in order. Of all the offices in the Washington administration, Hamilton's was the most challenging inasmuch as he inherited the financial disarray caused by the old government's impotence. Under the Articles of Confederation, the Congress could only make requests of money from the states and was thus forced to borrow and issue fiat money to pay for the war effort. Once the war was over, the lack of a taxing power made it impossible to pay back the debts contracted. The nation's abysmal credit in turn placed constraints on the growth of the country. The Washington administration also recognized that should an emergency arise such as war, the government would likely be unable to take necessary actions because of its finances. With all eyes on Hamilton, creditors anxiously waited for a solution.

Born out of wedlock in the West Indies, Hamilton was the perfect man for such a national undertaking as he was unaffected by any local prejudices. Whereas his nemesis Jefferson was first and foremost a Virginian, Hamilton viewed himself as a citizen of a promising new empire. Serving as an aide under General Washington in the

Revolutionary War, Hamilton gained the reputation as a problem solver. As an officer in Washington's army, Hamilton daily dealt with difficulties caused by the government of the Confederation. The army lacked the funds to properly clothe and feed its troops, and suppliers fled in the face of worthless paper promises from the Congress.

Hamilton realized that America's enormous debt was "the price of liberty."[13] He also realized that the paying of debts contracted was the cornerstone of public credit. "States, like individuals," wrote Hamilton, "who observe their engagements, are respected and trusted: while the reverse is the fate of those, who pursue an opposite conduct."[14] Of course, during the War for Independence not all debts were incurred by the Congress. The several states individually had accumulated large debts. And some states were much quicker to pay them off than others. Hamilton feared that the states less inclined to pay their debts could sabotage the credit of the whole. In addition, Hamilton envisioned a conflict between the states and the national government as both legislative sovereigns competed for tax money to pay the war debt.

In order to combat these problems and restore credit to the entire union, Hamilton proposed that the national government assume the revolutionary war debts of the states. Though Hamilton believed such a plan would "be a measure of sound policy and substantial justice,"[15] his critics became alarmed. States that had diligently paid down their debts protested inasmuch as their citizens would be taxed to pay the debts of states that had made no such efforts. Moreover, those who believed in the necessity of strong state governments to keep the national government in check sensed that Hamilton acted with a sinister motive. By assuming state debts, Hamilton would effectively tie men of means to the national government. Wealthy creditors would look to the national government rather than the state governments for payment, thus strengthening the former and weakening the latter. Hamilton admitted as much in his Report on Public Credit: "If all public creditors receive their dues from one source, distributed with an equal hand, their interests will be the same. And having the same interests, they will unite in the support of the fiscal arrangements of the government."[16]

But Hamilton wanted to go farther than debt assumption. He believed a funded national debt would assist in establishing public credit. By funded national debt, Hamilton envisioned the Congress setting aside a portion of tax revenues to pay each year's interest without an annual appropriation. Redemption of the principal would be left to the government's discretion. At the time Hamilton gave his Report on Public Credit, the national debt was $80 million. Though such a large figure shocked many Republicans who saw debt as a menace to be avoided, Hamilton perceived debt's benefits. "[I]n countries in which the national debt is properly funded, and the object of established confidence," explained Hamilton, "it assumes most of the purposes of money."[17] Federal stock would be issued in exchange for state and national debt certificates, with interest on the stock running about 4.5 percent. To Republicans the debt proposals were heresy. The farmers and planters of the South, who were predominantly Republican, owed enormous sums to British creditors and thus had firsthand knowledge of the misery wrought by debt. Debt, as Hamilton himself noted, must be paid or credit is ruined. High levels of taxation, Republicans prognosticated, would be necessary just to pay the interest on the perpetual debt. Believing that this tax burden would fall on the yeoman farmers and eventually rise to European levels, Republicans opposed Hamilton's debt program.[18]

To help pay the interest on the debt, Hamilton convinced the Congress to pass an excise tax[19] on whiskey. In *Federalist* No. 12, Hamilton noted that because "[t]he genius of the people will ill brook the inquisitive and peremptory spirit of excise law,"[20] such taxes would be little used by the national government. In power, the Secretary of the Treasury soon changed his mind and the tax on the production of whiskey rankled Americans living on the frontier. Cash was scarce in the West and the frontiersmen used whiskey as an item of barter. Westerners viewed the tax as an imposition from a national government that ignored their two greatest needs: navigation of the Mississippi and protection from Indian attacks. The paucity of good roads in the West made it almost impossible for the westerners to ship their produce to markets. Without navigation of the Mississippi, which was controlled by the Spanish, the farmers of the frontier were isolated. Add constant Indian attacks to the mix, and the frontiersmen felt that they should be exempt from the excise, which according to Western belief should only be levied by local bodies during national emergencies. There was resistance to the tax in the remote areas of Virginia, Kentucky, North and South Carolina, but the frontiersmen of Pennsylvania, because of their proximity to the seat of government in Philadelphia, caught President Washington's eye. In western Pennsylvania tax collectors were tarred and feathered, frontiersmen exchanged fire with soldiers from Fort Pitt, and eventually 7,000 western Pennsylvanians marched on Pittsburgh. Washington, recognizing that the Whiskey Rebellion was underway, nationalized 13,000 militiamen to quell the uprising. There were some peace negotiations between the national government and the rebels, but historians recognize that these "were a sham."[21] Though a localist at heart, Madison described the rebellion as "universally and deservedly odious" and only a few statesmen offered the rebels encouragement.[22]

Hamilton accompanied the army into western Pennsylvania in an effort to teach the frontiersmen to respect his tax collectors. Because no rebel army ever took the field and order was quickly restored, Hamilton's soldiers amused themselves by terrorizing the local inhabitants. Hamilton authorized the impressment of foodstuffs to feed his army knowing that civilians would soon be facing a harsh winter. A round-up-the-usual-suspects attitude led the soldiers to rouse a number of citizens from their homes for a forced march to Philadelphia. Two Pennsylvanians were eventually convicted of treason, but Washington pardoned them because both obviously suffered from mental disability and could not have orchestrated the uprising. Even with the end of the Whiskey Rebellion, the whiskey excise would never yield much more than the costs of enforcement. In short, the excise on whiskey was the least successful element of Hamilton's financial plan.

Another controversial part of Hamilton's plan to establish credit was his stand on full payment of securities issued by the Continental Congress. During the war the Congress issued negotiable instruments—essentially promises to pay in full at a future date—to fund much of the war effort. As more and more of this paper was issued, people believed that the government would probably never make good on the notes and consequently the value of the notes plummeted. Soldiers and farmers who were given the government's paper promises sold them for a fraction of face value. In order to establish public credit, Hamilton asserted that the securities had to be paid at face value. Republicans protested because this would mean that speculators who had purchased the securities for minimal amounts would reap huge profits, and the impoverished people who had originally received the securities would still be in the same impecunious position. Hence, Republicans proposed discrimination in payment. According to Republican calculation, speculators deserved no more than the current market value of the securities. Payment to original holders, on the other hand, would be at face value. Hamilton objected to discrimination. He observed that Congress, in issuing the securities, intended that they be negotiable—meaning "[l]egally capable of being transferred by endorsement or delivery."[23] Consistent with congressional intent, those who took by issue transferred the instruments to the speculators for market value. Thus, discrimination would be "inconsistent with justice," wrote Hamilton, "because in the first place, it is a breach of contract; in the violation of the rights of a fair purchaser."[24] And Hamilton was right. Though the Republicans' hearts were in the right place, a plan of discrimination would have been impossible to administer inasmuch as many of the securities had changed hands dozens of times. Sorting out who deserved what payment would have been too cumbersome. Moreover, no one forced the sale of the securities at prices below face value. Market participants simply acted in accordance with the prevailing market forces.

But this does not mean that the light of justice bathed Hamilton's proposal to pay all holders at face value. Jefferson noted that once Congress approved Hamilton's securities proposal this information spread among speculators who then bought up large amounts of the securities. Though Hamilton did not line his own pockets, many of his cohorts did. "Immense sums," wrote Jefferson, "were thus filched from the poor and ignorant and fortunes accumulated by those who themselves had been poor enough before. Men thus enriched by the dexterity of a leader, would follow of course the chief who was leading them to fortune and become zealous instruments of all his enterprises."[25] With the speculative frenzy Jefferson saw the ranks of the Federalist juggernaut expand at the expense of the common man.

Also on Hamilton's agenda was a national bank. Hamilton suggested a bank with a capital of $10 million and 25,000 shares of stock. The national government would own 5,000 shares and private investors the remaining 20,000 shares. Hamilton foresaw the bank issuing its own notes in amounts over its assets and the government borrowing from the national bank in time of need. To Hamilton a national bank was "an Institution of primary importance to the prosperous administration of the Finances, and would be the greatest utility in operations connected with the support of Public Credit."[26] The Secretary of the Treasury posited that gold and silver ought not be passed in payment of debts. Instead, gold and silver should be deposited in the Bank of the United States, where they could acquire "an active and productive quality."[27] Paper would circulate, the gold and silver would collect interest, and the bank would make loans far in excess of its reserves. The economy would benefit by the increase in the money supply and the notes issued would aid in tax collection inasmuch as they would replace the bulky, heavier specie. As Murray Rothbard has noted, the result of such a counterfeiting scheme is not real prosperity, but "ruinous cycles of boom and bust generated by expansions and contractions of the counterfeit bank credit."[28] And the Bank of the United States did create such a boom shortly after its doors opened for business.

Republicans fought creation of a national bank. Hamilton's bank[29] was to Jefferson and other Republicans but a conspiracy to "delug[e] the States with paper money instead of gold and silver."[30] Republicans understood that a paper money system vests the government with much power, whereas with a pure specie standard control rests in the free market. Without the ability to create paper money out of thin air, which leads to inflation, government must tax or borrow to fund its projects.[31] This keeps the government honest and, more importantly, defends the value of the laborer's wages. Though Republicans distrusted banks, mainly because of the large sums they owed to British creditors, opposition centered more on the constitutionality of the Bank of the United States.

Republicans perceived that a power grab was underway vis-à-vis a loose interpretation of the Constitution. The Constitution mentioned nothing about chartering corporations, but Hamilton argued that such a power was incident to sovereignty and that the Necessary and Proper Clause countenanced a national bank inasmuch as it was related to taxation, regulation of trade, borrowing, and the government's power to raise and support armies. Jefferson, taking a more restrictive view of the Constitution in his report to Washington on the bank, pointed out that under the Tenth Amendment what is not delegated to the national government is reserved. Jefferson feared departure from this basic principle would transform the government from a limited government approved by the people of the several states in the ratification process, to an omnipotent Leviathan more powerful than the centralized British government that oppressed the colonies. (Hamilton's and Jefferson's arguments will be more closely scrutinized in chapter 3.) Washington sided with Hamilton and the genie of loose constitutional construction happily left the confines of the bottle.

The final prong of Hamilton's financial plan, and the only prong not adopted at the time, was the Report on Manufactures. According to Hamilton, "not only the wealth; but the independence and security of a Country, appear to be materially connected with the prosperity of manufactures. Every nation with a view to these great objects, ought to endeavor to possess within itself all the essentials of national supply."[32] Though independence from foreigners concerning military and other necessaries seems to be a laudable goal, Hamilton's means to the end resembled a modern big-government approach to the problem. Government monetary support of certain industries, tariff walls (more aptly additional taxes on consumers), government grants to inventors, internal improvements, and assumption of the travel expenses of skilled foreigners who settled in the United States formed part of Hamilton's industrial vision for America.

Hamilton's industrial program illuminated yet another philosophical difference between Federalists and Republicans. Industrialization was contrary to the agrarian principles of the Republican South. Jefferson described farmers as "the chosen people of God"[33] and believed that the United States would be a virtuous land "as long as they are chiefly agricultural."[34] Staunch republican Ben Franklin described agriculture as the "only honest way"[35] to earn a living. Proponents of agrarianism[36] believed that by cultivating the land, the farmer could avoid the misery and poverty of the factory worker. The farmer would never grow rich, but at least he could support himself and have time to cultivate his interests as well as his crops. Moreover, as one who looked to no other man for his wages, the farmer was independent and the safest repository of republican liberty. Republicans envisioned the family farm dominating the continent as America expanded westward and believed an abundance of land would ensure an equal distribution of wealth upon which "private morality and public virtue alike depended."[37]

As for constitutional concerns about the Report on Manufactures, Jefferson feared that enactment of the proposal would set precedent and thus allow "Congress to take everything under their management which they should deem for the public welfare, and which is susceptible to the application of money."[38] But with the ideas of free trade gaining currency and the people's suspicion of the new national government, Congress declined to follow the Secretary of the Treasury's grandiose industrial plan.

As an astute politician, Hamilton knew where his financial plan and theories of constitutional interpretation would lead. The delegates in Philadelphia had prevented him from copying the British model of government under which Parliament may, to quote Dicey, "make or unmake any law whatever."[39] Hamilton had suggested the abolition of the state governments and the creation of a national government with the "power to pass all laws whatsoever."[40] Thwarted in his frontal assault, Hamilton simply infiltrated the new government and undertook to remove as many constitutional limitations as possible. Today, one is hard pressed to distinguish the authority of the American Congress and that of the British Parliament. Without question, Hamilton was successful in laying the groundwork for the present balance of national and state power.

The French Revolution

The strife sparked by Hamilton's financial plan grew in the wake of the French Revolution.[41] Americans, like other peoples of the Western world, were divided into opposing camps by the events in France. One can compare this divisiveness to the contrasting views toward Soviet Communism in the twentieth century, but such a comparison fails to convey the true antipathy between the American Francophiles and Anglophiles. By the end of the 1790s, Americans who ventured outside wearing the French cockade (a red, white, and blue ribbon) risked assault, as Federalists, sporting the black cockade, believed that a French army would soon be sailing for the United States.

During the opening days of the French Revolution, however, most Americans saw the events in France as an extension of the American Revolution. Likewise, many Britishers also saw the French Revolution as an extension of their Glorious Revolution. John Cartwright summed up the views on both sides of the Atlantic in 1789 when he wrote: "Degenerate must be that heart which expands not with sentiments of delight at what is now transacting in the National Assembly of France. The French, Sir, are not only asserting their own rights, but they are also asserting and advancing the general liberties of mankind."[42]

Even as the Jacobins known as the Mountain, the most radical of the French revolutionaries, toppled the more moderate Girondins, Republicans continued to emphasize the promise of the earlier phases of the Revolution. The revolutionaries had proclaimed new constitutions, abolished feudalism, and issued a Declaration of the Rights of Man and Citizen. Jefferson boasted that France "has been awakened by our revolution, they feel their strength, they are enlightened, their lights are spreading, and they will not retrograde."[43] Moreover, with American revolutionaries like Thomas Paine serving in the French Convention, Republicans reasoned that the French were guided by the Spirit of 1776 and *Common Sense*. The French added to such flattery by conferring honorary citizenship on Madison, Hamilton, and Washington.

In contrast to the Republicans, the Federalists concentrated on the darker side of the French Revolution. The revolutionaries murdered King Louis XVI, abandoned constitutions almost as quickly as they adopted them, confiscated private property, murdered 40,000 citizens and arrested 500,000 during the Jacobins' Reign of Terror, and replaced Christianity with a cult of reason.

Federalists especially feared the numerous democratic-republican societies that arose in the United States in support of the French

Revolution. Members of the societies addressed each other in the French fashion as "Citizen" and celebrated French military victories with grand feasts. Some societies raised money to equip French privateers. The societies fervently believed that if Europe's monarchs succeeded in crushing the French Revolution, the same coalition would turn on the United States. Nor were the ebullient societies shy about their sympathies. For example, during the 1794 Fourth of July celebration in Baltimore, the local society offered the following toast: "The national convention of France, and an emulation of their virtues by the American congress."[44] The Philadelphia Society toasted the Jacobins of the Mountain: "May tyranny be chained at its foot, and may the light of Liberty from its summit cheer and illuminate the whole world."[45]

Fearing they would soon be chained at the foot of the Mountain by Jefferson and the Republicans, Hamilton and the Federalists took umbrage at any positive mention of France. In this climate of distrust augmented by the French Revolution, Adams's and Jefferson's friendship was one of the first casualties. Thomas Paine's *The Rights of Man* had appeared in Britain as a response to Edmund Burke's criticism of the Revolution in his influential *Reflections on the Revolution in France.* Jefferson arranged for Paine's work to be reprinted in the United States and sent the book to a printer. Along with the book, Jefferson enclosed a personal note expressing pleasure "that something was at length to be publicly said against the political heresies which had of late sprung up among us, not doubting that our citizens would rally again round the standard of Common Sense."[46] Unbeknownst to Jefferson, the printer added the note as a preface to the book. Of course, the "heresies" Jefferson inveighed against referred in part to Adams's *Discourses on Davila* in which he assailed the French Revolution. Adams took offense at the preface and his friendship with Jefferson promptly cooled.

Foreign Entanglements

The divisiveness caused by the French Revolution increased as war erupted between France and Britain. The United States was bound by treaty to defend the French West Indies and prohibited from aiding the enemies of France. With the advent of war the treaties with France became liabilities. Hamilton, advising the president, proffered several arguments to prevent the United States from assisting France. Hamilton counseled Washington that the 1778 Treaty of Alliance could be suspended inasmuch as it was made with the deposed French king. Moreover, the Secretary of the Treasury argued that the alliance was defensive, and because France had started an offensive war against Britain, the United States was relieved of any duties under the treaty. Jefferson swiftly countered by pointing out that the treaty was between nations and could not be repudiated solely because of the French government's change in form. "Compacts between nation and nation," wrote Jefferson, "are obligatory on them by the same moral law which obliges individuals to observe their compacts."[47] After weighing Hamilton's and Jefferson's opposing views, President Washington prudently decided that neutrality would be the proper policy for the young Republic and he issued the Neutrality Proclamation of 1793. Though neutrality was the judicious course, Jefferson and other Republicans questioned Washington's authority to issue such a proclamation.[48] The Constitution, by vesting Congress with the power to declare war, sought to restrict the executive's authority in the realm of foreign relations. English history taught the Framers that untrammeled executive discretion often led the English people into unnecessary foreign wars.[49] In *Federalist* No. 69, Hamilton was careful to point out to critics of the Constitution that though the president was commander in chief of the armed forces, his power was much less than the king of Great Britain whose power "extends to the declaring of war and to raising and regulating of fleets and armies; all which by the Constitution under consideration would appertain to the Legislature."[50] With Hamilton perhaps adopting an opinion different from that in the *Federalist*, his former collaborator Madison perspicaciously warned that "[a]n assumption of prerogatives not clearly found in the Constitution & having the appearance of being copied from a Monarchial model, will beget animadversion equally mortifying to him [Washington] & disadvantageous to the Government."[51] Madison insisted that a system giving the people's representatives a voice in decisions regarding war and peace, as found in the Constitution, was far superior to one of executive discretion.

Though Jefferson lost the constitutional argument regarding the issuance of the proclamation, he did win two important concessions.[52] First, the word neutrality never appeared in the document. Instead, the proclamation simply declared that the United States would "pursue a conduct friendly and impartial toward the belligerent powers" and counseled Americans to avoid "aiding . . . or abetting hostilities."[53] Second, Jefferson washed his hands of the proclamation as best he could by suggesting that the proper party to draft the proclamation was the attorney general rather than the secretary of state. In the end, Republicans were none too happy with Washington's decision. According to

Madison, the proclamation "wounds the popular feelings by a seeming indifference to the cause of liberty."[54]

While the cabinet debated neutrality, the embodiment of the French Revolution landed in Charleston, South Carolina. Edmond Charles Genet, the new minister of the French Republic, brought to America a true taste of the Revolution that would forever damage the cause of France. Hamilton suggested that Washington should not receive Genet and attempted to tie reception of the minister to the validity of the treaties. Jefferson countered that the treaty provisions mentioned nothing about receiving ministers and that to refuse Genet would be an insult.[55] Washington sided with Jefferson on this matter. Genet would be received, but with little fanfare. Washington did not want to signal that the United States was prepared to aid France. Republicans hoped for at least words of support, but got nothing.

Genet had been raised in the shadow of Versailles, home of the French monarchy, and enjoyed a comfortable and eventful youth. His father was head of the Bureau of Interpretation in the Ministry of Foreign Affairs, and young Genet, following in his father's footsteps, could by age 12 read English, Swedish, Italian, and Latin. By age 13 he had translated Olof Celsius's *History of Eric XIV* from the Swedish and received a gold medal from the king of Sweden in appreciation of his work. Genet's eldest sister served Queen Marie Antoinette as *femme de chambre*. In this capacity she managed the Queen's social calender and kept track of the Queen's expenses. The Queen arranged for Genet to tour Europe in 1780, but he was forced to return early upon learning of his father's death. Genet immediately became chief of the Bureau of Interpretation and continued to serve the French government even as revolution engulfed the nation. Though he benefited from the royal family's patronage, this did not stop Genet's involvement with Girondin political forces. To help outfit revolutionary soldiers, Genet sold the gold medal given to him by the Swedish king. The Girondins eventually rewarded his patriotism by appointing him minister to the United States.

Before sailing to the New World, Genet received lengthy instructions from his government. Genet was to secure a commercial treaty with the United States, obtain advance payments of the American debt to France, outfit forces to march on Spanish possessions in the southeastern United States, incite rebellion in Canada, outfit privateers in American ports, and demand rigorous observance of existing treaties. In typical revolutionary fashion, Genet's overlords addressed his letter of accreditation to Congress and not the president, though the latter by the Constitution is empowered to "receive Ambassadors and other public Ministers."[56]

Such a blunder illustrated the imperfect French understanding of American institutions.[57]

In Charleston friendly crowds and local dignitaries greeted Genet. Governor William Moultrie encouraged Genet to begin outfitting privateers and before the Minister left Charleston he had commissioned *Républicain*, *Sans Culotte*, *Anti-George*, and *Patriote Genet* to prey on British shipping. Moultrie also supplied Genet with a list of men who might be useful to him in planning expeditions against Spanish possessions. As Genet traveled to Philadelphia, throngs of people greeted him and local officials in the Republican South treated the French Minister to banquets. With such spontaneous receptions Genet had no reason to believe that his mission would soon end in disaster. While in Richmond Genet learned of the Neutrality Proclamation and sped to Philadelphia. Citizen Genet received a cool reception from President Washington and was politely rebuked by Jefferson for using American ports to outfit privateers and sell captured prizes. Jefferson conceded that French vessels could enter American ports with their prizes, but equipping privateers without permission violated American sovereignty.[58] Genet protested that his actions were not prohibited by treaty and that commissioning privateers in neutral ports at times of war was perfectly acceptable. Though Jefferson originally described the Minister as "offer[ing] everything and ask[ing] for nothing,"[59] in a mere two months Jefferson would describe Genet as a "calamitous appointment" possessing "no judgment."[60]

Less than two weeks after his first clash with American officials over treaty interpretations, Genet learned that two American citizens serving on a French privateer had been arrested for violating American neutrality. Genet retained prominent Republican lawyers in Philadelphia to defend the men, and after a jury trial the sailors were acquitted. This incident only reinforced Genet's belief that he could overrule the policies of the Washington administration by appealing directly to the people. Though Jefferson politely suggested to the Minister that if he consulted the Constitution he would find that the people had vested the president with the power to execute the laws, Genet did not heed Jefferson's advice.[61] Viewing American and French politics as but variations of mob rule, Genet's conduct grew more reckless.

Eventually, a conflict over a privateer proved to be Genet's undoing. The *Little Sarah* was a British ship captured by the French in international waters and brought to Philadelphia to be outfitted as a privateer. Alexander Dallas, serving as the secretary of state of Pennsylvania, asked Genet to refrain from launching the privateer until Jefferson returned to

Philadelphia the next day. Genet became belligerent and threatened to "appeal from the President to the people."[62] Jefferson spoke with Genet and asked him to wait until Washington's return before taking any action. Though Genet made no promises, Jefferson assumed that the ship would stay. Hamilton, against Jefferson's will, ordered placement of artillery at a strategic point to prevent the ship from escaping. Jefferson strenuously argued against military action inasmuch as the French fleet was scheduled to arrive in Philadelphia at any moment and because he "would not gratify the combination of kings with the spectacle of the only two republics on earth destroying each other."[63] However, before the artillery was ready the privateer sailed. Washington was naturally incensed at Genet's actions and the cabinet unanimously agreed to demand his recall. Hamilton gleefully informed newspaper editors of Genet's threat to appeal to the people and news of Genet's conduct spread. At town meetings held across the country the people adopted resolutions supporting Washington and neutrality. The Genet debacle so embarrassed Jefferson that he attempted to resign his post, but Washington persuaded him to stay on. Madison recognized that Republicans, in the wake of Genet's misadventures, had to draw distinctions between themselves and the Minister and the French Republic. Otherwise "the enemies of France & of Liberty" would steer Americans toward monarchy and ultimately into the arms of Great Britain.[64] But in light of the Republicans' original embrace of Genet, Federalists found distinctions meaningless.

The Girondins had fallen from power in France and the Jacobins of the Mountain were more than happy to recall Genet.[65] Genet's replacement arrived in Philadelphia and asked President Washington for permission to arrest Genet and have him transported back to France. The magnanimous Washington, knowing that the guillotine awaited Genet in Paris, declined permission and let Genet remain in the United States. Genet eventually married Cornelia Clinton, the daughter of New York's governor, and settled down to a bucolic existence in upstate New York. He became an American citizen in 1804 and never returned to France. Though his mission was short-lived and unsuccessful, Genet changed the course of American politics. As Harry Ammon has observed: "The issues presented by the outbreak of the war between France and Great Britain, the French Revolution, and the Minister's conduct, compelled men to take sides. They could no longer function as independents deciding each question on its merits, for all political issues had to be evaluated in the light of a set of basic ideological commitments."[66] Thanks in part to Genet's conduct, the dream of a nation bereft of political parties died a quick death.

After Genet's recall, issues of foreign affairs continued to divide America. Relations between the United States and Great Britain had been strained since the American Revolution. Problems between the two nations centered on three main issues: British troops remaining in the American Northwest, a British definition of wartime contraband that effectively prevented French receipt of grain from the United States, and British restrictions on American commerce more onerous than those borne by the colonies before the Revolution. On top of this, the two sides were also at odds over such things as American confiscation of loyalist property during the Revolution and the British confiscation of American slaves. As tensions grew with each passing year, Americans and Britishers realized that unless something was done to resolve the differences war would likely result. But neither side seemed inclined to take the first step.

Britain alleged that troops remained in the Northwest in order to monitor the former colonies' adherence to the Treaty of Paris. The treaty provided that the soldiers would be withdrawn with "all convenient speed," but the two nations disagreed on the definition of convenience. In reality, the British were not monitoring American treaty compliance, but instead protecting the very lucrative fur trade. According to Samuel Flagg Bemis, the fur trade was amazingly profitable and was "a national asset well worth protecting."[67] Indians trapped and exchanged the pelts for British manufactured goods. Were the British to pull out, Americans would quickly fill their shoes and reap the profits from the trade. Furthermore, the British did not want to divulge to their Indian allies that they had ceded to the United States much of what was supposed to be Indian land. Officers manning the British forts were carefully instructed to never reveal the truth to the Indians lest they incite an uprising. Instead, the British encouraged Indian attacks on Americans who intruded on what was supposed to be Indian territory.

Lord Dorchester, the governor of Canada at the time, went so far as to advise the Indians that the United States and Britain would soon be at war, and if the Indians aided the British a new boundary line would be drawn giving the Indians as much land as they desired. As American General Anthony Wayne moved into the Ohio wilderness with approximately 2,000 disciplined troops, the British prepared the Indians for what the redcoats hoped would be a decisive battle. However, Wayne crushed the Indians at the Battle of the Fallen Timbers in August 1794, destroyed their crops, and scattered the tribes across the wilderness. The defeated Indians exchanged a large portion of their territory for $10,000 worth of annuities when they signed the Treaty of Greenville.

Wayne had attempted to offer the Indians peace without battle, but the British had the Indians so enraged that they never considered Wayne's proposals. Wayne later almost exchanged fire with British regulars, but he withdrew in order to avoid certain war.

As for general issues of commerce, Americans in 1776 thought that independence would mean the end of the British navigation laws and the beginning of an era of prosperity through trade. In actuality, independence meant an end to much of the lucrative trade with the British West Indies. American ships were also forbidden from trading with Canada and the Canadians forbidden to import American goods. American ships were permitted to carry American products to British ports, but not the goods of other nations. Moreover, American commerce continued to be dependent on the British. British merchants were quick to extend credit and British manufactured goods were superior to the French alternatives. Madison and other prominent Republicans had hoped to divert much trade to France by placing reciprocal restrictions on British shipping. Madison proposed high duties on the manufactured goods produced by nations having no commercial treaty with the United States (i.e., Britain), and reciprocal restrictions when these nations did not permit American ocean carriage of their goods. Madison felt the United States should demand "an equitable share in carrying our own produce; we should enter into the field of competition on equal terms, and enjoy the actual benefit of the advantages which nature and the spirit of our people entitle us to."[68] The Hamiltonians recoiled at the notion of cutting trade with Britain. Without the tariff revenue, Hamilton's entire financial program would fail. But Hamilton had little to worry about. Britain was so rooted in matters of trade in America that any proffered restrictions could not have been enforced. Also, increasing British depredations of American commerce appeared to require more stringent measures than those proposed by Madison.

As Britain warred with France, the British adherence to the principle of *consolato del mare*, under which they claimed the right to take enemy goods from neutral ships, caused Americans much consternation. Under a British Order in Council of November 6, 1793, British naval commanders were instructed "to stop and detain all ships laden with goods the produce of any colony belonging to France or carrying provisions or other supplies for the use of any such colony."[69] Around this time there were sundry American ships in the French West Indies because France had opened its colonies to American vessels. Within four months the British detained over 250 American ships. Crew members who were not left naked on West Indian islands were thrown into prison where many of them died of fever. News of this treatment incensed the public and war seemed closer than ever.

In an effort to preserve peace with Great Britain, four Federalist senators called upon President Washington and urged that he appoint a special envoy to hammer out differences with the British. They recommended Hamilton, but Washington rejected this choice. The President knew that many Americans distrusted Hamilton because of his affections for Great Britain. Instead, the President appointed John Jay and he was confirmed by the Senate in an 18-8 vote.

Like Hamilton, Jay was very pro-British in his political philosophy and also an avowed enemy of the revolution in France. Known for his conservatism, Jay was among the last of the Founders to believe that the colonies should break from the mother country. After the war, Jay asserted that the British were justified in holding their forts in the Northwest because of state impediments to the recovery of British debts. According to Bemis, such sentiments made Jay second only to Hamilton in the eyes of British leaders.[70]

Washington gave Jay full discretion in negotiating a treaty except for two points. First, Jay was forbidden to commit the United States to any agreement that would necessitate a breach of the treaties with France. Second, no treaty would be acceptable that did not grant American ships the rights to enter the British West Indies.

Jay negotiated with Baron Grenville and no minutes of the discussions were kept. If one considers avoidance of war with Great Britain as the ultimate aim of the Jay mission, then the treaty he negotiated was a success. But Jay gained this victory by completely acquiescing to the British view of the law of the sea. Jay accepted *consolato del mare* and the broad definition of contraband. Arguably, such a failure in this area was not Jay's fault. The United States had as a bargaining chip the threat that it might join other nations in armed neutrality to combat the British treatment of neutral vessels. Hamilton, however, informed George Hammond, the British minister to the United States, that the American government did not consider armed neutrality a serious option and thus weakened Jay's position. Hamilton's free exchange of information with Hammond has been described by one scholar as "in truth nothing less than a penetration of the highest councils" by agents and officials of a foreign power.[71]

The British did agree to leave their posts in the Northwest, compensate Americans for losses sustained under the Order in Council of November 6, 1793, and grant American ships of limited tonnage access to the West Indies. But there were no provisions protecting American sailors from impressment, compensating slave owners for property seized during the War for Independence, or prohibiting interference with Indians living in American territory. In sum, Jay perhaps saved the United States from war, but did little else to further American interests.

Once copies of the treaty arrived in the United States Washington called a special session of the Senate. The Senate quickly struck Article XII of the treaty, which concerned American access to the West Indies. The Article limited American ships to 70-ton vessels and enumerated items of tropical produce that could not be reexported from the United States. The Senate rightly found such restrictions too burdensome, but ratified the rest of the treaty by a vote of 20-10. The vote was sectional, with only two Southerners voting for the treaty. One more dissenting vote would have killed the entire treaty. Senators were prohibited from copying the treaty but the full text was soon published in the Philadelphia *Aurora*. The public, believing Jay could have obtained more concessions, quickly expressed displeasure. Riots ensued in several commercial centers and Jay was burned in effigy. In Boston a British merchant ship was mistaken for a privateer and the mob destroyed the vessel within minutes. In Philadelphia rioters attacked the home of the British minister. When Hamilton attempted to speak in favor of the treaty at public meeting, the crowd stoned him and forced him to flee the area.

Letters poured into Philadelphia urging President Washington to reject the treaty. Citizens of Clark County, Kentucky, informed the President that if he signed Jay's treaty "western America is gone forever—lost to the union."[72] A Virginia newspaper promised to petition the Virginia legislature "praying that the said state may recede from the Union, and be left under the government and protection of ONE HUNDRED THOUSAND FREE AND INDEPENDENT VIRGINIANS."[73] So disgusted was the House of Representatives with Washington that a vote to adjourn for a short time to wish the President a happy birthday was defeated 50-38. Moreover, Washington needed $90,000 from the House to implement the treaty. Though the Constitution gives the House of Representatives no role in making treaties, many Republicans sought to sabotage the Jay Treaty by refusing to appropriate the necessary funds. And inasmuch as the Constitution requires that all revenue bills originate in the House, the Republicans possessed a strong hand. In the end the Federalists rallied their forces and by a 51-48 vote the House appropriated the money. Madison, serving in the House at the time, described the Jay Treaty as an "insidious instrument" and yet another betrayal of France.[74]

Though Jay's name figures prominently in the history of the instrument, Bemis points out that "[m]ore aptly the treaty might be called Hamilton's Treaty," inasmuch as he would have accepted anything to secure the tariff revenue on which national credit depended.[75]

The abuse Washington received because of the Jay Treaty figured in his decision to step down as the election of 1796 approached. On Hamilton's advice, Washington did not announce his retirement until the last minute in order to prevent the Jeffersonians from mounting an extended campaign. Though Washington's Farewell Address warned of the "danger of parties," the election brimmed with partisanship aroused by the Jay Treaty. Hamilton, distrustful of the independent-minded John Adams, attempted to elevate the more pliant Thomas Pinckney to the presidency. But in the end Adams edged Jefferson by three votes and became the nation's second president.[76] As the candidate with second largest number of votes, Jefferson assumed the vice presidency.

At first it appeared that Adams might rise above partisanship in his administration, but after his initial meeting with the holdover cabinet, Adams quickly "returned to his former party views."[77] Of course, continued problems with France also explain why Adams leaned on pro-British Federalists rather than the pro-French Republicans. Within a month after taking office, Adams learned that the French had refused to receive the new American minister, Charles Cotesworth Pinckney. In addition, the French Directory—France's executive body—issued a decree of July 2, 1796, which declared that France would treat neutral vessels in the same manner as the British did. In essence, this gave French captains *carte blanche* to prey upon American shipping. Within one year after the ratification of the Jay Treaty, the French had captured or destroyed over 300 American vessels.

Adams called a special session of the Congress to consider measures to meet the new threat. The Congress convened on May 16, 1797, and Adams promptly addressed the body. French actions, according to Adams, had "to be repelled with a decision which shall convince France, and the world, that we are not a degraded people, humiliated under a colonial spirit of fear and sense of inferiority, fitted to be instruments of foreign influence."[78] Exercising his "indispensable duty to recommend effectual measures of defence,"[79] Adams suggested the need for naval vessels to accompany convoys of merchant ships as well as additions to artillery and cavalry should the French invade. Adams could not resist rankling Republicans by observing that "endeavors have been employed to foster and establish a division between the Government and people of the United States."[80] In effect, Adams accused Republicans of disloyalty. Later Republicans demanded Adams and the Federalists offer proof of the alleged treason,[81] but the Federalists saw no need to prove what to them was obvious. Both the Senate and House responded favorably to Adams's message, though Republicans in the House feared the speech made war inevitable.

Congress did act by appropriating funds to equip three frigates under construction, authorizing a salt and stamp tax to be implemented if necessary, and beefing up the inadequate American land defenses. The measures did little more than signal that the United States was aware of the French threat; were there to be a war, the United States was still unprepared. But most Americans hoped for a negotiated settlement.

Wisely, President Adams proposed a diplomatic mission to France. He spoke with Jefferson about the possibility of Madison and Elbridge Gerry joining Pinckney in Paris, but Madison did not want to make the journey. Had Madison accepted, President Adams would have needed a new cabinet inasmuch as all the holdovers threatened to resign if Madison was sent. The cabinet initially persuaded Adams to send a delegation made up entirely of loyal Federalists, dampening Adams's hopes that the mission would represent all parts of the union and differing political viewpoints. John Marshall and Francis Dana were to join Pinckney in Paris, but Dana withdrew from the mission because of poor health. Without consulting the cabinet, Adams offered Dana's spot to Elbridge Gerry, the one Republican Adams trusted. Complaining of Adams's choice, a number of Federalists remarked that "to distract the mission, a fitter person could not be found."[82] And in the end they were right as the French puppeteers pitted the Republican against the two Federalists.

Surprisingly, the French received the envoys and issued cards of hospitality. But chances of the mission's success soon dwindled. French Foreign Minister Talleyrand believed "the United States was of no greater consequence . . . than the Republics of Genoa or Geneva."[83] Talleyrand cared nothing for American interests, or French interests for that matter. He desired only to line his pockets and ensure a comfortable lifestyle. Historians estimate that in two years Talleyrand received 14 million francs from foreign envoys in exchange for favorable treatment from France. The three diplomats hoped Talleyrand would be partial toward the United States because he had lived in America in exile for two years. But Talleyrand developed a distaste for the United States during his short stay. President Washington had refused to receive him and Talleyrand generally found Americans to be crude people. Furthermore, Talleyrand like other French officials, viewed the

Jay Treaty as an attempted reconciliation with England and a betrayal of France. So long as it remained on the books, the United States could not be trusted.

Talleyrand's agents, known in Marshall's dispatches as X, Y, and Z,[84] demanded from the three Americans as a prerequisite for negotiation a bribe, a loan to France, and an apology for anti-French statements made by President Adams. Marshall and Pinckney were astonished by this behavior, but Gerry was more willing to consider the demands. The French, recognizing the division between the two Federalists and Gerry, exploited the situation and soon Marshall and Pinckney would hardly speak to the Republican. To exacerbate the situation Talleyrand habitually extended dinner invitations to Gerry alone and sought to negotiate with him while keeping Pinckney and Marshall in the dark. Convinced that success had eluded the mission, Marshall and Pinckney asked for their passports and prepared to return to the United States. Pinckney relocated to the south of France to better care for his daughter who was ill, and Marshall left Paris without saying goodbye to Gerry. Gerry remained in hopes of reaching a compromise once the two Federalist envoys left, but he did not succeed.

On March 4, 1798, the first of the envoys' dispatches arrived in the United States. Jefferson had interpreted the silence as "a proof of peace," but the dispatches disabused him of this rosy picture.[85] Adams made several bellicose statements after receiving the dispatches, causing congressional Republicans to demand full disclosure of Marshall's account of the affair. Many Republicans believed that after reading Marshall's correspondence in its entirety they could prove that the French government had not acted in an offensive manner. Federalists were only too happy to provide the Republicans with the rope to hang themselves. "The Jacobins want them," declared one Federalist, "[a]nd in the name of God let them be gratified; it is not the first time they have wished for the means of their destruction."[86]

Once the American public learned of the envoys' treatment, "millions for defense, not one cent for tribute" became the national cry.[87] Many Republicans soon acquiesced in the Federalists' war preparations "to wipe off the imputation of being French partisans."[88] Jefferson, however, still believed that President Adams's fiery speeches on French affairs were "in truth the only obstacle to negotiation."[89] Congress created the Department of the Navy and authorized the president to commission and arm 12 ships. Congress prohibited French ships from entering American ports unless in distress. Federalists also imposed a stamp duty, a direct tax on houses and slaves, a land tax, and

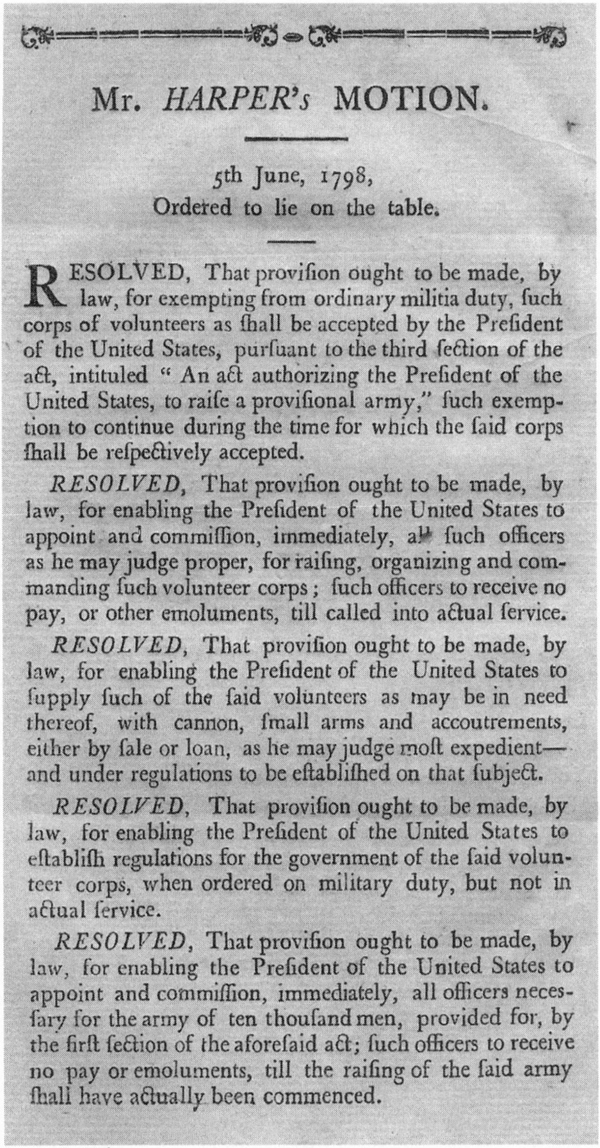

Mr. *HARPER's* MOTION.

5th June, 1798,
Ordered to lie on the table.

RESOLVED, That provifion ought to be made, by
law, for exempting from ordinary militia duty, fuch
corps of volunteers as fhall be accepted by the Prefident
of the United States, purfuant to the third fection of the
act, intituled " An act authorizing the Prefident of the
United States, to raife a provifional army," fuch exemp-
tion to continue during the time for which the faid corps
fhall be refpectively accepted.

RESOLVED, That provifion ought to be made, by
law, for enabling the Prefident of the United States to
appoint and commiffion, immediately, all fuch officers
as he may judge proper, for raifing, organizing and commanding fuch volunteer corps ; fuch officers to receive no
pay, or other emoluments, till called into actual fervice.

RESOLVED, That provifion ought to be made, by
law, for enabling the Prefident of the United States to
fupply fuch of the faid volunteers as may be in need
thereof, with cannon, fmall arms and accoutrements,
either by fale or loan, as he may judge moft expedient—
and under regulations to be eftablifhed on that fubject.

RESOLVED, That provifion ought to be made, by
law, for enabling the Prefident of the United States to
eftablifh regulations for the government of the faid volunteer corps, when ordered on military duty, but not in
actual fervice.

RESOLVED, That provifion ought to be made, by
law, for enabling the Prefident of the United States to
appoint and commiffion, immediately, all officers neces-
fary for the army of ten thoufand men, provided for, by
the firft fection of the aforefaid act; fuch officers to receive
no pay or emoluments, till the raifing of the faid army
fhall have actually been commenced.

Image 1.1   In the summer of 1798, Federalists began to prepare for war with
France and to squelch the Republican opposition, which they viewed as disloyal.
Courtesy of the South Caroliniana Library, University of South Carolina, Columbia.

an increase in the customs duties. The government resorted to borrowing, taking a $5 million loan at 8 percent that later made the Federalists look like wastrels.

Staunch Republicans opposed most of these measures because they feared standing armies and fiscal irresponsibility. Moreover, they believed that the war preparations would strengthen the commercial interests of the North at the expense of the South. Though Jefferson loathed the Federalists' taxes, he also found hope in them. He realized that only strong medicine would cure the people of war fever, and in a November 26, 1798 letter to Madison, he expressed his belief that with the levying of taxes "the Doctor is now on his way to cure [war hysteria], in the guise of a tax gatherer."[90]

The people needed strong medicine to return them to their senses. The streets of Philadelphia abounded with canards that French armies would soon land in the United States. Federalists accused Jefferson and his supporters of planning to link up with French forces once the invasion began. Southerners feared a slave rebellion as rumors spread that the French would land in the Carolinas and recruit slaves as the foot soldiers for their war of conquest. Tempers flared as Federalist and Republican partisans clashed on the streets. Fearing the American Jacobins would soon make their move, President Adams ordered a cache of weapons delivered to his home in Philadelphia. In an effort to rally the Federalist troops, Adams occasionally appeared in public in a military uniform with a sword at his side.

Alexander Hamilton happily fanned the flames of war as he urged that an army of 20,000 men be raised immediately. Fearing he had underestimated the danger, Hamilton later raised the figure to 50,000. George Washington, in retirement at Mount Vernon, let the administration know he would be willing to take charge of the army in this time of national crisis. Washington did assume command, but he was only a titular commander. Hamilton, serving as inspector general of the army, held the real power.

Of all the Federalists, Hamilton greeted war with the most excitement. Not only did he long to meet the forces of regicide on the battlefield, but he also saw the crisis as an opportunity to quell resistance to national power in the Southern states. When Virginia began to upgrade its neglected defenses, primarily in response to increased Indian attacks on its western border, Hamilton took this as a sign that Virginia was preparing to question the authority of the union.[91] Fortunately, cooler heads restrained Hamilton from marching on the Old Dominion. Hamilton also hoped to use his army to take Louisiana and Florida for the United States. Ever ambitious, he entertained dreams of pushing into South America as well.

Madison, writing to Jefferson, observed that "it is a universal truth that the loss of liberty at home is to be charged to the provisions against danger, real or pretended, from abroad."[92] Such has been the case throughout American history whenever a war or a supposed danger confronted the nation.[93] In 1798 Federalists in control of the government appreciated the French threat to the United States exemplified by the war at sea; however, the Federalists cooked up the drama of an invasion and Republican treachery in order to solidify their hold on the government. The Alien and Sedition Acts were passed that summer, and criticism of the national government became a crime. As is so often the case with war measures, the national government's threat to domestic liberty in 1798 far exceeded the machinations of foreign foes.

Chapter 2

Legislation and Persecution

The crisis of the Alien and Sedition Acts capped off the turmoil of the 1790s. Crafted in the summer of 1798, the Acts were the most illiberal legislation passed during the early national period. Ostensibly aimed at securing the home front as the Federalists braced for French invasion, the Acts served the much broader purpose of Federalist political hegemony. Through this legislation, the Federalists sought to restrain democratic-minded foreigners and silence all criticism of the national government. Procrustean conformity became the cardinal principle of Federalist politics.

Of course, a penal law is only as effective as its enforcement machinery. But fortunately for the Adams administration, the national judiciary was replete with loyal Federalists. The judges gave Republican defendants few favorable rulings, and the entire affair demonstrated, to put it charitably, that impartiality was not the brightest star in the judges' constellation.

Though draconian, the Federalists' program was not original. In the early 1790s, Great Britain enacted similar legislation in hopes of quelling support for revolutionary France. The British laws broadened the definition of treason, regulated public meetings, provided punishment for those defaming the government, created a reporting and licensing system for aliens, and provided for speedy deportations.[1] Prime Minister William Pitt (the Younger) used these laws to break up democratic societies and send newspaper editors to the Botany Bay penal colony. In the face of this persecution, a number of outspoken reformers departed for North America,[2] but quickly learned that the Federalists were great imitators of the British government.

The Naturalization Act

The Naturalization Act of 1798 was the first piece of legislation aimed at the crisis. Congress had twice before tackled the issue of naturalization.[3]

In 1790, Congress declared that foreigners would be eligible for citizenship after two years of residence in the United States. Responding to unrest in Europe and growing numbers of immigrants, in 1795 Congress increased the residency requirement to five years.[4] However, unlike the earlier laws, the 1798 Act was enveloped in controversy and did not receive wide support.

In April 1798, Federalists proposed that the House Committee on the Defense of the Country and for the Protection of Commerce should review the naturalization requirements. Fear abounded that foreigners residing in the United States would welcome the Directory's armies and swell their ranks after invasion. Of course, had 1798 witnessed a French invasion, a change in the naturalization law would have been inconsequential. Seen in this light, the congressional tinkering with naturalization appears to have been a waste of precious time. However, if one views the Naturalization Act as a means to weaken Jefferson's party, which had a large contingent of immigrants, then the Federalists' worries over citizenship make more sense. During debates on citizenship requirements, Federalists specifically pointed to the large number of naturalizations that had occurred prior to the previous election. Federalists hoped that changes in the naturalization law would stunt the growth of the Republican party, thus ensuring a Federalist victory in the elections of 1800.

Jefferson further speculated that the citizen bill was aimed at foreign-born statesmen. He especially feared for Swiss-born Albert Gallatin, who was the Republican floor leader in the House. "Their threats pointed at Gallatin," wrote Jefferson, "and it is believed they will endeavor to reach him by this bill."[5] Federalists indeed had their sights set on Gallatin, hoping to correct "the mistake which this country fell into . . . of admitting foreigners to citizenship."[6] Harrison Gray Otis of Massachusetts, just as Jefferson predicted, proposed amending the naturalization law so that only persons born in the United States could hold office in the national government. Robert Goodloe Harper of South Carolina wanted to extend the scope of Otis's amendment to the states, but later withdrew his proposal when reminded that the Congress had no power to set qualifications for state office.

Others saw constitutional problems in the original proposal because Otis's amendment would have created two tiers of citizenship. One class of citizens, the native born, would have been entitled to vote and hold office, while naturalized citizens would have enjoyed only the franchise. Otis believed that if Congress could deny citizenship to foreigners, which it surely could under the Constitution, then Congress could also modify the rights of citizenship. Abraham Venable of Virginia countered that once foreigners had been admitted as citizens, "Congress had not the power of declaring what should be their rights; the Constitution has done this."[7] And Venable was absolutely correct. For example, to be eligible to serve in the House of Representatives, the Constitution specifies: "No person shall be a Representative who shall not have attained to the Age of twenty five Years and been seven Years a Citizen of the United States, and who shall not, when elected, be an Inhabitant of that State in which he shall be chosen."[8] In effect, Otis was attempting to insert additional requirements in the above quoted language by an act of Congress rather than a constitutional amendment.

As Republican attacks continued, Samuel Sitgreaves of Pennsylvania persuaded Otis to withdraw his proposal. Sitgreaves averred that the better vehicle for preventing foreign influence in the government would be an alien law inclusive of the power to expel or apprehend aliens in times of danger. In the end, Federalists settled for a naturalization law raising the residency requirement to 14 years. This measure passed in a 41-40 vote.

Even with Otis's proposal off the table, Republicans refused to acquiesce. Gallatin protested against the naturalization bill's retroactive features. He thought the bill unfair because the increased residency requirement would apply to foreigners already residing in the United States as well as to new arrivals. Gallatin believed that persons residing in the United States before enactment of the 1795 law should remain under the more liberal five-year residency provision. High Federalists complained that because so many "Jacobins and vagabonds" had entered the country in previous years, the bill's retroactivity was necessary to preserve the integrity of the government.[9] However, High Federalist fears could not stop moderate Federalists with myriad foreigners living in their districts from joining the Republicans in abolishing the bill's retroactive features. In the end, aliens who resided in the United States before 1795 were allowed to take advantage of the five-year residency requirement. But to fall under the 1795 act, an alien was required to have already declared his intention of applying for citizenship and to complete the naturalization process four years after making the declaration.

After minor changes, the Naturalization Act of 1798 passed the Senate and was signed by President Adams on June 18. The main features of the new law required an alien seeking citizenship to prove that he had resided in the country for 14 years. Moreover, the act required the alien to spend five of the 14 years in the state or territory where the naturalization occurred and to have declared his intent to become a citizen five years before being naturalized.

The Alien Laws

With the citizen law in place, Federalists proceeded to deal with foreign influence. At first, the House lumped foreigners together without distinguishing between citizens of enemy nations and those of friendly nations. However, Congress eventually recognized a distinction and passed two acts: the Alien Enemies Act and the Alien Friends Act. The Defense Committee originally proposed giving the president the power during times of war or invasion to issue a proclamation expelling or apprehending citizens of the enemy. High Federalists thought the proposal too weak. John Rutledge of South Carolina argued that the United States could not wait for a declaration of war to deport Frenchmen. So long as French agents continued to operate in the United States, Rutledge argued, France would have no need for a formal declaration of war. Sitgreaves agreed, describing the French as "cankerworm[s]" bent on "corroding the heart of the country."[10]

Republicans, on the other hand, feared the proposal vested the president with too much discretion. Rather than the whim of the president, Matthew Lyon of Vermont hoped that foreigners residing in the United States "might depend on something more certain."[11] Gallatin described the bill as "grounded upon the principle that the President of the United States shall have the power to do by proclamation what ought to be done by law."[12] Others observed that France might retaliate against Americans in like fashion. Unpersuaded, the Federalists declared that the time of tranquillity had passed. Otis believed that in these turbulent times, "punishment ought not to depend upon the slow operations of a trial."[13]

As the bill took shape, it was directed at alien enemies—that is, citizens of nations at war with the United States. What drew the Republicans' fire were provisions punishing individuals for concealing aliens or inhibiting enforcement of the act. Offenders were to be punished "as by law is or shall be declared." Thus, a citizen harboring an alien enemy would be guilty of a crime, but ignorant of the punishment until Congress through legislation, or the president through proclamation, acted. Ignorance of the punishment aside, Republicans also complained that the portion concerning a presidential proclamation violated the Constitution's separation of powers. The very first words of Article I provide that "All legislative Powers herein granted shall be vested in a Congress of the United States."[14] By delegating to the president legislative power, the Federalists were again statutorily modifying the Constitution.

In light of Republican objections, the alien enemies bill was sent to a special committee. As the bill underwent modifications, the Federalists pushed through a temporary bill that dealt with both alien enemies and friends. The temporary measure (discussed below) gave the president arbitrary powers and so frightened Republicans that they clamored for passage of the Alien Enemies Act, which was a permanent measure. In the debates on what became the Republicans' Alien Enemies Act, only Representative Robert Williams of North Carolina questioned the Act's propriety. Unlike his Republican colleagues, Williams refused to accept that Congress possessed heightened powers at time of war or danger. Williams realized that "war powers" were but a branch of Hamilton's beloved implied powers. Because the Constitution gave the national government no power to summarily remove alien enemies, Williams opposed what became the Alien Enemies Act.

Williams cogent arguments aside, the Republicans' Alien Enemies Act was far better than the original proposal. It contained greater specificity, removed much of the president's discretionary power, and dispensed with criminal sanctions against citizens. Under the first section, all males 14 years old or older, citizens or subjects of a nation declared to be at war with the United States or involved in an invasion of the United States, could be apprehended or deported upon the president's proclamation. Alien enemies not "chargeable with actual hostility, or other crime against public safety" were allowed time to recover or dispose of their property within the United States as stipulated by treaty.[15] In the absence of a treaty these aliens had only as much time as the president would permit.

The second section spelled out the duties of law enforcement officers, thus depriving the executive of unbridled discretion. The section empowered state and federal courts to hear complaints against aliens dangerous to the public peace. Upon showing of sufficient cause the court could order deportation, imprisonment, or require the alien to provide a surety for his good behavior.

Unlike the Naturalization Act and the Alien Enemies Act, the Alien Friends Act originated in the Senate.[16] The Senate's legislation permitted the president to remove aliens posing a threat to national security. The determination of who was a threatening alien was left to the president; the bill did not provide for trial by jury. The bill also created a national registration system for aliens. Aliens residing in the

United States were required to obtain a permit, and aliens without permits could be imprisoned or fined. Similar to the original version of the Alien Enemies Act, the bill targeted citizens harboring aliens. Before permitting an alien to cross the threshold of his home, the citizen was to give written notice to a federal judge. Citizens who had not given the requisite notice could be fined. Polish writer Julien Niemcewicz, having firsthand knowledge of tyranny under the Russian Czar, described the Senate's bill as "conceived in a truly Turkish spirit, show[ing] to what point the administration attempts to adopt and imitate the arbitrary means of despots. There is nothing more proper than to be on guard against troublesome and dangerous foreigners, but indiscriminately to place under suspicion all foreigners comes from a desire more to rule than protect."[17] Jefferson concurred and described the Senate's handiwork as "a most detestable thing."[18] The West Indian–born Hamilton, on the other hand, approved of the effort against aliens and announced that "the mass ought to be obliged to leave the Country."[19] After modifications, the Senate in early June forwarded the bill to the House.

When the bill arrived, the House was considering an omnibus alien and sedition bill. In this omnibus bill, the House targeted aliens guilty of felonies or seditious practices in their country of origin, and citizens or aliens voicing criticisms of the national government. Jefferson believed that the Senate and House bills were "so palpably in the teeth of the constitution as to shew [the Federalists] mean to pay no respect to it."[20] The debates in the *Annals of Congress* indicate that the House originally preferred its omnibus bill to the Senate bill. However, events pushed the House toward the Senate's harsher prescription.

John Marshall returned from the failed mission to France and received a hero's welcome when he entered Philadelphia. Marshall's presence served to heighten anti-French sentiment throughout the city. At the same time, George Logan, a private citizen and loyal Republican, departed for France on an unauthorized peace mission. Federalists speculated that Logan carried with him information to aid preparations for a French invasion. These circumstances aside, the real catalyst behind the House's support of the Senate measure was the publication in the Philadelphia *Aurora* of a letter from Talleyrand to the American government. The letter, partly conciliatory and somewhat insulting, had not been released by the government. This led Federalists to conclude that Benjamin Franklin Bache, the *Aurora*'s editor, was a French agent.

Bache was the grandson of Benjamin Franklin and a master of political invective.[21] Bache traveled to France with his grandfather in 1776 and was educated in Europe. An enthusiastic supporter of the French

Image 2.1 An opponent of the Kentucky and Virginia Resolutions, John Marshall's dispatches from Paris persuaded many Federalists that the Alien and Sedition Acts were warranted. Courtesy of the Library of Virginia.

Revolution, Bache was one of the first journalists to publically criticize George Washington for his pro-British policies. Washington accused Bache of attacking him with "malignant industry, and persevering falsehoods . . . in order to weaken, if not destroy, the confidence of the

Public."[22] Abigail Adams described Bache as possessing "the malice and falsehood of Satan," and she repeatedly called for his arrest.[23]

On the floor of the House, Bache was accused of being "an agent of the French Directory."[24] And though Bache never disclosed from whom he received Talleyrand's letter, he was able to turn the tables on the Federalists. Bache alleged that the criticism of him for publishing the letter was but "a link of the chain of persecution by which it is attempted to injure the Aurora and muzzle the press."[25] To Bache, publication of the letter was necessary to dispel Federalist propaganda that the French were "decidedly hostile to this country."[26] Bache also exposed how the national government had removed a packet addressed to him from the mail. The packet had aroused suspicion because on the back was the seal of the French Foreign Ministry. Officials assumed they had evidence of a treasonable correspondence, but the packet contained more mundane matters: pamphlets on British politics written by an old friend of Bache. When Secretary of State Timothy Pickering finally returned the materials to Bache, the editor made the most of the government's debacle. But Secretary Pickering would later have his revenge.

Publication of the Talleyrand letter so incensed the Federalists that when the House reconvened they favored the Senate's alien friends bill over their own more moderate measure. The Republicans tried to assuage the Federalists' rage by appealing to the Constitution. Gallatin quoted the Tenth Amendment and pointed out that "no power is given by the Constitution to Congress to banish or remove alien friends."[27] Gallatin also feared that if the federal government assumed the power to deprive alien friends of liberty, then the citizen's liberty would be the next casualty. He cited the Slave Import Clause, which prohibited Congress from interfering with "[t]he Migration or Importation of such persons as any of the States now existing shall think proper to admit" before 1808,[28] and argued that migration referred to alien friends, while importation referred to slaves.

Federalists then rose and argued that removal of alien friends was within the national government's powers. The Federalists believed that if the national government through its war powers could remove alien enemies, then it could certainly reach alien friends. "If the Constitution prevented Congress from exercising these powers," asked Otis, "would such a constitution be worth a farthing?"[29] Without the alien laws, Otis continued, "foreign agents and domestic traitors" would be "vaulted into place and power."[30]

Samuel Sewall proffered four specific reasons why an Alien Friends Law was constitutional. First, Sewall appealed to the Preamble of the

Constitution ("We the People . . .") and argued that the United States as a sovereign nation had the inherent power to deal with aliens. Second, he turned to Congress's power to regulate interstate and foreign commerce and asserted that the removal of aliens was related to this enumerated power. Third, Sewall tried to seize the Slave Import Clause from Gallatin. Sewall interpreted the clause as delegating to Congress the power to oversee alien friends. At most, he argued, the Slave Import Clause prohibited the exercise of this power until 1808. Lastly, Sewall trotted out the General Welfare Clause and averred that Congress could pass any law so long as they deemed it for the general welfare of the nation.

Republicans quickly confronted Sewall's arguments. First, the Republicans noted that the Preamble, as its name indicates, is but an introductory statement to the Constitution and confers no power on the national government. Second, the Republicans considered the Commerce Clause argument and asserted that the alien friends bill was "not intended for any commercial purpose" and was "not related to aliens as merchants."[31] Third, the Republicans reiterated Gallatin's distinction between migration and importation, but were a bit uneasy over such a use of the clause inasmuch as the intent behind it pointed only at slavery, not alien friends. Finally, the Republicans turned to the General Welfare Clause. Section Eight of Article II provides that Congress may collect taxes and pay the debts for the "common Defence and general Welfare of the United States" and then goes on to enumerate Congress's powers.[32] Abraham Baldwin of Georgia argued that the General Welfare Clause had never been considered a part of legislative authority. If the clause did confer authority, Williams asked why an enumeration of powers followed. Such a specific list of Congress's powers would be but surplusage under the Federalist interpretation. Gallatin reasoned that the purpose of the general welfare language "was not to give a general power all together unconnected with the remaining part of the sentence, but to define the purposes for which taxes should be laid."[33] Specific arguments aside, Republicans feared that the Federalists' assertion of the inherent powers of sovereignty and the power to legislate for the general welfare would impair state government. State governments must "fall prostrate before [the national government]," proclaimed Baldwin, "as there will be no power left for them to exercise."[34]

In rebuttal, the Federalists brushed aside the Republicans' constitutional arguments as mere quibbles. William Gordon of New Hampshire observed that Congress had exceeded its enumerated powers on previous occasions, pointing specifically to the Bank of the United States, and he failed to see why Congress should not do so again. To Harper the argument that states controlled alien friends meant that "though we see the knife of the traitor held to our throats, we are to wait until the state governments will come in and snatch it away."[35]

The debate then shifted from constitutional concerns to the arbitrariness of the bill. Edward Livingston of New York observed that the United States had a plethora of vigilant magistrates and that there was no reason to hand the president arbitrary power. However, under the alien bill, "the President is empowered to make the law," explained Livingston, "to fix in his mind what acts, what words, what thoughts or looks shall constitute the crime contemplated by the bill."[36] Livingston also complained that the alien friends were stripped of basic due process requirements. "No indictment; no jury; no trial; no public procedure; no statement of the accusation; no examination of witnesses . . . no counsel for defense; all is in darkness," Livingtson said, "silence, mystery, and suspicion."[37]

Though Federalists were no doubt tiring of Republican objurgations, all took notice of Livingston's remarks concerning resistance. The states, Livingston proclaimed, should not submit to such unconstitutional measures. If they did "they would deserve the chains which these measures are forging for them."[38] Livingston further contended that "whenever our laws manifestly infringe the Constitution under which they were made, the people ought not hesitate which they should obey. If we exceed our powers, we become tyrants, and our acts have no effect."[39] Gallatin also believed that "the states and state judiciary would, indeed they must, consider the law as a mere nullity, they must declare it to be unconstitutional."[40] Defending the doctrine of resistance to unconstitutional laws, Gallatin described American independence as "a monument of that right."[41] But he later said that the Alien Friends Act was not sufficiently dangerous to merit a revolt.

The Federalists characterized Livingston's talk of resistance as the "French doctrine" and evidence of "the contagion of the French mania."[42] Federalists averred that only the judiciary could sit in judgment of acts of Congress. If anything, Livington's remarks stiffened the Federalist resolve and the alien friends bill passed the House by a 46-40 vote. Adams signed the bill into law on June 25, 1798. And though harsh, the bill was milder than the Senate's original version.

The first section empowered the president "to *order* all such *aliens* as he shall judge dangerous to the peace and safety of the United States, or shall have reasonable grounds to suspect are concerned in any treasonable or secret machinations against the government thereof, to depart out of the territory of the United States."[43] If the alien disobeyed the order to depart and had not obtained a license from the president permitting his continued presence, the alien could be imprisoned for three years and was barred from ever becoming a citizen. To obtain the prized license, the alien had to prove that "no injury or danger to the United States will arise from suffering the alien to reside therein."[44] The president could also require the licensee to post a bond and provide sureties. The license could be revoked by the president "whenever he shall think proper."[45]

The second section empowered the president to order deported any alien imprisoned under the Act. If an alien returned to the United States after deportation, he could be imprisoned "so long as, in the opinion of the President, the public safety may require."[46] The third section required ships' captains immediately upon arrival to report to customs officials concerning aliens on board. The captain had to report such things as the alien's name, age, country of origin, and occupation. Captains failing to follow this provision risked a fine and detention of their ships.

Under Section Four, the federal courts were given jurisdiction "of all crimes and offenses against this act."[47] Marshals and other officers were also required to execute the orders of the president under the Act. The fifth section graciously permitted an alien ordered to depart the United States to take with him as much of his property "as he may find convenient."[48] Property left in the United States "remain[ed] subject to [the alien's] order and disposal."[49] The final section provided that the Alien Friends Act would remain in effect for only two years.

The Sedition Act

With measures in place dealing with aliens, the Federalists prepared to confront domestic criticism of the government. "I wish the Laws of our Country were competent to punish the stirer up of sedition," wrote Abigail Adams to her sister, "the writer and Printer of base and unfounded calumny. This would contribute much to the peace and harmony of our Country."[50]

To the First Lady and other administration officials, harmony of the country was synonymous with Federalist reign. And to preserve their power, the Federalists appreciated the power of the press. Federalist newspapers outnumbered Republican papers, but the Federalists refused to underestimate Bache and his fellow travelers. Aware of Federalist objectives, Jefferson predicted early on that the goal of a sedition act would be "the suppression of the Whig presses."[51] Should the Federalists be successful, Jefferson feared that "republicanism will be entirely brow beaten."[52] Of course, the Federalists' desire for control was not purely selfish. Many Federalists believed that if Jefferson was elevated to the presidency and the Republicans achieved a majority in Congress, the American experiment with self-government would fail. In the words of Massachusetts Federalist Fisher Ames, power would be transferred "into the hands of men equally destitute of private virtue and public spirit."[53]

To avoid this fate, Federalists commanded unanimity. A divided people was inimical to sound government needed in time of crisis, and Americans who openly disagreed with the government were described as bereft of "loyalty, religion, conscience, or any other honorable motive."[54] Criticisms of President Adams's policy toward France were to Federalists but "audacious attempts to separate the people from the government."[55] Moreover, criticism of those elected to office ran counter to the Federalist theory of democracy.[56] The Federalists believed "the sovereignty of the citizen [was] to be exercised" only "at the elections."[57] After elections, the executive and legislators exercised authority and the people were to obey and support the government. The obligation to support the government included forbearance from political discourse meant to influence legislative or executive decision-making. Thus the administration considered the activities of the democratic-republican societies, whose avowed purpose was to push the government away from England and toward France, as a usurpation of power. "[E]very insurrection against the constituted authorities, *or* opposition to them," wrote Reverend John Thayer, "is a revolt of a part against the general will, by which those authorities exist, and is highly criminal."[58] The Federalists' view is difficult to fathom today considering that private lobbying is an integral part of politics. However, the Federalists believed that political deliberation outside the halls of Congress would empower special interests and dilute the franchise of the ordinary citizen. By limiting political discourse to the elected, the Federalists sought to ensure an equal voice for all.

So, in an effort to remain in power and restore their version of democracy, the Federalists pushed forward with a sedition bill. With Independence Day ceremonies fresh in the collective memory, the House of Representatives received the Senate's proposed bill on July 5, 1798. Republicans immediately moved that the Bill of Rights should be read before further proceedings, but Speaker Jonathan Dayton rejected the proposal on procedural grounds. In the alternative, Republicans moved to reject the bill. John Allen of Connecticut then rose and lambasted Republican opposition to the sedition bill. "If ever there was a nation which required a law of this kind," observed Allen, "it is this one." Allen instructed Republicans to examine "certain papers printed in this city and elsewhere and ask themselves whether an unwarrantable and dangerous combination does not exist to overturn and ruin the government by publishing the most shameless falsehoods."[59] Allen described an editorial in the New York *Time Piece* calling President Adams a "mock monarch" as "a conspiracy against [the] Government and people."[60]

Anticipating Republican appeals to the First Amendment, the Federalists proffered a definition of freedom of the press. According to Harper, freedom of the press meant that "a man shall be at liberty to print what he pleases, provided he does not offend against the laws, and not that no law shall be passed to regulate liberty of the press."[61] This definition was substantially in accordance with the common law understanding that the government could not place prior restraints upon the press, but could punish criminal utterances after publication.

Republicans jumped into the libertarian vanguard and asserted that the press should remain free to provide the people with important information. Nathaniel Macon of North Carolina appealed to the marketplace of ideas and observed that a falsehood printed in the *Aurora* would be contradicted in another paper, thus permitting the people to judge for themselves the truth or falsity of any statement. Gallatin pointed out that if the people were deprived of information, then the Federalists would also "render their right of electing nugatory."[62]

Turning to the Constitution, John Nicholas of Virginia "looked in vain amongst the enumerated powers . . . for authority to pass a law like the present; but he found what he considered an express prohibition against passing it."[63] Of course, by express prohibition, Nicholas meant the First Amendment: "Congress shall make no law . . . abridging freedom of speech, or of the press."[64] In light of the history of the ratification of the Constitution, the First Amendment coupled with the Tenth Amendment gave the Republicans much ammunition.

In 1787, proponents of the Constitution had argued during the ratification debates that a bill of rights was unnecessary because of the enumeration of powers. Alexander Hamilton in *Federalist* No. 84 asked: "For why declare that things shall not be done which there is no power to do? Why for instance, should it be said that liberty of the press shall not be restrained, when no power is given by which restrictions may be imposed?"[65] With such an understanding of the Constitution, the definitions of freedom of the press were irrelevant. Freedom of the press could mean no prior restraints, but to legislate concerning the exercise of this right Congress would still need to invoke an enumerated power.

In the face of Republican arguments, Otis fell back to inherent powers. He insisted that every government possessed the power to defend itself against "injuries and outrages which endanger its existence."[66] Otis mocked the Republicans' newly found libertarianism and pointed to state laws prohibiting sedition. He thought it hypocritical that the Republicans would tolerate such laws at home, but object to the national government simply following suit. Moreover, Otis claimed that a sedition law was necessary and proper to execute the government's powers. The Necessary and Proper Clause follows the enumerated powers and provides that Congress may "make all Laws which shall be necessary and proper for carrying into Execution the foregoing Powers."[67] Gallatin reminded him that the reference to "foregoing Powers" meant that he must *first* point to an enumerated power, something the Federalists were unable to do. Otis also appealed to a general federal common law of crimes, but Republicans dared him to point to constitutional provision to support his theory.

As with the Alien Friends Act, the Federalists were not receptive to Republican constitutional arguments. The House passed the Sedition Law on July 10 by a 44-41 vote. The first section prohibited combinations or conspiracies to oppose any measure of the national government. It also reached those who counseled or advised an insurrection or an unlawful assembly. Persons convicted under section one were guilty of a high misdemeanor and faced a prison term ranging from six months to five years. They could also be fined up to $5,000.

The second section punished persons who wrote, uttered, published, or printed "false, scandalous and malicious" statements about the national government with the intent to bring it "into contempt or disrepute."[68] This section also reached those who "stir[red] up sedition" or assisted "any hostile designs of any foreign nation against the United States."[69] Violators were to be tried and convicted in federal courts, and could serve up to two years in prison and be fined up to $2,000. The third section permitted the accused to offer the truth as a defense and provided for the jury to decide questions of law and fact. The final section provided that the Sedition Act would expire along with President Adams's term of office on March 3, 1801.[70]

Though to the modern reader the Sedition Act breathes tyranny, in some respects it gave libertarians all they had ever asked for: increased responsibilities for the jury and truth as a defense. Before the Sedition Act, the jury's sole function in a sedition case was to determine publication.

In other words, the jury determined whether the accused wrote or uttered the statement and the judge determined the statement's criminality. In England, the Fox Libel Act of 1792 changed this and put the entire matter before the jury. Libertarians in the United States believed this was a great improvement, a bulwark against wrongful conviction. As Leonard Levy has pointed out, this additional role for the jury had little effect because most prosecutions for criticism of the government are brought in times of public excitement.[71] Add to this the common practice of marshals, appointed during the Federalist reign, choosing the jurors in federal cases, and one can see just what odds a criminal defendant faced.

Furthermore, truth as a defense, long advocated by libertarians, proved to be virtually useless as well. This stemmed from the fact that one cannot prove the truth or falsity of opinion. And indictments for seditious utterances issued during the Adams administration largely targeted political opinion. For example, a writer indicted for calling President Adams a "mock monarch" could not begin to prove the truth of the statement. Of course, assuming evidence could have been offered pointing to Adams's monarchial tendencies, such an introduction of evidence would have only angered the Federalist jury and could possibly have formed the basis of a second indictment for sedition.

In the face of pyrrhic victory, Republicans reconsidered freedom of speech and advocated a broader definition of this fundamental right. An excellent example of the new thinking is St. George Tucker's annotated edition of Blackstone's *Commentaries*. Described as the "American Blackstone," Tucker was the preeminent legal theorist of the early 1800s. His annotated 1803 edition of Blackstone was the standard legal text used in the first half of the nineteenth century. In 1790, Tucker succeeded George Wythe as professor of law at William and Mary. According to Clyde Wilson, Tucker was dissatisfied with Blackstone because "it was suffused with the principles of a monarchial and aristocratic state that Americans had only recently repudiated."[72] Thus, Tucker set out "to republicanize Blackstone."[73] In the place of "no prior restraints," Tucker called for an "absolute freedom of the press."[74] He asserted that "[e]very individual, certainly, has a right to speak, or publish, his sentiments on the measures of the government: to do this without restraint, control, or fear of punishment for so doing, is that which constitutes the genuine freedom of the press."[75] However, Tucker and other Republicans recognized that the several states possessed a broad police power and in the absence of a state constitutional provision could restrict freedom of speech. Though Republicans did not urge passage of state sedition acts, they recognized the power of a state to pass such a measure. This Republican constitutionalism underscores that the Sedition Act controversy was essentially a question of federalism. Republicans prized individual liberty, but thought it best secured when power was exercised at the local level.

Image 2.2 Instrumental in crafting an American libertarian theory of free speech, St. George Tucker's commentary on the Constitution was rooted in Jeffersonian principles and served as a guide for several generations of American lawyers. Courtesy of the Library of Virginia.

Prosecution and Persecution

With the Alien and Sedition Acts in place, Federalists prepared to exercise their newly claimed authority. In some cases just the threat posed by the Acts sufficed. As early as May 3, 1798, Jefferson reported to his friend Madison that "[t]he threatening appearance from the alien bills have so alarmed the French who are among us, that they are going off. A ship, chartered by themselves for this purpose, will sail within about a fortnight for France, with as many as she can carry."[76] The administration did target some foreigners under the Alien Friends Act and Adams signed blank orders of deportation which were never used. But with the general exodus caused by the Act, the administration never needed to officially invoke it.

Sedition was a different story. At least 25 people were arrested for criticizing the government and approximately 14 were indicted. To understand the vehemence with which the Federalists attacked political opposition, one need only examine the accounts of sedition trials. The trials featured sycophantic judges and prosecutors who vigorously punished citizens holding heterodox views. The four trials examined here are simply illustrative of Federalist efforts to silence the opposition. In surveying Federalist tactics, this chapter will examine a prosecution under the common law, a prosecution of a member of Congress, a prosecution at the seat of government, and the only prosecution conducted in a Southern state. Though different in many respects, a common thread of arbitrariness runs through all four prosecutions. And as arbitrariness is antithetical to limited government, Republicans believed that the trials were but a taste of things to come. If nothing else, a study of the trials confirms just how precarious liberty under law was in the late 1790s.

Remarkably, disdain for the Republican press led Federalists to take legal action before passage of the Sedition Act. In the absence of a statute they relied on the common law. Three weeks before President Adams signed the Sedition Act, Benjamin Bache was arrested for seditious libel. But for the publication of the Talleyrand letter, the Federalists might have waited until the statute was in place. Bache was represented by able counsel, Alexander James Dallas and Moses Levy. In an appearance before District Judge Richard Peters, counsel sought a dismissal of the case for lack of jurisdiction. The attorneys argued that federal courts possessed no common law jurisdiction in criminal cases. They observed that the Constitution, which is the sole source of jurisdiction for the national government, mentions nothing about a common law of crimes.

Because all powers not expressly delegated to the national government are retained by the states, they averred that the states alone could prosecute seditious libel.

Dallas and Levy cited *United States v. Worrall*,[77] a case that had just been decided in April 1798. The government prosecuted Worrall for attempting to bribe Commissioner of Revenue Tench Coxe. Dallas and Levy, who had also represented Worrall, argued to Supreme Court Justice Samuel Chase[78] and Judge Peters that the indictment could not be sustained under the common law because the offense was not specified in the Constitution or statute. Chase, agreeing with Dallas and Levy, accepted the arguments and opined that the national government had no common law and thus Worrall could not be prosecuted. Peters disagreed, stating that the government had the power to prosecute any offense against its well-being.

Of course, Chase's opinion in *Worrall* did not help Bache. Judge Peters made clear he had not changed his mind since the *Worrall* decision; therefore, he instructed counsel to refrain from rehashing old arguments. Precedent certainly favored Peters's stance. At the time, Chase was the only Federalist judge to question the propriety of federal common law prosecutions.[79] His colleagues had accepted common law jurisdiction since 1793.[80] However, in 1812 the Supreme Court confronted the issue and held that in the absence of a statute enacted pursuant to Congress's enumerated powers, federal courts could not assume jurisdiction over criminal offenses.[81]

But the 1812 decision could not assist Bache in the summer of 1798. Peters set bail at $2,000 and demanded that two sureties each post $1,000 to ensure Bache's presence at the trial scheduled for the October term. Offended at the insinuation of attempted escape, Bache declared that he would "prefer death, as a victim, to a flight that would render his innocence suspected."[82] Unfortunately, Bache got his wish. Yellow fever struck Philadelphia and 3,500 city dwellers died that summer. Bache contracted the fever and died on September 10, 1798. Because Bache's case never came to trial, we do not know what writings formed the basis of the indictment. Deprived of a conviction, the Federalists soon set their sights on other Republican luminaries.

Once the Sedition Act was in place, the Federalists had no need for the common law. Matthew Lyon, a congressman from Vermont, became the first victim of the statute. Born in Ireland, Lyon learned about oppression at an early age. His father was put to death for participating in an uprising against the British government, and young Lyon soon resolved to emigrate to North America. Crossing the Atlantic in 1765,

Lyon paid for his passage by permitting the ship's captain to sell him on the auction block in New York. Hence, Lyon entered American life as an indentured servant. Lyon was an industrious boy and bought his freedom after one year of indenture. He then went to work at the Ethan Allen Iron Works in Connecticut and married Allen's niece. Lyon and his wife followed Allen to Vermont where he soon found himself in the midst of the American Revolution. In 1775, Lyon assisted the Green Mountain Boys in capturing Fort Ticonderoga and later participated in Richard Montgomery's abortive Canada campaign. Lyon's military career reached its nadir when he was court-martialed by General Horatio Gates for his inability to prevent a retreat. However, Lyon was later restored to the army. Rising to prominence after the war, Lyon was elected to Congress in 1796.

The freshman congressman immediately raised eyebrows when he opposed the custom of representatives personally attending the president's first message to Congress. He thought it a "boyish piece of business" and suggested that the practice be discontinued. Though Federalists dubbed Lyon "Ragged Mat the Democrat," in 1798 he earned another nickname, "Spitting Lyon." While chatting with colleagues in the House, Lyon opined that the Federalist representatives from Connecticut ignored the interests of their constituents and that if a Republican newspaper could be launched there, the Federalists would be exposed and tossed out of office at the next election. Roger Griswold, a Federalist from Connecticut, overheard these remarks and made a disparaging comment about Lyon's war record. Lyon immediately turned and spat in his face. The Federalists attempted to use this episode to expel Lyon from the House, but they fell short of the necessary two-thirds vote. Unfortunately, the incident did not end there. Three days later Griswold assaulted Lyon on the floor of the House. Approaching Lyon from behind, Griswold began to beat him with a hickory stick. In an attempt to defend himself, Lyon grabbed the tongs from the fireplace and a scuffle ensued. Other representatives broke up the fight but it will always be remembered as a low point in the history of the House of Representatives.

Unable to expel Lyon and thus deprive the Republicans of a crucial vote, in the fall of 1798 the Federalists turned to the Sedition Act. In October 1798 Lyon was home campaigning for the upcoming election when a federal grand jury sitting at Rutland, Vermont, indicted him on three counts. The first count dealt with a letter written by Lyon in which he accused President Adams of sacrificing the public welfare "in a continual grasp for power"; "thirst[ing] for a ridiculous pomp, foolish adulation, and selfish avarice"; and turning away office seekers who showed an independent spirit.[83] The second count accused Lyon of maliciously publishing a letter from an American in France who queried why Congress had not sent President Adams to "a mad house."[84] The third count was "for assisting, counseling, aiding, and abetting the publication of the same."[85] Lyon's attorneys could not make the journey to Rutland because of bad weather and thus Lyon proceeded without the aid of counsel. Supreme Court Justice William Paterson and District Judge Samuel Hitchcock presided over the trial.

At the beginning of the trial, the judges struck one juror who had reportedly said within earshot of the deputy sheriff that Lyon "would not, or should not, be condemned."[86] Lyon then challenged the seating of two jurors who he knew thought ill of him. One had even written a newspaper article "inveighing politically and personally against" him.[87] The judges struck the author of the article, but seated the other juror because Lyon could produce no evidence of prejudice.

Accounts of the trial indicate that the prosecution made quick work of its task. As to the first count, Lyon admitted writing and publishing the letter. Next, witnesses testified that Lyon at public meetings had read from the "mad house" letter and that the reading had caused a disturbance. The prosecution supported the final count by introducing evidence that Lyon's wife had delivered the "mad house" letter to a printer for publication. With its case concluded, the prosecution summed up the evidence for the jury and emphasized Lyon's evil intentions to defame the government of the United States.

At this point, Justice Paterson began to charge the jury. Lyon politely interrupted him and asked for an opportunity to present his case in chief. Justice Paterson, surprised that Ragged Mat the Democrat had anything to offer, directed him to proceed. Lyon's defense centered on the constitutionality of the Sedition Act, the innocence of the statements, and the truth of the statements. Lyon spoke for two hours, but his arguments undoubtedly suffered from his lack of legal training. He offered no witnesses in support of his first two arguments. To prove the truth of the statements, Lyon asked Justice Paterson whether he had "dined with the President and observed his ridiculous pomp and parade?"[88] Justice Paterson responded that he had dined with President Adams, but had observed "a great deal of plainness and simplicity."[89] Lyon then rested his case.

In his charge to the jurors, Justice Paterson made clear that they were to ignore Lyon's challenge to the constitutionality of the Sedition Act. "[U]ntil this law is declared null and void by a tribunal competent for the purpose," instructed Paterson, "its validity cannot be disputed."[90] He reminded the jurors that they were only to determine whether Lyon published the statements and whether he did so seditiously. After an hour's deliberation, the jury returned a verdict of guilty. The court imposed a four-month prison sentence and a fine of $1,000.

Lyon's confinement was especially difficult. Rather than being imprisoned at Rutland, the county of his residence, the marshal transported him to Vergennes, approximately 44 miles to the north. According to Lyon, his cell was "about sixteen feet long by twelve wide, with a necessary in one corner, which affords a stench about equal to the Philadelphia docks in the month of August."[91] The cell had one window with but "the iron bars to keep the cold out."[92] Thousands of Vermonters petitioned President Adams to pardon their duly chosen congressional representative. Adams refused, stating that "penitence must precede pardon."[93] But Lyon believed he had no reason to be penitent and his constituents agreed. In an effort to send a message to the Federalists, the people overwhelmingly reelected Lyon to the House while he was serving his prison term. Senator Stevens T. Mason of Virginia, as well as ordinary Vermonters, collected the money to pay Lyon's hefty fine. They reasoned that Lyon was suffering on behalf of all Republicans and thus all should contribute to payment of the fine.

On the morning of Lyon's release, rumors abounded that he would be arrested as soon as he stepped from the cell. The marshal had examined some of Lyon's letters written from prison and believed them seditious. To thwart the marshal, upon release Lyon announced "I am on my way to Philadelphia," and thus invoked his congressional privilege from arrest when traveling to Congress. Upon his arrival in Philadelphia, the Federalists tried to expel Lyon from Congress because of the sedition conviction. For the third time they failed to garner the necessary two-thirds majority. Rather than infer the people's displeasure from Lyon's reelection, the Federalists learned nothing from the affair. Their obstinacy would cost them the next election.

For a proceeding occurring in the outer reaches of the union, Lyon's trial garnered much publicity. However, Thomas Cooper's sedition trial in Philadelphia was a true spectacle. Attended by congressmen, members of the Adams administration, and the Philadelphia press, the trial was a national affair. Cooper was a multitalented lawyer and English radical who emigrated to the United States in 1794. A friend and follower of Dr. Joseph Priestly, Cooper has been aptly described by Dumas Malone as "a passionate advocate of political and intellectual freedom against tyranny in any guise, and an enthusiastic promulgator of what he believed to be the truth."[94] In England, Cooper had been a supporter of the French Revolution and had seen colleagues prosecuted for sedition. He hoped to find more tolerant climes in North America, but the Federalists proved themselves great imitators of the English.

Cooper first locked horns with the Federalists when he represented William Duane, Bache's successor at the *Aurora*. Duane had published a Senate electoral count bill which proposed to alter by statute, rather than constitutional amendment, the method of counting presidential electoral votes. Under the proposal, a Grand Committee of Thirteen would meet in secrecy to count the votes of the presidential electors. The Federalist-controlled House and Senate were each to choose six committee members, and the Federalist chief justice of the Supreme Court was to preside. The bill was a blatant attempt to steal the upcoming 1800 presidential election from Jefferson, and the bill's exposure in the *Aurora* angered the Senate. Accusing Duane of breaching the Senate's secrecy, a Senate Committee on Privilege declared him guilty of sedition. After the Senate commanded Duane to appear to explain himself, Duane retained Alexander Dallas and Thomas Cooper to provide a defense. The Senate resolved that Duane could have counsel, but it refused to permit Dallas and Cooper to inquire into the Senate's jurisdiction, which as a legislative body it clearly lacked. Cooper and Dallas declined to appear before the Senate with "gags" in their mouths and Duane chose to hide rather than proceed *pro se*. Powerless to capture Duane, the Senate abandoned emulation of star chamber and left Duane's prosecution to the judicial system.

Just weeks after his comment about the Senate's gag, Cooper was arrested for sedition. A handbill Cooper wrote five months earlier formed the basis of the prosecution. The handbill was in response to an attack on Cooper for criticizing the Adams administration while serving as the editor of the Sunbury and Northumberland *Gazette*. Cooper's detractor accused him of maligning the administration because President Adams had declined Cooper's request for an appointment as one of the agents arbitrating disputes over American and British debts. In the handbill, Cooper denied revenge as a motive inasmuch as his remarks on the administration were two years removed from the request. He next turned to the recent conduct of the Adams administration:

> Nor do I see any impropriety in making the request of Mr. Adams. At that time he had just entered into office; he was hardly in the infancy of political mistake: even those who doubted his capacity thought well of his intentions. Nor were we yet saddled with the expense of a permanent

navy, or threatened, under his auspices, with the existence of a standing army. Our credit was not yet reduced so low as to borrow money at eight percent. in time of peace, while the unnecessary violence of official expressions might justly have provoked war. Mr. Adams had not yet projected his embassies to Prussia, Russia and the Sublime Porte, nor had he yet interfered, as President of the United States, to influence the decisions of a court of justice—a stretch of authority which the monarch of Great Britain would have shrunk from . . . .[95]

For the above criticism, the government indicted Cooper. Justice Chase and Judge Peters presided over Cooper's trial. Defending himself, Cooper first tried to get the court to subpoena President Adams and other high officials. The court refused, fearing the resourceful Cooper would attempt to put President Adams on trial. Denied his star witness of executive folly, Cooper then asked for more time to obtain authenticated copies of some of the President's addresses. The court gave Cooper three days, but the administration proved uncooperative in supplying material. Cooper received no succor from the court and his trial proceeded.

Attorney General William Rawle opened the case for the government and accused Cooper of "publish[ing] a false, scandalous and malicious attack on the character of the President . . . with an intent to excite the hatred and contempt of the people of this country against the man of their choice."[96] Rawle argued that the jury should make an example of Cooper to deter future licentiousness. He attributed Cooper's handbill to "the basest motives" and accused Cooper of violating his sacred duty of citizenship—support of the government.[97] Rawle called but one witness and elicited testimony that Cooper had expressed pride in authoring the handbill. After a soliloquy on the evils of the handbill, Rawle rested the prosecution's case.

Cooper assured the jury he would prove that the statements in the indictment were true, that the statements were made without malicious imputation, and that his motives were pure. Cooper challenged the Rawle's assertion about the duties of citizenship. "But this confidence [in the government] ought not to be unlimited," said Cooper, "and need not be paid up in advance; let it be earned before it be reposed . . . ."[98] As Cooper mounted his defense, it was clear that he was not speaking merely to the court. The defense was more of an indictment of President Adams and a message to the people to support Jefferson and the Republicans in the election that was only months away. Cooper questioned how political opinions could be tested in courts of law and predicted that the government's prosecutions would produce "conviction neither in the mind of the sufferer nor of the public."[99]

Cooper next went through the allegedly seditious writing. Turning first to the "infancy of a political mistake" remark, he asked whether upon taking the oath of office a president is cloaked with infallibility. "I know that in England the king can do no wrong," said Cooper, "but I did not know till now that the President of the United States had the same attribute."[100] As for doubting the capacity of President Adams, Cooper observed that almost half the people in the election of 1796 had chosen Jefferson. Cooper questioned whether half the nation had been guilty of seditious behavior for their ballots. Cooper also attempted to prove the truth of his statements concerning a standing army, navy, and debt. As Cooper read from several newspapers, the court observed that normally a defendant would be permitted to read only from authenticated documents. But because Cooper was *pro se* the court was lenient.

After Cooper presented his case and Rawle enjoyed a short rebuttal, Justice Chase charged the jury. Chase observed that it was "necessary to the peace and welfare of this country, that these offences should meet with their proper punishment, since ours is a government founded on the opinions and confidence of the people."[101] Chase instructed the jury that if a person criticizes public officials "he effectually saps the foundation of the government."[102] Chase postulated that the national government could "only be destroyed in two ways; the introduction of luxury, or the licentiousness of the press."[103] In essence, Chase made clear that Cooper was guilty of the latter and that a guilty verdict would vindicate the government in the eyes of the citizenry.

Chase eventually moved from his Federalist civics lessons to the law of the Sedition Act. He charged that all Rawle had to prove was publication and malicious intent. Publication was clear and Chase reminded the jury that Cooper had admitted publication to a witness. He then moved to intent and asserted that Cooper's "conduct showed that he intended to dare and defy the government, and to provoke them, and his subsequent conduct satisfies my mind that such was his disposition."[104] After examining the seditious statements, Chase further declared the handbill was "intended to mislead the ignorant, and inflame their minds against the President, and to influence their votes on the next election."[105] Lastly, Chase shot down Cooper's defense of truth and instructed the jury that Cooper "must prove every charge he has made to be true; he must prove it to the marrow."[106]

So charged, the jury likely feared that a verdict of not guilty would have earned them arrest for sedition. Chase—seldom impartial—got the verdict he desired. He fined Cooper $400 and sentenced him to six months in prison. "I do not want to oppress," Chase said as he sentenced Cooper, "but I will restrain, as far as I can, all such licentious attacks on the government of the country."[107]

Those unfamiliar with Justice Chase might believe his conduct outrageous. However, during Cooper's trial Chase was on his best behavior. He controlled his temper, and his political sermon to the jury was fairly typical of the day. Judges often viewed jury instructions as lessons in citizenship as well as explanations of the applicable law in the case. Fortunately, the final sedition trial discussed here, that of James Thomson Callender, presents a more accurate view of Justice Chase.

Callender was born in Scotland in 1758.[108] An ardent Scottish nationalist, Callender fled to the United States in 1793 to avoid prosecution for his radical pamphlet, *Political Progress in Britain*. Upon arriving in Philadelphia, Callender lent his pen to the Republican press and produced numerous articles on Hamilton's financial plan and the danger of British influence. In his *History of the Year 1796*, Callender charged Hamilton with dipping into the public till and secret meetings connected with this impropriety. In answering Callender's charges, an embarrassed Hamilton admitted to an adulterous affair and blackmail, but denied any misuse of public funds. For humiliating their leader, Hamilton's myrmidons in the government designated Callender for prosecution under the Alien and Sedition Acts. In order to escape the Alien Friends Act, Callender became a naturalized citizen. He then relocated from Philadelphia to Richmond in hopes of avoiding prosecution under the Sedition Act. Though Callender found the political atmosphere in Virginia much more hospitable, he could not escape Justice Chase.

Chase was scheduled to hold court in Richmond, and while in Maryland a friend gave him a copy of Callender's *The Prospect before Us*. According to Callender's pamphlet:

> The reign of Mr. Adams has been one continued tempest of malignant passions. As President, he has never opened his lips, or lifted his pen without threatening or scolding; the grand object of his administration has been to exasperate the rage of contending parties, to calumniate and destroy every man who differs in opinion. . . . The object of Mr. Adams was to recommend a French war, professedly for the sake of supporting American commerce, but in reality for the sake of yoking us into alliance with the British tyrant. . . . He was a professed aristocrat; he had proved faithful and serviceable to the British interest.[109]

Chase seethed after reading Callender's attack on Adams. He described Callender's pamphlet as "a libel so profligate and atrocious, that it excited disgust and indignation in every breast not wholly depraved."[110]

He lamented that Callender had not been hanged and promised to punish Callender if Republican Virginia was "not too depraved to furnish a jury of good and respectable men."[111]

A grand jury indicted Callender for 20 offensive passages appearing in *The Prospect before Us*, and Chase prepared to silence another Republican journalist. Philip Norborne Nicholas, George Hay, and William Wirt, all prominent attorneys in Virginia, volunteered to defend Callender in the only prosecution under the Sedition Act brought in a Southern state. The three attorneys soon understood why Judge Peters said he "never sat with [Justice Chase] without pain, as he was forever getting into some intemperate and unnecessary squabble."[112]

Callender pled not guilty and his lawyers immediately moved for a continuance till the next term so they could procure material witnesses and documents. Chase denied the motion but did postpone the trial for five days. When the court reconvened, Hay renewed the motion for a postponement, arguing that it was the custom in Virginia for the accused to be tried during the succeeding term of court. Hay clearly hoped to get a more favorable judge, but Chase was anxious to try Callender. Hay also argued that Callender's statements were opinion and not triable. Chase became angered at this line of argument and proclaimed that "[a]ny falsehood, however palpable and wicked, may be justified by this species of argument."[113] Chase then ordered the marshal to call the jury. Nicholas attempted to challenge the seating of a juror who had reportedly expressed hostile opinions on *The Prospect before Us*. Nicholas wanted to ask all jurors whether they had formed and delivered an opinion on the pamphlet, but Chase refused his request. Chase would only ask the jurors whether they had formed or delivered an opinion on the indictment. As the jurors had not read the indictment, their answers were, of course, "no." The Federalist jury, with an openly hostile juror, was sworn.

Though the prosecution was charged with proving intent to defame along with maliciousness and publication, the prosecutor in his opening statement attempted to shift the burden to Callender. The prosecution asserted that unless Callender could prove truth in all parts of the publication the jury had to return a guilty verdict. The prosecutor then called nine witnesses in order to prove that Callender authored *The Prospect before Us*. With this established, the prosecutor attempted to introduce the pamphlet, but Hay objected because the pamphlet was not specifically mentioned in the indictment. Passages from the booklet were quoted, but the indictment, which must be precise, made no mention of the title of the pamphlet. After a lengthy argument, Chase permitted the prosecution to introduce the pamphlet into evidence. The prosecution then discussed *The Prospect before Us* and concluded its case.

The first witness called during Callender's case in chief was John Taylor of Caroline. Before Nicholas could ask a question, Chase demanded to know what the defense intended to prove. Nicholas replied that they hoped to prove that Callender was justified in calling Adams an aristocrat. Chase required Nicholas to submit in writing the proposed questions, but Nicholas objected that no such onus was placed on the prosecution. After heated comments, Chase declared that Taylor's testimony was inadmissible. According to Chase, evidence of truth that did not go to the whole charge was improper. Nicholas replied that it was common practice to call different witnesses to prove different parts of a statement, but Chase rejected this. Chase feared the examination of Taylor would cause much embarrassment for the President. As with Cooper's trial, Chase wanted to keep the accused on the defensive.

Not permitted to call witnesses, Wirt rose and argued to the jurors that as the triers of law and fact they could find the Sedition Act unconstitutional. Chase stopped Wirt, instructed him to sit, and delivered an opinion on the function of the jury. Chase refused to permit the jury to assume power greater than the national legislature. When counsel attempted to present contrary arguments to the court, Chase interrupted them and insisted on referring to Callender's attorneys as "young gentlemen." Insulted and by Chase's remarks, Hay sat down and refused to proceed even though Chase promised not to interrupt again.

Denied the opportunity to present a meaningful defense, Callender's counsel rested their case. After two hours' deliberation, the jury returned a verdict of guilty. Chase fined Callender $200 and sentenced him to nine months' imprisonment.

Republicans would not forget Chase's conduct during Callender's trial. In 1804–05, Chase was impeached by the House and tried in the Senate. Five of the eight articles of impeachment dealt with the Callender trial.[114] The Senate did not convict, thanks largely to the ineptness of John Randolph, who managed the case for the House of Representatives. Randolph was not trained in the law and was no match for Chase's attorney Luther Martin. In addition, Vice President Aaron Burr's desire that the trial be political rather than a strictly legal matter hurt the Republicans' efforts.[115]

Callender died in 1803, but he probably would not have testified against Chase had he lived. After the Republicans won the election of 1800, Callender expected to be rewarded for his work and prison time. Callender wrote Madison, Jefferson's secretary of state, demanding the

Richmond postmaster's position. Callender believed he had "gone to desperate lengths to serve the party," and expressed fear that Jefferson would "sacrifice me, as a kind of scapegoat to political *decorum* as a kind of compromise to federal feelings."[116] Jefferson declined to make the appointment, and a vengeful Callender offered his services to the Federalists. It was Callender who first published a detailed account of the Sally Hemings story.

* * *

Though the Sedition Act prosecutions were few in number, by targeting writers and editors like Callender, the Federalists made the most of these efforts. Information was scarce in the early Republic, and the Federalists attempted to hamstring the opposition press. Hoping to leave the people with only pro-administration newspapers, the Federalists sought to monopolize the marketplace of ideas. In retrospect, the Federalists waited too long to carry out their plans. Adams had barely defeated Jefferson in 1796, and the Republican press dared even criticize George Washington.

Though many Republicans did temper their comments in response to the Acts and prosecutions, the Whig tradition was firmly rooted in the United States. And the right to offer opinion on the conduct of public officials was a cardinal principle of this tradition.[117] In the winter of 1798, Whiggery joined with subsidiarity and a belief in the common man to give substance to protests against the Acts and prosecutions. Engendering the Kentucky and Virginia Resolutions, this combination would eventually end the decade-long reign of the Federalists.

CHAPTER 3
THE PRINCIPLES OF 1798

In the waning months of 1798, the legislatures of Kentucky and Virginia voiced their objections to the Federalists' Alien and Sedition Acts. Introduced by John Breckinridge, the Kentucky Resolutions were adopted by the state House of Representatives on November 10, 1798, and by the state Senate on November 13, 1798. One month later, John Taylor of Caroline offered similar resolutions in the Virginia legislature. The state House of Delegates approved the Virginia Resolutions on December 21, 1798, and the state Senate concurred three days later. Unbeknownst to contemporaries, the drafts of the Kentucky and Virginia Resolutions were prepared by Thomas Jefferson and James Madison, respectively. The involvement of a sitting vice president and the Father of the Constitution indicates the severity of the situation. The Republican Party was replete with philosophers, jurists, and essayists—most of whom were familiar with the core concepts of the Constitution. Rather than deferring to others, Jefferson and Madison took it upon themselves to contest Federalist dogma. In but a few hundred words, the Kentucky and Virginia Resolves explained the fundamental principles of the Constitution and challenged the rationale of the Alien and Sedition Acts. Though written over two centuries ago, the Resolves' insights into the American experiment with self-government remain instructive as we continue to debate the proper roles of the state and national governments.

The story of the Kentucky and Virginia Resolutions begins on June 27, 1798, the day Vice President Jefferson left Philadelphia. When he departed the sedition bill was still under discussion, but Jefferson knew that the Federalists had the numbers to ensure its passage. His presence would accomplish nothing. Upon entering his beloved Virginia, Jefferson was greeted as a hero. At Fredericksburg, an artillery company announced his return, and local dignitaries held a lavish feast in his honor. From Fredericksburg, Jefferson traveled to Montpelier,

Madison's residence, and the two friends no doubt talked about measures to check the national government's latest encroachment on state powers. In his waning years, Jefferson posited that Republican luminaries might have met at Monticello to discuss penning a set of resolves. Jefferson speculated that John Breckinridge, Wilson Cary Nicholas, and James Madison were in attendance, but feared he was "misremember[ing]" the details.[1] Most scholars agree that no such meeting took place,[2] and we will most likely never know exactly what happened in the summer of 1798. Rightly fearing incarceration would result if they were connected to the Kentucky and Virginia Resolutions, Jefferson and Madison left few written records during these tense times.

In fact, Madison's authorship of the Virginia Resolves was not revealed until 1809 when in the Richmond *Enquirer* John Taylor of Caroline acknowledged Madison's role. In 1814, Taylor in his *An Inquiry into the Principles and Policy of the Government of the United States* revealed in a footnote Jefferson's authorship of the Kentucky Resolutions, but the public paid little attention to this unsupported assertion. Seven years later the Richmond *Enquirer* repeated the fact of Jefferson's authorship. Joseph Cabell Breckinridge, believing his father the author, wrote Jefferson and requested that he deny the story. Jefferson replied that the *Enquirer* article was correct, yet he offered palliative comments on John Breckinridge's "zeal and talents."[3] Jefferson's desire to lessen the blow to Joseph Cabell coupled with advanced age likely led to faulty recollection of the meeting at Monticello.

Though the details of the planning phase of the Kentucky and Virginia Resolutions elude us, the choice of state legislatures as the vehicles of protest is not shrouded in mystery. Jefferson fervently believed that the state governments "were the true barriers of our liberty in this country."[4] Madison also recognized the states' role in limiting the national government. In *Federalist* No. 51, he described the horizontal and vertical checks and balances established by the Constitution and plainly stated that the state and national governments "will controul each other; at the same time each will be controulled by itself."[5] The check of the state governments on the national government was a major selling point of the Constitution. In the Virginia ratifying convention, for example, friends of the Constitution emphasized that the state legislatures would "be a powerful check" on Congress.[6] Of all people, Alexander Hamilton eloquently expressed the idea in *Federalist* No. 28. According to Hamilton, it was an "axiom" of the American system of government "that the state governments will in all possible contingencies afford complete security against invasions of the public liberty by national authority." He continued by postulating that should the national government pose a danger, the states could "at once adopt a regular plan of opposition, in which they can combine all the resources of the community. They can readily communicate with each other in the different states; and unite their common forces for the protection of their common liberty."[7]

In a little-known episode just before the Sedition Act crisis, Jefferson, responding to the actions of the grand jury of the federal circuit court sitting in Richmond, followed Hamilton's wisdom in *Federalist* No. 28 and laid much of the foundation on which the Kentucky Resolves would be built. In the spring of 1797 the grand jury formally accused Samuel Jordan Cabell, who was the congressional representative from Jefferson's district, of seditious libel under the common law. The first of its kind, the indictment was a precursor to the assault mounted a year later against Benjamin Bache. Cabell had sent a letter to his constituents denouncing the Adams administration and was subsequently indicted for "endeavoring at a time of real public danger, to disseminate unfounded calumnies against the happy government of the United States, and thereby separate the people therefrom; and to increase or produce a foreign influence, ruinous to the peace, happiness, and independence of these United States." Jefferson drafted an anonymous petition to the Virginia House of Delegates in which he called for the punishment of the offending jurors. In the petition, Jefferson viewed the federal grand jury's actions as violating the "natural right" of free correspondence, interfering with the affairs of Congress, and putting "the legislative department under the feet of the Judiciary."[8]

Though James Monroe suggested that Jefferson send his protest to Congress rather than to the state legislature, Jefferson rapidly dismissed such an idea. In rejecting Monroe's advice, Jefferson explained that the national government was claiming powers not delegated under the Constitution and thus "seiz[ing] all doubtful ground. We must join in the scramble, or get nothing." Moreover, Jefferson understood the federal character of the union was at stake. He continued his letter to Monroe by observing that "it is of immense consequence that the States retain complete authority as possible over their own citizens," rather than bowing to a "foreign jurisdiction."[9] Clearly, one year before the Kentucky Resolutions, Jefferson understood the very real threat of centralization and believed that the proper place to rally Republican forces was at the state level.

Nevertheless, the role of the state legislatures should not lead to the conclusion that the movement against the Alien and Sedition Acts had

Image 3.1 Thomas Jefferson drafted the Kentucky Resolutions of 1798 and led the nonviolent Revolution of 1800. Courtesy of the Library of Virginia.

no grassroots origin. On the contrary, local meetings were held throughout the union and the people affixed their signatures to sundry petitions. In resolutions passed at these gathering, the people described it as their duty to "remonstrate in a decent and constitutional manner, with firmness and decision against laws, made in violation of the constitution." Seldom did these resolutions mince words, as the people declared the Acts "tyrannical" and "afford[ing] just cause for alarm."[10] Moreover, many of these gatherings attracted sizeable crowds. In Lexington, Kentucky, for example, a meeting was scheduled at a local church to consider the Acts, but had to be moved to the town square because 5,000 citizens—twice the population of Lexington—assembled.[11] Republican leaders welcomed the mass gatherings, but believed that random protests would not be as effective as a coordinated effort instituted in the various state legislatures. Hence, Jefferson and Madison began work on what would become the Kentucky and Virginia Resolutions.

The Compact

Jefferson began his draft of the Kentucky Resolves by declaring that the states were "not united on the principle of unlimited submission to their general government." Instead, the states by a "compact . . . constituted a general government for special purposes."[12] Madison's Virginia Resolutions, though beginning with a statement of attachment to the union, also described the Constitution as a "compact to which the States are parties."[13] By compact, Jefferson and Madison meant an agreement or contract between independent parties, giving rise to rights and obligations.[14] Thinking in terms of compacts would have been very familiar to the Revolutionary generation. In protesting against assumptions of power by Parliament, the colonists repeatedly appealed to the "principles of the English Constitution, and the several charters or compacts" in order to vindicate their rights.[15] Indeed, American colonists could trace the centrality of compacts in the New World back to 1620, when the Pilgrims entered into the Mayflower Compact by which they established a "civil Body Politic" and agreed to be bound by its laws.[16]

Though the compact theory of the Constitution has fallen from favor in modern times, Jefferson scholar Dumas Malone has observed that in the late eighteenth century "this view of [the Constitution] was widely held."[17] Proponents of ratification of the Constitution often described it as a "compact . . . between several sovereign and independent societies already formed and organized."[18] Others, however, denied the compact theory. James Wilson, for example, in the Pennsylvania ratifying convention declared that "it cannot be said, that [the Framers] thought they were making a compact, because I cannot discover the least trace of a compact in that system."[19] Wilson's assertion was based on the belief that the people of the nation were to ratify the Constitution. Pointing to the preamble, Wilson declared that "from [the people's] ratification alone it is to take its constitutional authenticity."[20]

At first blush, Wilson's argument is convincing. The preamble does provide that "We the People of the United States ... do ordain and establish this Constitution for the United States of America." However, an examination of Madison's *Notes of the Debates in the Federal Convention* dispels this simplistic understanding. The preamble of the first draft of the Constitution read as follows:

> We the People of the States of New Hampshire, Massachusetts, Rhode-Island and Providence Plantations, Connecticut, New-York, New-Jersey, Pennsylvania, Delaware, Maryland, Virginia, North-Carolina, South-Carolina, and Georgia, do ordain, declare, and establish the following Constitution for the Government of Ourselves and our Posterity.[21]

Once it dawned on the Framers that all states might not ratify, the preamble was altered and assumed its present form. The debates in no way indicate that a change in theory took place; the Framers never contemplated one great national act of ratification.[22] The Philadelphia Convention further decided that the ratifications of nine states would put the Constitution into effect among the states so ratifying. This was a wise decision inasmuch as North Carolina and Rhode Island did not ratify until long after the other 11 states. Placing the preamble in the context of ratification clearly demonstrates that the American people, acting as one body, did not ratify the Constitution.

Of course, caution must be used when describing the Constitution as a compact between the states. As recognized by Madison in his Report of 1800, the term "states" has three different meanings: (1) territories occupied by political societies, (2) governments established by the political societies, and (3) "the people composing those political societies, in their highest sovereign capacity."[23] According to Madison, it was in this third sense that the states ratified the Constitution. Though some might accuse Madison of splitting hairs by emphasizing that *the people of the several states*, rather than *the people of the nation*, ratified the Constitution,[24] such a distinction was critical to the Revolutionary generation. As Gordon Wood has observed, the question of where sovereignty resided "was at the heart of the Anglo-American argument that led to the Revolution."[25]

Sovereignty is the supreme power of governance. The British believed that sovereignty resided in Parliament, which could make laws binding on all subjects of the crown. The colonists, on the other hand, believed that sovereignty resided in each colonial legislature.[26] After achieving independence, the theory of sovereignty further developed and Americans rejected the idea that an artificial body such as a legislature could possess supreme power. Rather than each state legislature possessing ultimate power, Americans realized that people of each state were the sovereign authority and had delegated to their elected representatives certain powers. Thus, we often say that the people of the several states posses *ultimate* sovereignty and their chosen representatives possess *governmental* or *legislative* sovereignty.[27] The question of sovereignty posed no problem under the Articles of Confederation because the confederation Congress's power did not extend to individuals. For example, as mentioned in the opening chapter, the Confederation government could not lay taxes; it could only make requisitions of the state governments. However, with the Constitution of 1787 the question again arose. After much study and debate, the Framers created a system in which the people of the several states delegated power to two governmental sovereigns: the national and state governments. "The Federal and State Governments are in fact but different agents and trustees of the people," wrote Madison in *Federalist* No. 46, "instituted with different powers, and designated for different purposes."[28] By ratifying the Constitution in separate conventions, the people of each state took a portion of the power originally delegated to their state governments and transferred this power to the national government.[29] The powers possessed by the state governments before the Constitution, and not affected by the Constitution, remained with the state governments. At the time of the American Revolution this division of power had been unthinkable—Parliament was either sovereign in all aspects of law-making or it was powerless to legislate for the colonies. But with the Constitution, governmental sovereignty was divided.[30] This division of power and creation of a national government occurred in the several state conventions and was effective only between the states choosing to ratify the Constitution, thus making the states in their highest sovereign capacities parties to the compact.

Enumerated Powers

After describing the Constitution as a compact, Jefferson observed in his draft of the Kentucky Resolutions that the states delegated to the national government only "certain definite powers."[31] Madison's Virginia Resolutions declared that the national government's powers were "limited by the plain sense and intention of the instrument constituting that compact; as no further valid than they are authorized by the grants enumerated in the compact."[32] In 1787–88, as friends of the Constitution lobbied the several states to ratify, they repeatedly stressed the document's enumeration of powers. Much blood and treasure had been expended for the right of the separate colonies, which became independent states, to govern themselves. Because the Articles of Confederation secured each state's right of self-government, Americans were hesitant to swap the Articles for another system. Moreover, the Articles were often viewed with pride rather than embarrassment. "The Confederation," reminded Patrick Henry on the floor of the Virginia ratifying convention, "the despised government, merits . . . the highest encomium: it carried us through a long and dangerous war; it rendered us victorious in that bloody conflict with a powerful nation; it has secured us a territory greater than any European monarch possesses."[33] Of course, Henry and other Anti-Federalists realized that the Confederation was deficient, especially regarding commerce and foreign affairs. But viewing liberty as "the greatest of all earthly blessings," they preferred to live with the Confederation's weaknesses rather than risk all with a new constitution.[34]

Even those less sanguine than Henry about the efficacy of the Confederation feared that the Constitution delegated too much power to the national government. Melancton Smith, speaking to the New York ratifying convention, admitted that the Framers of the Articles "too much restricted the powers of the general government." However, he feared that with the Constitution of 1787 "it is now proposed to go into the contrary, and a more dangerous extreme—to remove all barriers, to give the new government free access to our pockets, and ample command of our persons."[35] Similarly, Elbridge Gerry, a member of the Philadelphia Convention, refused to sign the Constitution because "some of the powers of the legislature are ambiguous, and others indefinite and dangerous," thus presenting the national government with ample opportunity to expand its powers.[36] This perceived ambiguity was a central theme in most Anti-Federalist newspaper essays of the day.[37]

Faced with these objections, proponents of the Constitution sought to assure Americans that they were not trading the Articles for an omnipotent national government. "[T]he powers of the federal government," Madison explained in the Virginia ratifying convention, "are enumerated; it can only operate in certain cases; it has legislative powers on defined and limited objects, beyond which it cannot extend its jurisdiction."[38] Picking up where Madison left off, Francis Corbin reminded the Virginia Anti-Federalists that "the internal administration of government is left to the state legislatures, who exclusively retain such powers as will give the states the advantages of small republics, without the danger commonly attendant on the weakness of such governments."[39]

Though these arguments carried the day and the Constitution was ratified, the states demanded amendments to ensure Congress would not claim undelegated powers. In its ratification message, Massachusetts insisted on "certain amendments and alterations . . . [to] more effectually guard against an undue administration of the federal government."[40] Massachusetts recommended "[t]hat it be explicitly declared that all powers not expressly delegated by the aforesaid Constitution are reserved to the several states."[41] South Carolina, New Hampshire, New York, and Rhode Island made similar demands.[42]

In response to the states' call for various amendments and Jefferson's insistence "that a bill of rights is what the people are entitled to against every government on earth,"[43] Madison, elected to the first Congress, began work on amendments once the body convened. Madison maintained that he had "always been in favor of a bill of rights; provided it be so framed as not to imply powers not meant to be included in the enumeration."[44] Congress soon drafted 12 amendments and submitted this bill of rights to the states. The preamble of the bill of rights recognized that the states had "expressed a desire, in order to prevent misconstruction or abuse of [the national government's] powers, that further declaratory and restrictive clauses should be added."[45] Perhaps the most important such clause was the twelfth amendment submitted (tenth ratified): "The powers not delegated to the United States by the Constitution, nor prohibited by it to the States, are reserved to the States respectively, or to the people."[46] For Jefferson, the Tenth Amendment quickly became "the foundation of the Constitution."[47]

In light of the arguments made in favor of ratification, the concerns expressed by the states, and the addition of the Tenth Amendment to the Constitution, the Resolutions' emphasis on enumerated powers was their least controversial element. As Herbert Storing has observed, all friends of the Constitution agreed that "the new general government w[ould] possess only the powers specifically granted to it, which [we]re no more than required to deal with national concerns."[48]

Assumption of Undelegated Powers

Despite the nearly universal agreement on enumerated powers, Jefferson and Madison in their respective resolutions proclaimed that the national government had exceeded the bounds of the Constitution on numerous occasions. Jefferson averred that a broad construction of the Constitution's provisions "goes to the destruction of all limits prescribed."[49] Madison expressed "deep regret, that a spirit has in sundry instances, been manifested by the federal government, to enlarge its powers by forced constructions of the constitutional charter which defines them." The end result of such a construction, Madison explained, would be a consolidation of the states "into one sovereignty" and a transformation of "the present republican system . . . into an absolute, or at best a mixed monarchy."[50] By inveighing against assumption of powers, Jefferson and Madison no doubt had in mind misuse of the General Welfare Clause and the Necessary and Proper Clause. As discussed in the previous chapter, the Federalists appealed to both as they pushed the Alien and Sedition Acts through Congress.

In his Report to the Virginia Assembly on the Virginia Resolves, Madison paid special attention to misuse of the General Welfare Clause. The Virginia Resolutions specifically stated that this language was "copied from the very limited grant of powers in the former articles of confederation" to ensure against misconstruction.[51] "[I]t will scarcely be said," Madison observed in his Report, that the common defense and general welfare language found in the Articles of Confederation was "ever understood to be either a general grant of power" or to permit the Confederation Congress to escape the Articles' enumeration of powers.[52] Echoing arguments made by Abraham Baldwin and Albert Gallatin in the House as they fought the Alien Friends Act, Madison noted that the Framers would have been foolish to enumerate powers if "general welfare" was the measure of congressional powers.[53]

The Virginia Resolutions did not specifically mention the Necessary and Proper Clause, but Jefferson's Kentucky Resolutions did. By the Necessary and Proper Clause, the Framers ensured that Congress could exercise all powers incident to the enumerated powers. During the national bank controversy in 1791, Hamilton advocated a broad reading of the clause.[54] "If the end be clearly comprehended within any of the specified powers," Hamilton advised, "& if the measure have an obvious relation to that end . . . it may safely be deemed to come within the compass of national authority."[55] And as a bank, in Hamilton's mind, had some relation to Congress's powers to tax, borrow money, regulate trade, and raise armies, he thought it was constitutional. Jefferson, on the other hand, argued that "necessary" was not tantamount to "convenient." To the Sage of Monticello, "necessary" encompassed only "those means without which the grant of power would be nugatory."[56] Like a broad interpretation of the General Welfare Clause, Jefferson feared that a Hamiltonian reading of the Necessary and Proper Clause "would swallow up all the delegated powers, and reduce the whole to one power."[57]

While Jefferson's remarks on assumption of powers evince great concern, Madison's go further and one can sense a feeling of betrayal. Hamilton and others, who would later be known as members of the Federalist party, joined with Madison in the late 1780s to lobby for ratification. As discussed above, these friends of the Constitution stressed the very limited nature of the national government. But once in power, many proponents of the Constitution seemed to forget their earlier assertions. The Constitution, Madison complained during the bank controversy, in "its adoption was brought about by one set of arguments, and . . . is now administered under the influence of another set."[58] Of course, Madison knew there would at times be good faith disagreements over the extent of national government's powers. George Washington, in presenting the proposed Constitution to the Confederation Congress, noted that the Philadelphia Convention found it "difficult to draw with precision the line between those rights which must be surrendered, and those which may be reserved."[59] If the text of the Constitution did not settle the matter, Madison determined early on that "[i]n controverted cases, the meaning of the parties to the instrument, if collected by reasonable evidence, is a proper guide."[60] Jefferson was in accord with Madison on this point, stating that the Constitution should be interpreted "according to the true sense in which it was adopted by the States, that in which it was advocated by its friends, & not that which its enemies apprehended."[61]

Nonetheless, strict constructionists realized that unforeseen circumstances might render the enumerated powers insufficient to deal with a great national object.[62] Rather than confer on the national government additional powers through construction, they believed that amendment was the proper course of action. "Had the power of making treaties, for example, been omitted, however necessary it might have been," Madison instructed supporters of the national bank, "the defect could only have been lamented, or supplied by an amendment of the Constitution."[63] This was the common understanding at the time of ratification.[64]

The ultimate danger from amendment by construction and the accompanying assumption of power, as Madison noted in the Virginia Resolutions, was consolidation. To Republicans, consolidation meant a government "which should have the sole and exclusive power, legislative, executive, and judicial, without any limitation."[65] In other words, an end to the experiment of divided governmental sovereignty. At the time of ratification, many Anti-Federalists claimed the Constitution established a consolidated government, but the friends of the Constitution attempted to refute this argument by pointing out that the states, not a national body, were to ratify the Constitution, and that the states retained their legislative sovereignty over most objects of lawmaking except for foreign policy and trade.[66] With assumption of undelegated powers via the Alien and Sedition Acts, some Republicans no doubt believed that the Anti-Federalists had been correct. Madison could only champion the text and clear intent of the state ratifying conventions as he watched the centralizers twist the Constitution beyond recognition. As Lance Banning has speculated, "had [Madison] actually foreseen how Hamilton and others would interpret and employ the Constitution, the Virginia delegation to the Constitutional Convention might have had a third non-signer."[67]

The Alien and Sedition Acts

From the general principles of the Constitution, the Kentucky and Virginia Resolutions turned to the Alien and Sedition Acts. Jefferson fired his first shot at the latter. In the second Resolve, he observed that the Constitution had given Congress the power to punish but a few crimes such as treason, counterfeiting, and piracy. This coupled with the Tenth Amendment, in Jefferson's view, rendered void Congress's attempt to punish criticism of the national government.

In the third Resolve, Jefferson analyzed the Sedition Act as a regulation of speech rather than a criminal law. He observed that the states "retain[ed] . . . the right of judging how far licentiousness of speech and of the press may be abridged without lessening their useful freedom."[68] Recognizing that the First Amendment also encompassed freedom of religion, Jefferson apprehended that congressional interference with one component of the Amendment would open the door for violation of the other.

The fourth, fifth, and sixth Resolves dealt with the Alien Friends Act. Jefferson began by asserting "[t]hat alien friends are under the jurisdiction and protection of the laws of the state wherein they are."[69] Appealing once again to the Tenth Amendment, he denied that the national government could assume power over alien friends. Next, Jefferson turned to the Slave Import Clause and contended that attempts to remove alien friends would be tantamount to prohibiting migration itself. As David Mayer has recognized, Jefferson's use of the clause demonstrates that he "was not above resorting to ingenious constitutional arguments when making the case for the limitation of governmental powers."[70] Finally, Jefferson assailed the Act on due process grounds. Jefferson thought it repugnant to the Constitution that the president could remove an alien based on suspicion alone. Not only did this deny the alien his right to a public trial, the confrontation of adverse witnesses, etcetera, but it also "transferr[ed] the power of judging any person . . . from the courts to the President of the U[nited] S[tates]."[71] Such a transfer, Jefferson feared, vested Adams with too much power inasmuch as the president already possessed full executive authority as well as a veto on legislative enactments.

Madison's Virginia Resolutions, which were less wordy than Jefferson's endeavor, made many of the same arguments. Madison found the Sedition Act especially odious because it attacked "that right of freely examining public characters and measures, and of free communication among the people thereon, which has ever been justly deemed, the only effectual guardian of every other right."[72] He ended his short discussion of the Acts by observing that precedents contrary to the Constitution would be fatal to other rights as well.

The Remedy

After concluding that the Alien and Sedition Acts were outside the bounds of the Constitution, Jefferson and Madison turned to the remedy. Early in the first Kentucky Resolve, Jefferson reasoned:

> that whensoever the General government assumes undelegated powers, its acts are unauthoritative, void, and of no force: that to this compact each state acceded as a state, and is an integral party, its co-states forming, as to itself, the other party: that the government created by this compact was not made the exclusive or final judge of the extent of the powers delegated to itself; since that would have made its discretion, and not the constitution, the measure of its powers; but that as in all other cases of compact among parties having no common judge, each party has an equal right to judge for itself, as well of infractions as of the mode and measures of redress.[73]

By declaring the Acts void, Jefferson borrowed yet again from Alexander Hamilton. In *Federalist* No. 33, Hamilton counseled that acts of the national government "which are not pursuant to its constitutional powers . . . will [not] become the supreme law of the land. These will be merely acts of usurpation and will deserve to be treated as such."[74] This, in a nutshell, was Jefferson's position as well.

Returning to this controversial topic in the eighth Resolve, Jefferson observed that were officials to abuse delegated powers, "a change by the people would be the constitutional remedy." However, upon an assumption of undelegated powers, "a nullification of the act is the rightful remedy: that every State has a natural right in cases not within the compact . . . to nullify of their own authority all assumptions of power." "Nevertheless," Jefferson continued, Kentucky "from motives of regard and respect for its co-states, has wished to communicate with them on this subject" as the states are "solely authorized to judge in the last resort of the powers exercised under [the compact]."

Jefferson further ventured that unconstitutional acts "unless arrested at the threshold, necessarily drive these states into revolution and blood." In turn, monocrats would use such an uprising to demonstrate that "man cannot be governed but by rod of iron." As for those who might think that he was overreacting, Jefferson reminded them that "free government is founded in jealousy, and not in confidence; it is jealousy not confidence which prescribes limited constitutions. . . . [I]n questions of power, then, let no more be heard of confidence in man, but bind him down from mischief by the chains of the constitution." Jefferson closed the eighth resolve by predicting that each state would "take measures of its own for providing that [the Alien and Sedition Acts], nor any others of the general government not plainly and intentionally authorized by the constitution, shall be exercised within their respective territories."[75] Jefferson provided for a committee of conference and correspondence to communicate the Kentucky Resolves to the several state legislatures.

This was not the first time that Jefferson had raised the possibility of the states taking measures to prevent unconstitutional national enactments from operating in their territories. As early as 1792, when he learned of plans to open a branch office of the first Bank of the United States in Richmond, Jefferson became irate. Writing to Madison, Jefferson suggested that the legislature declare that "[t]he power of erecting banks and corporations was not given to the general government" and that any person who recognized the bank as legitimate would be guilty of treason. The proposed legislative enactment, according to Jefferson, should state that "whosoever shall do any act under colour of the authority of a foreign legislature whether by signing notes, issuing or passing them, acting as director, cashier or in any other office relating to it shall be adjudged guilty of high treason and suffer death accordingly."[76] Rather than attempting to calm his friend, Madison responded that Jefferson's objections to the branch office "seem unanswerable."[77]

Madison's brief Virginia Resolves did not call on state legislatures to pass laws preventing enforcement of the Alien and Sedition Acts.

The Virginia Resolves simply declared that

> in case of deliberate, palpable, and dangerous exercise of other powers, not granted by the said compact, the States who are parties thereto, have the right and are duty bound, to interpose for arresting the progress of the evil, and for maintaining within their respective limits, the authorities, rights and liberties appertaining to them.[78]

Madison expressed confidence that the states would join with Virginia "in declaring, as it does hereby declare, that the [Alien and Sedition Acts], are unconstitutional."[79] The Virginia Resolutions concluded by asking the governor to transmit the Resolutions to the several state legislatures as well as Virginia's congressional delegation.

At this juncture with nullification in the forefront, one must remember that Jefferson's and Madison's drafts of the Resolutions underwent various changes before they were adopted. The changes to the former were significant, but the changes to the latter were minor. As the mover of the Kentucky Resolves, John Breckinridge was much more than Jefferson's "transmitting angel."[80] Once Governor James Garrard of Kentucky urged the legislature to consider a "protest against all unconstitutional laws and impolitic proceedings" of the national government,[81] Breckinridge was at the center of the drive to pass a set of resolves. Breckinridge had not been in direct communication with Jefferson, but received Jefferson's draft from Wilson Cary Nicholas, who had planned to deliver the draft to Republicans in the North Carolina legislature. Federalist electoral victories in the Tarheel state persuaded Nicholas to seek a more receptive audience for Jefferson's draft and he then turned to Breckinridge in Kentucky.

For the most part, Breckinridge adhered to Jefferson's draft except for three key changes. First, Breckinridge struck the term "nullification" from the Kentucky Resolutions. This change was undoubtedly made to aid passage of the Resolutions, but one should not give the change too much weight. Though the official Kentucky Resolves did not mention "nullification," Breckinridge unabashedly used the term in his speech before the committee of the whole. "I hesitate not to declare it as my opinion," cried Breckinridge "that it is then the right and duty of the several States to nullify those acts, *and to protect their citizens from their operation.*"[82] However, he implied that nullification would be proper only if Congress ignored the remonstrances of the states and refused to "expunge their unconstitutional proceedings from the annals of the United States."[83]

Image 3.2 The author of the Virginia Resolutions, James Madison later rebuked South Carolinians for their support of nullification. Courtesy of the Library of Virginia.

In the second substantive change, Breckinridge deleted Jefferson's call for the states to thwart the enforcement of the Alien and Sedition Acts. For meaningful nullification, state obstruction was a necessary component. Without state action, the national government could continue to enforce the Acts, thus proving the states weak and ineffective.

Once Breckinridge decided to jettison the nullification language, it naturally followed that the language of resistance should be expunged.

In the final substantive change, Breckinridge deleted Jefferson's call for a committee of conference and correspondence to foster communication among the states, which Hamilton had suggested in *Federalist* No. 28. Such committees were commonly used during the American Revolution, and Jefferson's choice of this mode of communication "suggest[s] a Revolutionary parallel."[84] With Breckinridge's change, the legislature merely transmitted the Kentucky Resolutions to the state's congressional delegation and asked that the governor transmit the Resolutions to the several state legislatures.

Madison's Virginia Resolutions underwent changes both on the way to Richmond and in the legislature. Serving again as an intermediary, Wilson Cary Nicholas showed Jefferson a copy of Madison's draft several weeks before Taylor introduced the Resolves in the Virginia House of Delegates. Jefferson suggested that "instead of the invitation to cooperate in the annulment of the acts," Madison's draft should be changed "to make it an invitation 'to concur with this commonwealth in declaring, as it does hereby declare, that the said acts are, and were ab initio, null, void and of no force, or effect.' "[85] In the House of Delegates, Jefferson's insertion drew much fire. Opponents of the Virginia Resolutions believed that declaring acts of Congress null and void was "dangerous and improper; inasmuch as they had, not only a tendency to inflame the public mind; . . . but they had a tendency to sap the very foundation of the government, by producing resistance to its laws."[86] Just before the Virginia Resolutions passed the House of Delegates, John Taylor moved to have Jefferson's insertion struck and the Resolutions simply declared the laws unconstitutional. At the same time Taylor proposed another change. In his draft, Madison had written that the "states alone are parties" to the compact. Many Republicans objected to "alone" because they believed that the states (as legislative sovereigns) and the people of the several states were the real parties to the compact.[87] They argued that "Congress is a creature of the states and of the people"[88] inasmuch as the states were represented in the Senate and the people in the House. Taylor agreed with his Republican colleagues and the word "alone" was dropped. Virginia's confusion over who were the parties to the compact was not settled until 1800 when Madison prepared his famed Report and explained that by "states" he meant the people of the several states.

Unfortunately, the moderating efforts of the legislatures still do not reveal exactly what Jefferson and Madison or Kentucky and Virginia intended to accomplish with the Resolutions. Were they nullifying the Alien and Sedition Acts or simply protesting and urging other states to join? The question presents many complications and scholars wrestling with the intent behind the Resolutions have observed that "[a]mbiguity appears to have been built into the very heart of the principles of '98."[89] Indeed, after he finished his draft of the Kentucky Resolves, Jefferson sent a copy to Madison and urged that Virginia "should distinctly affirm all the important principles they contain, so as to hold to that ground in the future, and leave the matter in such a train as that we may not be committed absolutely to push the matter to extremities, and yet may be free to push as far as events will render prudent."[90] Jefferson, despite the fervent rhetoric about state officials prohibiting enforcement of unconstitutional acts, apparently wanted to avoid an early clash with the national government, yet hoped supporters would rally around the Resolutions to permit some form of victory.

Even if one can overcome the Resolutions' ambiguities, any attempt to determine their true meaning must begin by carefully distinguishing between the principles espoused by Kentucky and those by Virginia. Though the two sets of Resolves share much in common, the differences are critical. First, under Jefferson's compact theory each state contracted with every other state in forming the Constitution, whereas Madison viewed the compact as resulting from the collective action of the several states. This distinction becomes important in a consideration of nullification. Jefferson's draft of the Kentucky Resolutions was clear that a state acting alone could nullify an unconstitutional act of Congress. Though Breckinridge deleted the word "nullification," he kept Jefferson's version of the compact theory, which logically permits one state to act alone in redressing unconstitutional acts. Hence, the transmittal of the Kentucky Resolves to the co-states in both the draft and Breckinridge's version seems to have been but an act of courtesy and not necessity. The Virginia Resolutions are more vague on this subject, but it certainly appears that Madison anticipated collective action of the states.

Related to nuances in the compact theory of Jefferson and Madison is the distinction between a state convention and state legislature. Shortly after the Virginia Resolutions were adopted, Madison reminded Jefferson that in undertaking acts of constitutional significance a mere legislature "is [not] the legitimate organ especially as a Convention was the organ by which the compact was made."[91] For this reason, Madison used generalities in the Virginia Resolutions to shield the legislature against "the charge of Usurpation in the very act of protesting agst the usurpations of Congress."[92] Considering the esteemed place occupied by state conventions in Madison's constitutional thought, he did not intend the Virginia Resolutions as a nullification of the Alien and Sedition Acts.[93] If Madison ever contemplated something similar to nullification, the act would have required conventions of the several states. The debates in the Virginia House of Delegates support the proposition that Madison was not attempting to nullify the Alien and Sedition Acts via the Resolves. Proponents repeatedly stressed that the Virginia Resolutions did not contemplate measures to prevent enforcement of the Alien and Sedition Acts. Instead, the Resolutions were meant "to produce a temper in Congress for a repeal."[94] If Congress did not oblige, John Taylor speculated that in accordance with Article V of the Constitution the states might compel a constitutional convention.[95]

Jefferson eventually accepted Madison's distinction between a legislature and a convention,[96] but in his draft he clearly stated that state officers would thwart enforcement of the Acts. Jefferson's use of the Kentucky legislature rather than a convention might have been influenced by John Taylor. In June of 1798, presumably while Jefferson was composing the Kentucky Resolutions, Taylor wrote to Jefferson and suggested that "[t]he right of the State governments to expound the constitution, might possibly be made the basis of a movement towards its amendment."[97] Taylor had advocated a role for the states in constitutional interpretation as early as 1794, when he published a pamphlet suggesting that "the state legislatures have at least as good a right to judge of every infraction of the constitution as Congress itself."[98] Impressed with Taylor's pamphlet, Jefferson ensured that excerpts from it were printed in the *National Gazette*.

By following the lead of Taylor and recognizing a nullifying power in the state legislatures, Jefferson attempted to add potency to the state governments' check on the national government.[99] Jefferson feared that giving the national government the exclusive power to interpret the Constitution would lead to arbitrary government. As John Taylor later wrote in his *Construction Construed and Constitutions Vindicated*, "a jurisdiction limited by its own will, is an unlimited jurisdiction."[100]

In sum, we can only speculate on the intended effect of the Kentucky and Virginia Resolutions. Of the three versions discussed, Madison's Virginia Resolves were the most moderate. Though vague, Madison was not attempting to nullify the Alien and Sedition Acts. Under his theory of the Constitution no state legislature or aggregation of legislatures could nullify acts of the national government. Breckinridge's Kentucky Resolutions occupied the middle ground. By omitting the term

Image 3.3 John Taylor of Caroline introduced Madison's Virginia Resolutions into the Virginia House of Delegates. Courtesy of the Library of Virginia.

"nullification" and the call for states to prevent enforcement of the Acts, Breckinridge moderated Jefferson's fiery message. However, Breckinridge's assertions on the floor of the Kentucky House of Representatives that states could nullify congressional enactments cloud the meaning of the official Kentucky Resolutions. Finally, Jefferson's draft of the Kentucky

Resolutions was the most radical of the three. Jefferson declared that a single state could nullify acts of Congress and that state officials should prevent enforcement of the voided laws. Believing the Constitution of enumerated powers was endangered, Jefferson's draft contemplated extraordinary steps to preserve the proper division of legislative sovereignty.

Response of the States

As 1799 dawned, any further action by Virginia and Kentucky hinged on the response of the other states. Jefferson and Madison were no doubt disappointed when they learned that not one state legislature responded favorably to the Resolutions. Nine states north of the Potomac put their objurgations in writing, and seven of the nine transmitted a response to Kentucky and/or Virginia.[101] The Southern states did not respond at all. Viewed as a whole, the responses made four points. First, the legislatures attacked the doctrine of nullification/interposition. New Hampshire, for example, declared "[t]hat the state legislatures are not the proper tribunals to determine the constitutionality of the laws of the general government; that the duty of such decision is properly and exclusively confided to the judicial department."[102] Second, the responding states opined that the Alien and Sedition Acts were "within the powers delegated to Congress" and also "promotive of the general welfare of the United States."[103] Third, the various legislatures—in High Federalist fashion—rebuked Virginia and Kentucky for daring to criticize the national government. The Massachusetts legislature refused to "admit the right of the state legislatures to denounce the administration of that government to which the people themselves, by a solemn compact, have exclusively committed their national concerns."[104] Finally, the responding legislatures feared that the principles of the Resolutions would tear the union asunder. According to the New York Senate, the doctrines of the Resolutions were "inflammatory," and threatened "the Constitution of the United States, and the principles of their union."[105]

At the same time as the states were responding to the Kentucky and Virginia Resolutions, the House of Representatives considered petitions praying for repeal of the Alien and Sedition Acts. After a lengthy discussion of the Acts, the Federalist majority in the House concluded that they had acted within their powers and that it was inexpedient to repeal the measures.[106] Alexander Hamilton, hoping Congress would use the army to uphold the Alien and Sedition Acts, also weighed in on the Resolves. Hamilton saw the Resolves as an attempt "to unite the state legislatures in a direct resistance to certain laws of the Union" and believed that Kentucky and Virginia were stockpiling arms as a "means of supporting [the Resolves] by force." Even if peace was achieved with France, Hamilton suggested that the military "should for the present be kept on its actual footing" in order to counter any domestic resistance to the laws.[107] In the face of criticism of the Resolutions and further pronouncements that the Acts were both expedient and constitutional, Jefferson and Madison realized that Republicans needed to answer the challenge of the Federalists.

Principles Renewed

On August 23, 1799, Jefferson wrote to Madison and emphasized "[t]hat the principles already advanced by Virginia and Kentucky are not to be yielded in silence." Jefferson hoped both states would take some form of concerted action. Envisioning a rejoinder to the states that expressed opinions on the Resolves, Jefferson suggested a protest and "reservation of the rights resulting to us from these palpable violations of the constitutional compact," and a conciliatory statement that Virginia and Kentucky were attached to the union and "willing to sacrifice . . . every thing except those rights of self government." However, if the co-states refused to "rally with us around the true principles of our federal compact," Jefferson believed that Kentucky and Virginia should secede from the union. He advocated that Kentuckians and Virginians should "server ourselves from that union we so much value, rather than give up the rights of self government which we have reserved, and in which alone we see liberty, safety, and happiness."[108]

Though an extreme step, the idea that a state might leave the union was not heterodox in the 1790s. For example, three states in their messages signifying ratification of the Constitution stated that powers could be resumed if the national government became oppressive. In the words of the Virginia ratifying convention: "the powers of government may be reassumed by the people whensoever it shall become necessary to their happiness."[109] Some resolves passed at the local level during the summer of 1798 also mentioned the possibility of resuming the delegated powers. Fox example, the freeholders of Prince Edward County, Virginia, observed that in cases of abused powers, the people had a duty "to resume the delegated power, to call their trustees to an account, to resist the usurpation, extirpate the tyranny, to restore their sullied majesty, and prostituted authority, to suspend, alter, or abrogate those laws, to punish their *unfaithful* and *corrupt servants*."[110]

As the author of the Declaration of Independence, Jefferson accepted the theory of secession long before the Sedition Act crisis.[111] However, Jefferson believed that such a step should not be taken "for light and transient causes." In fact, during the previous summer when Jefferson learned that John Taylor was beginning to question the value of the union, he promptly took up his pen and counseled his friend against secession. Although Jefferson agreed with Taylor that "we are completely under the saddle of Massachusetts and Connecticut, and that they ride us very hard," he urged patience. Jefferson assured Taylor that Republicans would "see the reign of witches pass over, their spells dissolved, and the people recovering their true sight, restoring their government to its true principles." He further warned that if the union was reduced "to Virginia and North Carolina, immediately the conflict will be established between representatives of these two States, and they will end by breaking into their simple units."[112] Moreover, during this same period Jefferson described the union in a letter to Madison as "the last anchor of our hope, and that alone which is to prevent this heavenly country from becoming an arena of gladiators."[113] The change in Jefferson's thought that took place between the summer of 1798 and that of 1799 was undoubtedly due to the Sedition Act prosecutions and the responses of the Northern states to the Resolutions. The theories of the Constitution advanced by the Federalists so frightened Jefferson that he drew parallels to 1776. Believing that consolidation of the states was imminent, in August 1799 Jefferson concluded that the anchor of union had been transformed into a millstone around the neck of self-government.

Madison, no doubt disturbed by his friend's hastily sketched thoughts on secession, traveled to Monticello to temper Jefferson. No record exists of what the two men discussed, but Madison's moderating influence evidenced itself in Jefferson's letter of September 5, 1799, to Wilson Cary Nicholas. Like the earlier letter to Madison, Jefferson urged that Kentucky and Virginia engage in a general plan of action. The plan outlined by Jefferson mirrored that developed in the Madison letter except for one major point. Jefferson retreated from his earlier idea of a reservation of rights "not only in deference to [Madison's] judgment, but because, as we should never think of separation but for repeated and enormous violations, so these, when they occur, will be cause enough in themselves."[114] Jefferson further declined to draft anything in order to "avoid suspicions" and "because there remains . . . a mass of talents in Kentucky sufficient for every purpose."[115]

In November 1799, Kentucky reaffirmed the principles announced in 1798. We do not know who drafted the Kentucky Resolutions of 1799, but Wilson Cary Nicholas, having just communicated with Jefferson regarding concerted action, and John Breckinridge, having recently been elected speaker of the state House of Representatives, likely played instrumental roles. The Kentucky Resolves of 1799 began by describing the union as "conducive to the liberty and happiness of the several States." Kentucky averred that it would "be among the last to seek its dissolution," but feared that a disregard of the enumerated powers would end in a despotism. The Resolves tackled the assertion of the Northern legislatures that the Supreme Court was the final arbiter of the Constitution. According to the Kentucky legislature, this would make "the discretion of those who administer the government, and not the *Constitution*" the measure of powers. Showing no hesitation, the legislature declared "*Nullification*" the remedy for unauthorized acts of the national government. However, the legislature quickly inserted ambiguity into the Resolves by promising to "bow to the laws of the Union," while at the same time "oppos[ing] in a constitutional manner, every attempt . . . to violate that compact." The legislature concluded the Resolves by entering "its solemn PROTEST" against the Alien and Sedition Acts.[116] Even with the use of the term "nullification," the Kentucky Resolutions of 1799 were overlooked because of the death of George Washington. With the union in mourning and the newspapers filled with eulogies, scant attention was paid to yet another set of resolves.

Declining to pass resolutions, Virginia instead chose to release a formal report. Elected to the House of Delegates in the spring of 1799, Madison chaired the committee designated to respond to the arguments of the Northern states. In his famed Report of 1800, Madison analyzed the Virginia Resolutions line by line and delved into much of the Constitution's history. Recognizing that the judiciary could also "exercise or sanction powers beyond the grant of the Constitution," Madison defended state interposition.[117] However, this remedy was only to be exercised in cases of usurpations "deeply and essentially affecting the vital principles" of the Constitution. Evidently the Alien and Sedition Acts did not so affect the Constitution inasmuch as Madison averred that Virginia was merely protesting the Acts. In essence, Madison claimed broad, nebulous power for the states, yet at the same time denied that Virginia was exercising its right of interposition.[118]

Revolution of 1800

For its constitutional commentary and statement of principles, the Report became an integral part of the Republicans' campaign literature. Jefferson thought so highly of the Report that he practically begged James Monroe in February 1800 to forward an official copy so it could be reproduced and distributed to Republican leaders throughout the union.[119] With the election of 1800 fast approaching, Jefferson could think of no better document that could distinguish the Federalist and Republican views of the Constitution.

Though the Republican victories in the election, which resulted in a 24-seat majority in the House of Representatives, were certainly tied to the presentation of their principles to the people, one should not forget the Federalists' debacles. Evincing contempt for public opinion, the Federalists ignored the growing discontent with high taxes, debt, and the Alien and Sedition Acts. Against the wishes of his Hamiltonian advisors, President Adams sent another peace mission to France which eventually bore fruit. With the French threat and the resulting patriotic zeal dissipating, Federalists had trouble justifying a continuation of their high-handed policies.

Adams's efforts for peace and his decision to demobilize Hamilton's army split the Federalist Party. Angry at Adams's independence, Hamilton devised a scheme to elevate Charles Cotesworth Pinckney to the presidency. Hamilton urged Federalist electors to support equally Adams for president and Pinckney for vice president. Figuring South Carolina, Pinckney's home state, would overwhelmingly support a favorite son thus ignore the equal votes instruction, Hamilton believed Pinckney would be elected president while a disgraced Adams would assume the lesser office. Adams realized the intent behind the equal-support scheme and dismissed Secretary of War James McHenry and Secretary of State Timothy Pickering, both of whom served as Hamilton's eyes and ears in the administration. Never short on temerity, Hamilton urged McHenry and Pinckney to "take with you copies and extracts of all such documents as will enable you to explain both Adams and Jefferson."[120]

To further damage Adams in the eyes of Federalists, Hamilton penned his *Letter from Alexander Hamilton, Concerning the Public Conduct and Character of John Adams, Esq., President of the United States*. In this 54 page pamphlet, Hamilton decried the sending of a peace mission to France and concluded that Adams was unfit for the presidency. Two hundred copies of the screed were printed and one copy found its way into Republican hands. Republican newspaper editors, thankful to Hamilton for his literary endeavor, reprinted the most virulent passages of the pamphlet.

Though he hated Adams, Hamilton was not willing to accept a Republican administration. In the spring of 1800, New York held elections for the state legislature and Republicans made marked gains. This newly constituted legislature would be charged with choosing presidential electors, and Hamilton feared that this would all but secure a President Jefferson. Writing to New York Governor John Jay, Hamilton suggested that the lame-duck Federalist legislature be reconvened and a new election law passed which would ensure that New York's electors were good Federalists. Hamilton observed that there were objections to such a measure, but "in the times like these in which we live, it will not do to be over-scrupulous."[121] Realizing that such skulduggery could throw his state into rebellion, Jay declined to act on Hamilton's advice.

Despite a bitter campaign and warnings that a vote for Jefferson was a "sin against God,"[122] Jefferson and Aaron Burr tied with 73 electoral votes each, with Adams receiving 65 votes and Pinckney 64. The tie between Jefferson and Burr could have been prevented had Republicans arranged for one elector to cast his vote for someone other than Burr. But many feared that the election would be close and hence Republican electors were understandably skittish about throwing away votes. The tie between Jefferson and Burr threw the election into the House of Representatives, where each state's delegation received one vote and a majority of all states was necessary to elect a president. Refusing acquiesce in Jefferson's election, Federalists in the House cast their votes for Burr and thus prevented Jefferson from receiving a majority of nine states. Vote after vote, Jefferson received eight electoral votes, Burr six, and two states were divided. Had it not been for the efforts of Maryland Representative Joseph Hopper Nicholson, the Federalists would have been one state closer to electing Burr. A loyal Republican, Nicholson was bed ridden with an illness and had himself carried several miles through the snow so he could be in the House for the votes. Maryland—with Nicholson present—was evenly divided. Without him, the Federalists could have had their way.

Jefferson feared that the Federalists were determined to maintain the gridlock. Writing to Madison, he observed that many Federalists "openly declare that they will prevent an election, and will name a President of the Senate, *pro tem.* by what they say would only be a *stretch* of the constitution."[123] The Federalists, Jefferson speculated, would then give the government to this official or to John Jay or John Marshall.

The tide turned when Republican Samuel Smith informed Federalist leaders that Jefferson was not inclined to dismiss Federalist members of the civil service for political reasons. Upon hearing this news, James Bayard, Delaware's sole representative, urged his fellow Federalists to relent. A number of Federalists were still opposed to a Jefferson presidency, but the rumors abounding that their usurpation would be met by rebellion and a constitutional convention likely caused a change in heart. On the thirty-sixth ballot, Federalist congressmen from Maryland and Vermont declined to vote, an act that put these two states in Jefferson's column. South Carolina and Delaware abstained, and Jefferson was elected to the presidency.

The hated Sedition Act expired at midnight on March 3, 1800—the moment before Jefferson assumed office. The new chief executive terminated all pending prosecutions and pardoned those persons convicted under the unconstitutional Act. "[T]he Revolution of 1800," Jefferson would later write, "was as real a revolution in the principles of our government as that of 1776 was in its form; not effected indeed by the sword, as that, but by the rational and peaceable instrument of reform, the suffrage of the people."[124]

Jefferson's comparison of the two revolutions was no mere rhetorical flourish. To Jefferson, both revolutions were built on similar principles. In the American Revolution, the people of the colonies fought for the right to govern themselves. They refused to accept that Parliament was sovereign in all matters. Jefferson in 1774 declared sundry acts of Parliament "void" and "inauthoritative."[125] "Let no act be passed by any one legislature," Jefferson lectured George III, "which may infringe on the rights and liberties of another."[126] In the Revolution of 1800, the people of the states fought for the right to govern themselves. They refused to accept a Federalist version of the Constitution that ignored the division of legislative sovereignty. As in 1774, Jefferson pronounced as void the acts of a national legislative body and warned of consolidation as Congress infringed on the authority of state legislatures.

The people's earlier support for the Federalists' wartime measures, Jefferson believed, was an inaccurate depiction of their true character. Writing to Thomas Lomax, Jefferson observed that the people's "virtuous feelings have been played on by some fact with more fiction; they have been the dupes of artful maneuvers, and made for a moment to be willing instruments in forging chains for themselves." The 1800 elections satisfied Jefferson that the revolutionary spirit was not dead and that "[t]he body of the American people is substantially Republican."[127]

* * *

Though the Revolution of 1800 was peaceful, the doctrines invoked on the road to the election contemplated more than mere ballots. Jefferson and Madison—through nullification and interposition—sought to provide the states with a mechanism to defend the reserved powers. Though neither state nullified a federal law and both took pains to emphasize that the Resolutions were only protests, the Principles of '98 were much more than a political platform. Jefferson would never have broached the topic of secession if he had considered the Resolutions as mere tools of party politics. But because of Republican electoral victories in 1800, Jefferson and Madison had no need to further define the meaning of the Kentucky and Virginia Resolutions. This fateful task would be taken up by another generation.

Chapter 4

Influence of the Resolutions

The Federalist party withered and died in the years after the Revolution of 1800. High Federalism was throughly discredited and the Principles of 1798 were embraced by Republicans across the nation. But the death of the party of Hamilton and Pickering did not mean an end to conflict between the states and national government. The two legislative sovereigns continued to clash over the extent of the delegated powers. In these situations, the Resolutions were often quoted and put forth as definitive authority. On other occasions, the Resolutions were not cited, but the words and actions of the states involved evinced an understanding of the concepts underlying the Resolutions.

Though the South is most often associated with the Principles of '98, all parts of the union have proclaimed and embraced the truths expressed in the Resolutions. Ironically, in the years after the Revolution of 1800, states north of the Potomac became staunch defenders of the reserved powers in the face of questionable policies pursued by Presidents Jefferson and Madison.[1] Some of these controversies involved mere protests on the part of state authorities, and others involved more belligerent confrontations in which troops were marshaled and bayonets fixed. Pitting state authority versus national authority, these episodes demonstrate the depth of Americans' belief that the people are better governed by state and local assemblies having close ties to the citizenry.

The Olmstead Case

One of the first notable clashes between state and national power after the Jeffersonian ascension occurred in Pennsylvania. The dispute can be traced back to a decision of the Appeals Commission of the Confederation Congress that overturned award of a Pennsylvania state admiralty court. The state court decision held that Gideon Olmstead and his three associates were entitled to only a portion of the prize money for their efforts in capturing a British ship during the

American Revolution. (The state of Pennsylvania also received a portion.) Believing that the Commission had impermissibly overturned findings of fact made by a state jury, Pennsylvania refused to comply with the Commission's decision. Though self-interest obviously played a role in Pennsylvania's behavior, it did have a tenable legal argument that the Commission overstepped its bounds. Trial by jury in admiralty cases was a unique feature of Pennsylvania state law. In most other states such matters were handled via a bench trial with the judge serving as the fact finder. Though the state act creating the admiralty court provided that final decisions could be appealed to the Confederation Congress, a supplemental act prohibited any review of a jury's findings of fact.

For years Olmstead sought to enforce the Commission's decision. He litigated the matter in state courts and petitioned the state legislature, but all to no avail. In 1802, Olmstead's fortunes seemed to change. Federal District Judge Richard Peters issued an order requiring that Pennsylvania's portion of the prize proceeds, which were in the hands of executrixes of former State Treasurer David Rittenhouse, be handed over to Olmstead.

Still contending that the original jury's findings of fact could not be reversed, Pennsylvania declared Judge Peters's decision "null and void," and accused him of "illegally usurp[ing] and exercis[ing]" jurisdiction.[2] The state legislature averred that "it hath become necessary for the general assembly of Pennsylvania, as the guardians of the rights and interests of this commonwealth . . . to prevent any future infringements on the same."[3] The state legislature passed a bill requiring the governor "to protect the persons and properties of [Rittenhouse's executrixes] from any process whatever issued out of any federal court in consequence" of Judge Peters's order. In the face of Pennsylvania's defiance, Judge Peters declined to issue any compulsory process. With Jefferson serving as chief executive of the United States and the Republicans' attempts to rein in Federalist judges through impeachment and the repeal of the Judiciary Act of 1801, Judge Peters likely reasoned that he would receive little assistance in enforcing his decree.

There the matter rested for five years until the 82-year-old Olmstead petitioned the Supreme Court for a writ commanding Judge Peters to enforce his order. After hearing arguments, the Supreme Court ruled in favor of Olmstead. Denying that state legislatures possessed the power "to determine jurisdiction of the courts of the union," the Court concluded by issuing a mandamus ordering Judge Peters to enforce his decree.[4]

Enforcement of the decree, however, was not a simple matter. The governor of Pennsylvania called out the state militia to protect the executrixes. The Pennsylvania legislature passed resolutions promising to

> cheerfully submit to the authority of the general government, as far as that authority is delegated by the constitution of the United States. But, whilst they yield to this authority, when exercised within Constitutional limits, they trust they will not be considered as acting hostile to the General Government, when, as guardians of the State rights, they can not permit an infringement of those rights, by an unconstitutional exercise of power in the United States' court.

The legislature further "lamented . . . that no provision is made in the constitution for determining disputes between the general and state governments by an impartial tribunal." Accordingly, the resolution instructed Pennsylvania's congressional delegation "to use their influence to procure an amendment" to cure this oversight in the Constitution.[5] In the meantime, the legislature suggested that Congress appoint a commissioner to negotiate with the state to reach a peaceful solution to the controversy.

Judge Peters issued process against the Rittenhouse executrixes on March 24, 1809. When John Smith, the U.S. marshal, attempted to serve process, General Michael Bright and a division of Pennsylvania militiamen blocked his way. Smith took down the names of as many soldiers as he could, and then summoned a 2,000-man *posse comitatus* to assist in upholding national authority. At the same time, a federal grand jury indicted General Bright for obstructing justice. Three tense weeks passed without incident. Rather than confronting the militiamen, Marshal Smith waited for an opportune moment to sneak into the house and serve his papers on the executrixes. Service having been accomplished, Marshal Smith then placed both under arrest.

Realizing that the tide was turning in the national government's favor, Governor Simon Snyder sought the intervention of President James Madison who had just recently succeeded Thomas Jefferson. Expecting some succor from the author of the Virginia Resolutions, Governor Snyder was "consoled with the pleasing idea, that the Chief Magistracy of the Union is confided to man who . . . is so intimately acquainted with the principles of the Federal Constitution, and who is no less disposed to protect the sovereignty and independence of the several States." Madison responded that he was "unauthorized to prevent the execution of a decree sanctioned by the Supreme Court of the United States, [and] expressly enjoined, by statute, to carry into effect any such decree where opposition may be made to it."[6] Shortly after this exchange, the state supreme court denied a petition for a writ of habeas corpus aimed at winning the executrixes' freedom. The denial of the writ proved to Governor Snyder that further resistance was futile. After waiting 31 years, Olmstead finally received the funds due to him. General Bright and eight of his militiamen were convicted of treason in the federal district court, but were pardoned by President Madison. With this pardon, the Olmstead affair came to an end.

The Embargo

While the Olmstead case was in its final stages of litigation, another controversy brewed between the states and the national government. The beginnings of this controversy can be traced to renewed hostilities between Great Britain and France. In the midst of yet another war, both countries engaged in economic coercion that affected much of the world. As a result of edicts from the belligerents, American merchant vessels were put in peril each time they left the safety of American waters. "The whole world is thus laid under interdict by these two nations," observed President Jefferson, "and our vessels, their cargoes and crews are to be taken by the one or the other, for whatever place they may be destined, out of our own limits."[7] As the depredations on American commerce grew worse, President Jefferson recalled that in the early 1790s before the Jay mission to Great Britain, Madison had proposed high duties on British manufactured goods and reciprocal restrictions on British ocean carriage of American goods. The restrictions were never enacted, but Jefferson and Madison continued to believe that this type of economic coercion was an efficacious alternative to war. Consequently, President Jefferson recommended that Congress enact an embargo.

The Non-Importation Act, which prohibited importation of certain British goods, was already on the books, but this was a relatively mild measure. In his message to Congress, Jefferson cited the "great and increasing danger with which our merchandise, our vessels and our seamen are threatened on the high seas and elsewhere from the belligerent powers of Europe." Accordingly, Jefferson suggested "an immediate inhibition of the departure of our vessels from ports of the United States."[8] A France and Great Britain deprived of American grain, cotton, and tobacco, Jefferson believed, would quickly learn to respect the rights of neutral ships.

Jefferson sent his embargo message to Congress on December 18, 1807, and within a few hours the Senate, in secret session, passed the Embargo Act. The House of Representatives acted three days later and

President Jefferson signed the measure into law on December 22. The Act, in pertinent part, laid an embargo "on all ships and vessels in the ports and places within the limits or jurisdiction of the United States...bound to any foreign port or place, except vessels under the immediate direction of the President."[9] Supplementary acts were passed in January, March, and April 1808, aimed at coasting vessels, fishing ships, and others engaged in smuggling.

Congress also passed stiff penalties for those violating the embargo whereby vessels and cargoes could be forfeited for minor ministerial infractions. One of the most controversial provisions of the Enforcement Act dealt with the use of the U.S. Navy. Republicans had long feared standing armies and the use of the military in enforcing civil law, but put aside these concerns in what they perceived as a great time of national danger. Commanding officers of the armed vessels of the United States were authorized by statute to stop and search any domestic or foreign ship within the jurisdiction of the United States if the officers had "reason to suspect" the ship was engaged in a violation of the embargo.[10] Similarly, customs officials were "authorized to detain any vessel...whenever in their opinions the intention is to violate or evade any provisions of the acts laying an embargo."[11] With such measures, Congress and the President conveniently ignored that the Fourth Amendment, which was meant to protect the people "against unreasonable searches and seizures" provided that no search warrant would issue absent "probable cause"—a much higher standard than suspicion or mere opinion.[12]

The embargo proved to be a very unpopular measure among the American people, but especially in New England where a large portion of the population earned a living via foreign commerce. Because of the embargo, cotton and tobacco prices fell, sailors sat idly on the docks, ships rotted in the wharves, and warehouses were suddenly empty. New Englanders wryly observed that the Embargo Act should have been titled "an act for the better encouragement of the British Colonies in America" inasmuch as so many skilled seamen emigrated to Canada to ply their trade. President Jefferson made matters worse by failing to address the nation and explain why so many were made to suffer.

With distress increasing each day the embargo remained in effect, defiance of the people also grew.[13] In April 1808, Jefferson declared that a state of insurrection existed in the Lake Champlain area where huge rafts transported American foodstuffs into Canada from Vermont and New York. Reaping handsome profits from the smuggling, armed gangs thought nothing of using force against law enforcement officials.

Jefferson instructed the insurgents "to disperse and retire peaceably to their respective abodes" and "command[ed] all officers having authority, civil or military. . . to quell and subdue such insurrections or combinations, to seize upon all those therein concerned."[14] The militia was called out, and in one clash almost 40 smugglers and soldiers were wounded.

Though a federal district court concluded that the embargo was constitutional,[15] the lower house of the Massachusetts legislature refused to accept "that in a free country there is any stage at which the constitutionality of an act may no longer be open to discussion and debate." Otherwise, "our constitution would be nothing but a name—nay worse, a fatal instrument to sanctify oppression, and legalize the tyranny which inflicts it."[16] Accordingly, both houses of the legislature resolved that the Embargo Act and the legislation supplementing it were "unjust, oppressive and unconstitutional, and not legally binding on the citizens of this state." However, the legislature recommended that aggrieved parties "abstain from forcible resistance."[17] Delaware likewise declared that the embargo was "an invasion of the liberty of the people, and the constitutional sovereignty of the State governments."[18] Governor Jonathan Trumball of Connecticut reminded his state that

> Whenever our national legislature is led to overleap the prescribed bounds of their constitutional powers, on the State Legislatures, in great emergencies, devolves the arduous task—it is their right—it becomes their duty, to interpose their protecting shield between the right and liberty of the people, and the assumed power of the General Government.[19]

Spurred by Governor Trumball's message, the Connecticut general assembly declared that the Embargo Act was "incompatible with the constitution of the United States." In light of embargo's unconstitutionality, the general assembly refused "to assist, or concur in giving effect" to enforcement of the embargo, and prohibited "persons holding executive offices" in Connecticut from aiding national officers with enforcement duties.[20] Shortly after Connecticut's resolutions, the legislature of Rhode Island also invoked its right "to interpose for the purpose of protecting [the people] from the ruinous inflictions of usurped and unconstitutional power." Describing the embargo as "tyrannical," the legislature promised "to be vigilant in guarding from usurpation and violation, those powers and rights which the good people of this State have expressly reserved to themselves, and have ever refused to delegate."[21]

As Jefferson's second term approached its end, it became clear that rather than coercing Great Britain and France, the embargo was instead coercing the American people. Want, insurrection, and protests convinced Congress that continuance of the embargo was untenable. Just days before President Jefferson left office, he signed a bill repealing the embargo, permitting trade with the rest of the world (with the exception of Britain and France), and permitting the chief executive to reopen trade with whichever belligerent ceased to interfere with American shipping.

The War of 1812

Though rid of the embargo, James Madison's presidency began with Britain and France still plundering neutral commerce. In 1811, a number of young men who had grown weary of inaction were elected to Congress. Among them were John C. Calhoun and Langdon Cheves of South Carolina, Henry Clay of Kentucky, and Felix Grundy of Tennessee. These "War Hawks" as John Randolph described them, advocated military measures to deal with British contempt for American rights. On June 18, 1812, Congress sent President Madison a declaration of war, which he signed the same day. Unbeknownst to Americans, one day earlier Britain had revoked its decrees sanctioning the raiding of American shipping. But without modern communications, American leaders did not learn that the principal cause of the declaration of war had been removed.

The United States entered the War of 1812 as an unprepared and divided country. Congress had made no efforts to raise the necessary funds to prosecute a war, and the commercial states had voted overwhelmingly against the declaration of war. Peace and trade with Great Britain were essential for the prosperity of these states; New England merchants and ship owners were willing to suffer impressment and harassment from the British so long as there was money to be made. And with Britain and France at each other's throats, profits were astronomical for those not adverse to risk. Slogans like "free trade and sailors' rights," though stirring the patriotism of other sections, had little effect in the commercial and maritime states. Federalist New England also recognized that the War Hawks had their eyes set on Canada. If the conquest of Canada was successful, Federalists feared that this would strengthen the Republican party by adding more agrarian states to the union. Hence, to Federalist New England, the war was but an "act of baseness, corruption, treachery, and malignity" that would eventually "unveil to the people at large the real character of our rulers."[22]

The first clash between the states and national government over the war came when General Henry Dearborn, by authority of President Madison, instructed Massachusetts and Connecticut to supply militia forces for defense of the coast. Under the Constitution, the state militias could be called into national service "to execute the Laws of the Union, suppress Insurrections and repel invasions."[23]

Governor Caleb Strong of Massachusetts asserted that the states retained the power to determine whether any of the three contingencies existed and he doubted whether the circumstances then existing warranted use of the militia. Governor Strong then asked the Massachusetts Supreme Court for an advisory opinion. After considering the matter, the court agreed with Governor Strong that the commanders in chief of the several state militias had a right to determine whether any of the three exigencies enumerated in the Constitution existed. The judges reasoned that

> [a]s this power is not delegated to the United States by the Federal Constitution, nor prohibited by it to the states, it is reserved to the states, respectively; and from the nature of the power, it must be exercised by those with whom the states have respectively entrusted the chief command of the militia.[24]

To hold otherwise, feared the court, "would place all the militia . . . at the will of Congress, and produce a military consolidation of the states, without any constitutional remedy against the intentions of the people, when ratifying the Constitution."[25]

Following Massachusetts's lead, the Connecticut legislature adopted a special report on the matter. The legislature's report began by expressing a "deep interest in [the union's] preservation," but then turned to first principles.[26]

> But it must not be forgotten, that the state of Connecticut is a FREE SOVEREIGN and INDEPENDENT state; that the United States are a *confederacy* of states; that we are a confederated and not a consolidated republic. The governor of this state is under a high and solemn obligation, "*to maintain the lawful rights and privileges thereof, as a sovereign, free and independent state,*" as he is "*to support the constitution of the United States,*" and the obligation to support the latter, imposes an additional obligation to support the former.[27]

Calling out the militia for purposes other than those stated in the Constitution, averred the legislature, "would be not only the height of injustice to the militia, . . . but a violation of the constitution and laws of this state, and of the United States."[28] Use of the militia in an "offensive war," concluded Connecticut, was never contemplated by the state ratifying conventions.

Vermont and Rhode Island both supported the stand taken by their sister states. Governor Martin Chittenden of Vermont even went so far as to order the recall of some militia units serving in a neighboring state. Resolutions were introduced in Congress demanding the impeachment of Governor Chittenden, but no formal proceedings followed. Chittenden's spirit, however, infected militia units from other states. Once the push for Canada began, some companies of militia refused to cross the border. General Stephen Van Rensselaer in October 1812 moved on Queenstown with regulars and militia. Accompanying him as far as the border, New York militia units informed the general that they "were enlisted to protect their state, not to invade foreign territory."[29] The militia watched as 230 Americans suffered casualties and 764 were captured.

Queenstown was but one of many American military debacles, and as the war dragged on Congress considered a conscription bill. The Constitution gives Congress the power to raise armies and navies, but says not a word about drafting citizens into service. Borrowing a page from Alexander Hamilton's play book, Republicans justified conscription by appealing to implied powers. Daniel Webster of Massachusetts, however, sounded more like a Virginia states' rights advocate when he spoke against the draft. "Where is it written in the Constitution," asked Webster, "in what article or section is it contained, that you may take children from their parents, and parents from their children, and compel them to fight the battles of any war in which the folly or the wickedness of government may engage it?" If the bill passed, Webster declared it "the solemn duty of the State Governments to protect their own authority over their own militia, and to interpose between their citizens and arbitrary power."[30] Heeding Webster's advice, the legislature of Connecticut described the proposed conscription as "not only intolerably burdensome and oppressive, but utterly subversive of the rights and liberties of the people of this state, and the freedom, sovereignty, and independence of the same."[31] The conscription bill never passed, but in its stead Congress enacted a "Bill in regard to the Enlistment of Minors." Rising to combat what it believed to be a usurpation of power, Connecticut passed a measure which required state judges to discharge on a writ of habeas corpus all minors drafted without the consent of their parents or guardians.[32]

Connecticut, like the rest of New England, had avoided much of the danger and suffering that goes with war. Great Britain had not blockaded New England ports and troops had not occupied New England territory. This changed in the summer of 1814 when the British occupied a portion of Maine and a general invasion of New England seemed likely. The same states that had refused to supply militia for what they called "Mr. Madison's War" now demanded that Madison send troops to defend the coastline. But there was little Madison could do for New England. The President had just watched the British burn the White House and Capitol on August 24, and many speculated that his government would soon fall.

The Hartford Convention

Under these circumstances, Massachusetts invited the other New England states to send delegates to a convention to be held at Hartford. In its message, Massachusetts accused the national government of "fail[ing] to secure to this Commonwealth, and as they believe, to the eastern section of this union, those equal rights and benefits which were the great objects of its formation."[33] Not only did Massachusetts look for some coordination of a defense policy with other New England states, but it also wanted "to lay the foundation for a radical reform of the national compact, by inviting a further convention, a deputation from all the States in the Union."[34]

In December 1814, delegates from Massachusetts, Connecticut, Rhode Island, and scattered counties in New Hampshire and Vermont met in Hartford. The Hartford Convention has been vilified as the first step toward a separate New England confederacy, and others have defended it as necessary for the self-defense of the region. Whatever the case, a secessionist spirit had been growing in New England since the Louisiana Purchase. "I have no hesitation myself in saying," wrote Roger Griswold, "that there can be no safety to the Northern States *without a separation from the confederacy*. The balance of power under the present government is decidedly in favor of the Southern States; nor can that balance be changed or destroyed."[35] Former Secretary of State Timothy Pickering concurred in the need for secession: "The principles of our Revolution point to the remedy,—a separation. That this can be accomplished without spilling one drop of blood, I have little doubt."[36] Pickering did not propose to break all ties with the Southern states, but hoped to "preserve a useful friendship, which without such separation would infallibly be destroyed."[37] John Quincy Adams, the son of the former president and a future president himself, firmly believed that "[t]he Hartford Convention was to the Northern confederacy precisely what the Congress of 1774 was to the Declaration of Independence."[38]

Indeed, the Hartford Convention did resolve that the New England states should "adopt all such measures as may be necessary effectually to protect the citizens of said States from the operation and effects of all the acts which have been or may be passed by the Congress of the United States, which shall contain provisions . . . not authorized by the Constitution."[39] However, the bulk of the final resolutions adopted were in the form of proposed amendments to the Constitution. The Convention recommended that slaves no longer be counted for purposes of representation; that new states be admitted to the union only with the concurrence of two-thirds of both houses of Congress; that all embargos be limited to 60 days; that measures interdicting foreign commerce require the concurrence of two-thirds of both houses; that declarations of war require the concurrence of two-thirds of both houses; that no naturalized citizen be eligible to hold any civil office of the United States; that the president be limited to one term; and that a "President not be elected from the same state two terms in succession."[40] The delegates also asked that Congress return taxes paid by the New England states so that they could "be empowered to assume upon them-selves the defence of their territory against the enemy."[41]

Without question, the delegates hoped to weaken the power of the predominantly Republican states of the South and embark on a program of self-defense, but whether secession was seriously discussed at Hartford is unclear. Though delegates in attendance were much more moderate than the Pickering faction of the Federalist party, Samuel Eliot Morison has observed that "[e]very Federalist paper of Boston but one promoted [secession] as a platform for the Hartford Convention," and that Harrison Gray Otis, one of the driving forces of the Convention, toyed with treating the Madison administration as having abdicated power.[42]

Fortunately, the United States and Britain signed the Treaty of Ghent while the Convention was in session, removing the main grievance of New England before the delegates returned home. Though we can only speculate what New England would have done had the war continued, we do know that many New Englanders openly advocated "a truce or separate peace" with Britain.[43] Governor Strong of Massachusetts had in the months before the Treaty opened secret talks with British General Sir John Sherbrooke on the subject of an armistice. London instructed Sir John that if Madison did not accept the Ghent Treaty, he had author-ity to make peace with New England and provide logistical support to

New England's militia if American forces intervened. Had the United States and Britain been unable to agree on terms that December, severance of the union might have followed.

The Carolina Doctrine

The early 1800s were replete with fiery resolutions and outright resistance to national laws, but no state adopted a formal process of nullification until 1832 when South Carolina voided the Tariffs of 1828 and 1832. Though nationalists equated South Carolina's nullification with treason, the Carolinians pointed to the Kentucky and Virginia Resolutions as authority for their actions. South Carolina, the nullifiers urged, was merely building on the sound foundation laid by Jefferson and Madison. The Carolinians also pointed to New England's actions during the crisis of the embargo and war when arguing the case for a state negative on oppressive national laws. In the end, this nullification proved successful as it prompted Congress to lower the tariff duties. But South Carolina's actions also brought the United States to the brink of an internecine war.

A. The Negro Seamen Act

South Carolina, like the New England states, was no stranger to conflict with the national government. In the years before the nullification controversy, South Carolina dueled with the national government over the state's restrictions on black seamen. In late 1822, the South Carolina legislature passed an "Act for the Better Regulation and Government of Free Negroes and Persons of Color," often known as the "Negro Seamen Act."[44] Under the Act, free black mariners employed on domestic or foreign vessels visiting South Carolina ports were confined to prison, at the ship captain's expense, until the vessel was ready to sail. If the captain failed to retrieve the black seaman from the gaol, the seaman could be sold into slavery.

The impetus behind the Negro Seamen Act was the uncovering of a planned slave rebellion in the summer of 1822. A free Charleston mulatto named Denmark Vesey, who had purchased his freedom after winning a lottery, was the organizer. By all accounts, Vesey was an intelligent man and could stir a crowd with his oratory. Along with his chief lieutenant, an Angolan sorcerer known as Gullah Jack, Vesey planned to seize the city of Charleston and then either set sail for San Domingo, or try to hold the city until slave reinforcements could be procured. The conspirators were betrayed when a house servant reported to his master that he had been approached and asked to join the conspiracy. A show of force convinced Charleston slaves to abandon the rebellion, but the Charleston aristocracy never forgot this brush with disaster. With the Negro Seamen Act, the aristocracy hoped that by limiting their slaves' contact with free persons of color, the spread of radical ideas and plans of insurrection could be stopped.

The enforcement of the Negro Seamen Act caused much distress for ship owners employing large numbers of black mariners. Ships from the West Indies often visited Charleston, and in one case authorities imprisoned the entire crew of a British sloop during the captain's absence. Stratford Canning, the British minister in Washington, demanded intervention of the national government, and President John Quincy Adams attempted to persuade South Carolina's congressional leaders to exert their influence to put an end to the imprisonments. Enforcement of the law was discontinued for a short while, but not because of the President's efforts. The harbor master had grown weary of keeping tabs on the occupants of all ships entering the harbor and had ceased reporting the arrival of black mariners to the sheriff.

Implementation of the Negro Seamen Act resumed in the summer of 1823 when the influential South Carolina Association pressured local law enforcement officials. The sole function of the South Carolina Association was to ensure that all laws regulating slaves and free blacks were observed to the letter. The Negro Seamen Act was a favorite of the Association and members gladly kept an eye on all vessels docking in Charleston.

One of the first mariners to be taken into custody once enforcement resumed was Henry Elkinson, a British subject of Jamaican birth. The British consul, realizing that the chief executive had failed to quash the Act, turned to the federal judiciary and arranged for an attorney to challenge the Act in federal circuit court. Elkinson's attorney petitioned Justice William Johnson for a writ of habeas corpus, or, in the alternative, a writ of de homine replegiando. Interestingly, defense of the Negro Seamen Act was undertaken by the South Carolina Association, not the state attorney general.

The Association's lawyers argued that South Carolina, as a sovereign state, did not and could not surrender the right of self-preservation. South Carolina, the Association contended, retained the power to regulate its domestic institutions. Regulation of the state's slave population was within the state's broad police power, and therefore any national law to the contrary was unconstitutional. Justice Johnson rejected this line of argument, describing it as "asserting the right to throw off the federal constitution at . . . will."[45] Justice Johnson then turned to the specific provisions of the Constitution that he believed prohibited statutes such as the Negro Seamen Act. First, Justice Johnson pointed to Congress's power to regulate interstate and foreign commerce—a power he described as "paramount and exclusive."[46] Observing "that the navigation of ships has always been held, by all nations, to appertain to commercial regulations,"[47] Justice Johnson accused South Carolina of trespassing in an area belonging exclusively to the national government. Next, Justice Johnson adduced the national government's power to make treaties, and contended that the state's regulations were "an express violation of the commercial convention with Great Britain of 1815."[48]

However, after declaring the Negro Seamen Act "unconstitutional and void," Justice Johnson announced that he could not provide Elkinson a remedy. Under the Judiciary Act of 1789, federal courts could issue a writ of habeas corpus only when the prisoner was in federal custody. Because Elkinson was in the state gaol, a writ could not issue. As for the writ of de homine replegiando, which normally dealt with the repossession of chattels, Justice Johnson concluded that it could not issue against the sheriff because Elkinson was a freeman, but that it could issue against the sheriff's vendee if Elkinson were sold into slavery. Hence, Justice Johnson's conclusions of law regarding the Act were dicta, and South Carolina treated them as such by continuing the Act's enforcement.

In 1823, South Carolina exempted U.S. naval vessels and foreign vessels from the Act so long as black mariners stayed on board their ships. The state legislature also replaced the enslavement provisions with corporal punishment and banishment. Disappointed that the national government could not protect black seamen from the operation of South Carolina's laws, British consuls began direct negotiations with state officials. Off and on, the Negro Seamen Act continued to be a thorn in the state department's side until the eve of the War Between the States.

B. The Tariff

In the wake of South Carolina's refusal to cease enforcement of the Negro Seamen Act, another controversy with the national government arose. This time the dispute involved not the peculiar institution, but the tariff. The tariff controversy that erupted in the early 1830s can be traced back to the War of 1812.[49] Not long after peace was secured, Congress passed a tariff bill to protect domestic manufacturers. At the time of the war, the United States had few manufacturing facilities. Citizens earned livelihoods either in agriculture or the carrying trade, and manufactured goods were imported from Great Britain. The embargo and nonintercourse measures, enacted just before the war, had cut off this trade with Britain, and as a result a number of domestic manufactories came into existence to meet the demand for manufactured goods. When the war ended, the owners of these manufactories feared that the resumption of trade with Great Britain would cut their profits and in some cases drive them out of business.

The war had kindled much patriotism in the South and West, and Congress was more than willing to come to the aid of domestic manufacturers. "Should the present owners be ruined, and the workmen dispersed and turned to other pursuits," the young War Hawk John C. Calhoun told the House of Representatives, "the country would sustain a great loss."[50] Calhoun also feared that in case of another war with Britain, the United States would again find itself deprived of much needed manufactured goods. To avoid this difficulty that war would bring, Calhoun offered two solutions: a strong navy or domestic manufactures. "By the former," explained Calhoun, "we could open the way to our markets; by the latter, we bring them from beyond the ocean, and naturalize them."[51] Calhoun admitted that had the United States "the means of attaining an immediate naval ascendency," the protective tariff would have been unnecessary.[52] But because it would be many years before the United States could challenge Britannia on the high seas, Calhoun believed that immediate protection for domestic industry was the proper course.

Less nationalistic members of Congress challenged Calhoun's defense of the protective tariff. "I hold as a sound general rule," remarked Representative Thomas Telfair, "that no other higher duties should be laid than are both necessary and proper for the purposes of revenue."[53] Under the Constitution, Congress may lay duties "to pay the Debts and provide for the common Defence and general Welfare of the United States."[54] As previously discussed, the general welfare language was not understood at the time of ratification to a be a general grant of power unrelated to the enumerated powers. Protection of industry is nowhere mentioned in the Constitution, and therefore Telfair argued that tariffs could only be laid for revenue purposes and that the interest of the manufacturer could be regarded only as "an incidental consideration."[55]

However, as early as 1789 the first Congress had placed duties on goods "for the support of the government, for the discharge of debts of the United States, and the encouragement and protection of

manufacturers."[56] In 1789 the ratification debat
one's memory, and the mention of protection in t
indicates that protection was not outside the boun
Of course, one could also argue that protection w
the bill and incidental to the other two valid cons

Constitutional concerns aside, Telfair also cont
1816 would hurt consumers by forcing them to
imported goods, and that protection would give ri
powerful industrialists who would reap inordinate profits and exert
undue influence in the government. Telfair and other free traders ultimately lost the debate, and the Tariff of 1816, averaging 25 percent of
the value of imported goods, was approved by both houses of Congress.[57]

With the nation prospering in the first few years after the war, the
tariff was a not a major issue. However, the Panic of 1819 changed this.
Americans again learned of the dangers of paper money, and the second
bank of the United States, chartered in 1816, made more enemies when
its extensive role in Western land speculation was exposed. State banks
began to call in their loans, the money supply was cut in half, and
debtors found it almost impossible to pay creditors as a result of the
deflation. The South, as a large importer of manufactured goods, felt the
pain more than any other section. Once-affordable goods were out of
reach, and the Tariff exacerbated the situation. At the same time,
exhausted soil led to decreasing cotton yields. World cotton prices fell
and crops that brought over 30 cents per pound in 1818 brought less
than a dime per pound by the late 1830s.

Though discontent with protection was growing, in 1824
Congress increased the tariff to an average of $33^1/_2$ percent of the
value of imported goods. This action in the face of Southern suffering
sparked formal resolutions. South Carolina, for example, resolved
"[t]hat it is an unconstitutional exercise of power on the part of
Congress, to lay duties to protect domestic manufacturers."[58] Virginia
reaffirmed its resolution of 1798, denied that Congress could protect
industry, and described the tariff as "highly oppressive and partial in its
operation."[59]

Never one to shy away from controversy, Thomas Cooper inserted
himself into the middle of the tariff debate in 1827. Speaking at an
antitariff meeting in Columbia, South Carolina, Cooper fired a rhetorical shot that was heard throughout the union. Cooper denounced the
tariff as

> a system, whose effect will be to sacrifice the south to the north, by
> converting us into colonies and tributaries—to tax us for their own

emolument—to claim the right of disposing of our honest earnings—
to forbid us to buy from our most valuable customers—to irritate into
retaliation our foreign purchasers, and thus confine our raw material to
the home market—in short to impoverish the planter, and to stretch the
purse of the manufacturer.[60]

Because of this unjust system, Cooper concluded, "we shall 'ere long be
compelled to calculate the value of our union; and to enquire of what
use to us is this most unequal alliance."[61] According to Dumas Malone,
the secession of the South "from an unprofitable Union certainly
received its first extensive advertising as a result of this speech."[62]

The response to Dr. Cooper's rhetoric and similar sentiments
expressed throughout the South was not compromise, but yet another
increase in the tariff. In 1828, Congress raised duties to 50 percent of
the value of imported goods. This so-called Tariff of Abominations
caused South Carolinians to think seriously about Cooper's inquiry.
James Hamilton, Jr., soon to be governor of South Carolina, suggested
that nullification was the proper remedy. For precedent, Hamilton cited
"the authority of Jefferson and Madison, sustained by the finding of the
almost unanimous votes of the Legislatures of Virginia and Kentucky,
canonized, at once by the Catholic faith of the great republican party of
our country."[63]

However, the election of Andrew Jackson to the presidency and
Calhoun to the vice presidency persuaded many that extreme measures
were unnecessary. Writing to Jackson in the fall of 1828, Senator Robert Y.
Hayne explained that South Carolinians would look to Jackson "as a
PACIFICATOR" even though Jackson believed that protective tariffs
were constitutional.[64] In his first inaugural address, Jackson declared
that a tariff "with a view to revenue" rather than protection would be
within "the spirit of equity, caution, and compromise in which the
Constitution was formed."[65] In his first annual message, Jackson again
spoke to tariff reform. The President observed that the national
debt would soon be paid off and that "[a] reduction, therefore, of the
existing duties will be felt as a common benefit, but like all other legislation connected with commerce, to be efficacious and not injurious it
should be gradual and certain."[66]

Unfortunately, Jackson's words did not translate into action and the
old general showed little leadership as South Carolina's patience waned.
Vice President Calhoun had privately embraced nullification in 1827
when he observed to Littleton Walker Tazewell that Northern insistence
on the tariff "admits of but one effectual remedy, a veto . . . on the part
of the states."[67] Calhoun, like many of his Southern compatriots, had

Image 4.1 Thomas Cooper suffered persecution under the Sedition Act and later played a key role in the nullification controversy. Courtesy of the South Caroliniana Library, University of South Carolina, Columbia.

come down from the patriotic high created by the War of 1812 and the fear of a future conflict with Great Britain. The nationalism that was in vogue for a short time in the South gave way to increased feelings of sectionalism. Believing that they had made concessions to the Northern interest in order to serve the greater good in the postwar years, Southerners of the 1820s searched their memories for instances of Northern reciprocity. Recalling none, many Southerners again embraced the doctrines of strict construction and localism.

Though embracing the idea of state veto in his private correspondence, Calhoun realized that in most cases elections would serve to check tyrannical rulers. However, when unjust measures did not operate equally on all citizens or all sections, Calhoun believed that an added safeguard of nullification was necessary. Tariff supporters challenged Calhoun's assertions on the operation of the tariff by pointing out that all consumers, Northern and Southern, paid an increased price for goods because of the duties. Contending that all shared an equal burden, they argued that state veto, under Calhoun's own theory, was unnecessary. To this Calhoun replied that "[t]he very act . . . which imposes the burdens on consumers gives to the labour of one section the power of recharging and more than recharging the duty, while to the other it is a pure unmitigated burden, which cannot be shifted to the shoulders of others."[68] In other words, Northerners occupied a position "like that of a pensioner of government, who pays say ten dollars in taxes and receives one hundred in pension money."[69]

Calhoun's analysis of the effects of the tariff was sound, but a few South Carolinians believed that the tariff was even more pernicious than Calhoun admitted. The firebrand George McDuffie crafted his "forty-bale theory" whereby he claimed that the planter, rather than the consumer, was the party hurt by the tariff laws. In the case of a duty of 30 percent, for example, McDuffie averred that the planter received less money for his cotton because merchants paid the 30 percent duty on manufactured goods at the customs house and passed only 10 percent on to consumers. The merchant recovered the other 20 percent from the British, who accounted for this sum by paying Southern planters less for their cotton. Hence, McDuffie believed that "by the legerdemain of this nefarious system,"[70] Southern planters were cheated out of 40 bales of cotton for every 100 bales sold. The 40-bale theory was not based on sound economics, but it did serve to agitate crowds when McDuffie spoke on the operation of the tariff system.

In November 1828, on the eve of Jackson's election to the White House, Calhoun agreed to write a detailed explanation of South

Carolina's position on the tariff and possible measures for combating the perceived injustice. Interestingly, Calhoun requested that his friends obtain two items to assist him: (1) a report on the country's imports and exports, and (2) a copy of the Kentucky Resolutions. That Calhoun deemed the Kentucky Resolutions indispensable in writing the *South Carolina Exposition* is not surprising. As Calhoun scholar Clyde Wilson has observed, Calhoun began his career as, "and always considered himself to be, a Jeffersonian Republican."[71]

Calhoun began the *Exposition* with the constitutionality of the protective tariff. Like the opponents of the Tariff of 1816, Calhoun argued that Congress's power to lay duties was "granted as a tax power for the sole purpose of revenue—a power in its nature essentially different from that of imposing protective or prohibitory duties."[72] Observing that the Constitution authorizes states to impose duties with the consent of Congress, Calhoun argued that such a procedure was the only legitimate mechanism for protecting manufacturers. Northern states could petition Congress for permission to levy their own duties, but they could not force Southern states to bear the bulk of the burden of protection. Otherwise, a nationwide protective tariff made South Carolinians "serfs of the system—out of whose labor is raised not only the money paid into the Treasury, but the funds out of which are drawn the rich rewards of the manufacturer and his associates in interest."[73]

Calhoun also feared that the protective tariff would lead to a trade war in which European nations would refuse to buy Southern staples inasmuch as the high duties deprived the Europeans of much of the American market. Free trade, Calhoun argued, would enable the South to prosper. But this prosperity would result "not by the oppression of our fellow-citizens of other States, but by our industry, enterprise, and natural advantages."[74]

Turning next to the nature of the union, Calhoun recognized the division of legislative sovereignty between the state and national governments.

> Our system, then, consists of two distinct and independent Governments. The general powers, expressly delegated to the General Government, are subject to its sole and separate control; and the States cannot, without violating the constitutional compact, interpose their authority to check, or in any manner to counteract its movements, so long as they are confined to the proper sphere. So, also, the peculiar and local powers reserved to the States are subject to their exclusive control; nor can the General Government interfere, in any manner, with them, without violating the Constitution.[75]

Careful to distinguish between legislative and ultimate sovereignty, Calhoun observed that the latter "resides in the people of the States respectively."[76] This ultimate sovereignty would be threatened, continued Calhoun, if the Supreme Court were held to be the final authority on constitutional construction. Such a power for one of the branches of the national government "would, in effect, divest the people of the States of their sovereign authority, and clothe that department with the robe of supreme power."[77]

Though Calhoun denied that the Supreme Court was the finial arbiter of the Constitution, he recognized the Court's role in protecting the national government should the states usurp power. However, he did not believe that the Supreme Court, as a branch of the national government, could or should protect the states from national usurpations. In earlier writings, Calhoun posited that the state supreme courts could protect state exercise of reserved powers if the Judiciary Act of 1789 were amended to prohibit appeal from state to federal courts. With such a change to the Judiciary Act "the practical consequence would be, that each government would have a negative on the other, and thus possess the most effectual remedy, that can be conceived against encroachments."[78]

This remedy was abandoned for nullification most likely because a change to the Judiciary Act would have required a majority in Congress, while nullification could be accomplished by a single state. Consequently, in the *Exposition* Calhoun contended that "it would seem impossible to deny to the States the right of deciding on infractions of their powers, and the proper remedy applied for their correction. The right of judging, in such cases, is an essential attribute of sovereignty— of which the States cannot be divested without losing their sovereignty itself. . . ."[79]

Basing the nullifying power on ultimate sovereignty, Calhoun naturally preferred a convention over the state legislature. "When convened," wrote Calhoun, "it will belong to the Convention itself to determine, authoritatively, whether the acts of which we complain be unconstitutional. . . ."[80] The calling of a convention would be "highly favorable to calm investigation and decision" inasmuch as the electoral preparation would be a solemn occasion with much deliberation among the people.[81] If the convention nullified a law within the limits of South Carolina, a higher authority—a convention of three-fourths of the states—could be summoned to determine whether the national government should enjoy the contested power. If this constitutional convention conferred the power on the national government, South Carolina would have to obey, or secede from the union.

The *Exposition* also anticipated many of the arguments that would be made against nullification. For example, Calhoun expected that many might object to state veto because there was no specific provision in the Constitution authorizing a state to nullify a federal law. To this Calhoun replied that neither was there an express provision authorizing the Supreme Court to declare a duly enacted law unconstitutional. Nevertheless, tariff advocates had repeatedly referred to the Court as the final arbiter. Calhoun also expected that his opponents would argue that nullification would lead to anarchy and disunion. He answered this objection by pointing out that "[i]t is impossible to propose any limitation on the authority of governments, without encountering, from the supporters of power, this very objection of feebleness and anarchy."[82] Appealing to history, Calhoun observed that "the opposing parties—the advocates of power and of freedom—have ever separated" on the issue of limited government.[83]

The South Carolina legislature made some changes to the *Exposition* and ordered 5,000 copies to be printed. Calhoun's authorship was kept secret, though many speculated about his role. Calhoun's observations about the difficulty and solemn nature of calling a convention proved to be perspicacious. A two-thirds majority of the state legislature was needed under the state constitution to call a convention, and the nullifiers fell far short of this in 1828 and 1830. In 1831, the nullifiers formed the States Rights and Free Trade Association of South Carolina. The Association's purpose was to educate and persuade the electorate of the necessity of a state convention. Governor Hamilton, elected vice president of the Association at its first meeting, spoke of the "vital importance of having our associations thoroughly organized forwith, throughout the State, and in a condition of perfect preparedness."[84] Hamilton predicted that his fellow citizens would join the Association by the thousands and questioned how any South Carolinian could "love the Federal Government more in its injustice, than they love their own poor state in its suffering."[85]

While Hamilton planned a statewide campaign for nullification, Calhoun in July 1831 issued his Fort Hill Address in which the Vice President publicly embraced state interposition. Calhoun recognized that many South Carolinians had considered his early nationalism "to be my greatest political fault," but he assured his fellow citizens that he was dedicated to protection of the reserved powers.[86] It is difficult to estimate the influence of the Fort Hill Address on the push for a convention. Calhoun was a major player in South Carolina politics, but one should not neglect the groundwork laid by Thomas Cooper, perhaps the

Image 4.2 John C. Calhoun viewed nullification as firmly grounded in the text and spirit of the Kentucky and Virginia Resolutions. Courtesy of the South Caroliniana Library, University of South Carolina, Columbia.

state's most influential nonelected official. Cooper served as the president of the South Carolina College in the 1820s, and in this capacity he repeatedly warned his students of the dangers of consolidation and touted the rights of the states. Cooper sang the praises of a national government "with powers strictly limited, under the authority delegated by independent states" and a Constitution which could "be altered and amended by an appeal to them, and in no other way."[87] Cooper had accused Calhoun and other Republicans of "forg[etting], in most part, the principles that originally characterized" the party, and of "acquiesc[ing] in one encroachment after another."[88] This school master of states' rights, to borrow a phrase from Dumas Malone, was no doubt pleased that the former nationalists had come over to his way of thinking, but nonetheless remained skeptical of their motivations.

With the state's elite well-versed in republican political theory and the evils of the tariff, the States Rights and Free Trade Association published numerous tracts targeted toward skilled laborers and farmers who were less familiar with the doctrines of Calhoun and Cooper. For example, in "A Catechism on the Tariff for the use of Plain People of Common Sense," the Association explained that "[i]t is in no case our interest to pay three days labor for an article which we can get for two, whether we pay the additional price to our neighbor, or to a foreigner. The cheaper we buy, the more we can afford to buy."[89] Summarizing Adam Smith's principles on division of labor, the tract continued:

> The actuating principle of commerce, is to bring articles wanted at home, and which cannot be raised profitably at home, from countries where these articles are plentiful and cheap. Thus, we import silver from South-America, and sugar from Cuba into Pennsylvania, in return for wheat flour. While the Spaniards sell the sugar which they can raise, cheaply, for the flour which they cannot.[90]

After a discussion of the delegated powers and the constitutionality of protection, the tract described a nullification as "a mere declaration of legal fact, and a refusal to conform to an unauthorized act of an agent who has exceeded his powers."[91] An unconstitutional act of Congress could be no more binding on a South Carolinian "than on the King of France."[92]

South Carolina's unionists floundered as the States Rights and Free Trade Association attracted men of all classes to its standard. The unionists never overcame their Federalist-like disdain for pandering to the masses and their cause stagnated. While the Association reached out to rich and poor alike, unionists concentrated on their aristocratic brethren—a small fraction of the state's electorate. This lack of managerial acumen meant that a state convention was certain to occur.

The unionist cause was also hurt because they could advance no remedy likely to bring a change in the tariff laws. Unionist leaders agreed that "[t]he doctrine of Free Trade is a great fundamental doctrine of civilization,"[93] but their theory of the Constitution gave South Carolinians two ineffectual options: (1) a test case presented to the Supreme Court, or (2) a constitutional amendment prohibiting protective tariffs. As for the former, the Supreme Court under John Marshall was decidedly nationalistic and unlikely to strike down the protective tariff. As for the latter, the Constitution requires two-thirds of both houses of Congress to propose amendments to the states, or two-thirds of the state legislatures applying to Congress for a convention. If the Southern congressional representatives could not garner a 51 percent majority to repeal the tariff, then they certainly could not muster a super majority to propose amendments. Likewise, with the North benefiting from the tariff, two-thirds of the legislatures would never petition Congress for a convention.

Conceding that the tariff was oppressive and offering no relief, the more successful unionist strategy was an appeal to nationalism. Unionist leaders like Daniel Huger accused the nullifiers "of exchanging Washington's legacy for a ledger, or reducing patriotism to dollars and cents."[94] But the nullifiers were also successful in appealing to history and the legacy of revolutionary heroes.[95] The States Rights and Free Trade Association proclaimed that if South Carolina submitted to the protective system "let us at once dismantle the many monuments erected to our proud ancestors—let us obliterate every trace of the glorious contest of '76—for then we will have no further business with the memory and honor of those names and times."[96] George McDuffie compared Northern tariff advocates to "the English oppressors of our ancestors"[97] and urged South Carolinians "to contemplate the conduct of our ancestors . . . when placed in similar circumstances."[98]

In the summer of 1832, Congress passed a new tariff bill. The average rate was reduced to 25 percent of the value of imported goods. However, rates on iron, woolens, and cottons remained at the 50 percent level. To make matters worse in the Carolinians' eyes, the national treasury expected to enjoy a surplus in the 1830s as a result of the retirement of the debt from the War of 1812. As much as they loathed protection, South Carolinians were willing to be taxed to pay their portion of the war debt. But with debt retirement on the horizon, the tariff became even more unpopular.

With the principle of protection reaffirmed in the Tariff of 1832, the people of South Carolina voted overwhelmingly in October 1832 for nullifier candidates. Governor Hamilton called the new legislature into special session, and, as expected, two-thirds of both houses voted for a state convention. A special election for convention delegates was held on November 12, and the Convention met on November 19. Upon the motion of Judge C.J. Colcock, Governor Hamilton was elected president of the Convention and was given the authority to appoint a select committee of 21 to report on a course of action. The handful of unionists present introduced a resolution stating that the Convention was incompetent for wielding sovereign power because delegates were chosen based on a "compound ratio of population and property."[99] The Convention, however, refused to consider the resolution and proceeded with its business.

Reporting back on November 22, the Committee presented the Convention with four documents: (1) the Committee's report drafted by Robert Y. Hayne, (2) an address to the people of South Carolina written by Robert J. Turnbull, (3), an address to the people of the United States composed by Calhoun and revamped by McDuffie, and (4) an ordinance of nullification written by William Harper. The various documents recounted the adoption of the Tariff of 1816, the steady increase in the duties, the economic objections to the tariff, and the constitutional issues raised by protection. The documents emphasized that South Carolina had not rushed to a convention. The state legislature had adopted resolutions and the state's representatives in Congress had made South Carolina's concerns known to the nation—all to no avail. "We cannot again petition," the Committee report concluded, "it would be idle to remonstrate, and degrading to protest. In our estimation it is now a question of Liberty or Slavery."[100]

Nonetheless, the documents did not breathe a hatred for the union of states. The Convention, for all of its fiery rhetoric, accepted that union was beneficial. "We still cherish that rational devotion to the Union," the Convention explained, "by which this State has been pre-eminently distinguished, in all times past."[101] However, an "idolatrous devotion, which would bow down and worship Oppression and Tyranny, veiled under that consecrated title—if it ever existed among us," the Convention continued, "has now vanished forever."[102] In other words, South Carolina remained loyal to the old union created by the Constitution of 1787, the union James Madison described as "a feudal system of republics,"[103] but rejected the concept of union in which the states were but administrative subdivisions of a consolidated government. In the words of Thomas Cooper, South Carolina wanted to "keep the Constitution of the United States, such as the [Philadelphia] convention left it, pure and undefiled."[104]

Though framing the controversy as a question of liberty or slavery, the Convention informed the nation that South Carolina was "willing to make a large offering to preserve the Union."[105] South Carolina would accept "that the same rate of duty may be imposed upon the protected articles that shall be imposed on the unprotected, provided that no more revenue be raised than is necessary to meet the demands of the Government for Constitutional purposes."[106] In the absence of such a compromise, South Carolina would prohibit enforcement of the tariff. And if the national government chose to use force to collect the tariff revenue, South Carolina "prefer[red] that the territory of the State should be the cemetery of freemen than the habitation of slaves."[107]

Viewing themselves as acting in the spirit of their forefathers, the delegates reserved the first lines of the signature portion of the ordinance of nullification for the seven members of the Convention who had fought in the American Revolution. By signing the ordinance, these old patriots along with rest of the delegates declared the tariffs of 1828 and 1832 "null, void, and no law, nor binding upon this State, its officers or citizens." However, to give Congress an opportunity to lower the duties, the Convention provided that the ordinance would not go into effect until after February 1, 1833. The ordinance further provided that the legislature should enact such measures as necessary to implement it, prohibited an appeal to the Supreme Court of the United States of any matter pertaining to the ordinance, and required that all men holding civil or military office in the state (excluding the legislature) take an oath to obey and execute the ordinance. The ordinance ended by threatening secession if the national government took any coercive measures. "[T]he people of this State," the ordinance averred, "will thenceforth hold themselves absolved from all further obligation to maintain or preserve their political connection with the people of the other States, and will forthwith proceed to organize a separate government."[108] South Carolina had put into operation the theory of the Kentucky and Virginia Resolutions.

Following the Convention, Hayne resigned as a United States senator and Calhoun resigned as the vice president.[109] The former was elected governor and latter was appointed to the Senate. As vice president, Calhoun had often been unable to support his state with the vigor which he thought South Carolina's cause deserved. But as a senator,

Calhoun would be able to defend nullification and at the same time participate in efforts to reach a compromise on the tariff.

Aside from the appointments of Calhoun and Hayne, the legislature was busy passing measures to enforce the ordinance.[110] The legislature chose to eschew a belligerent brand of nullification, and instead sought to channel cases into the South Carolina court system. With the Replevin Act, the legislature gave merchants who refused to pay duties on imported goods recourse to the courts. By filing a replevin action, the merchant could recover goods detained for nonpayment of the tariff. A judge and jury, sworn to uphold the ordinance, would find the protective tariff unconstitutional and order the goods to be turned over to the merchant. If a United States customs officer refused to relinquish the goods, local law enforcement officials could seize the personal property of the federal customs officer and hold the property until the goods were delivered to the merchant. Also, persons arrested by federal officials for failure to pay duties were authorized to petition a state court judge for a writ of habeas corpus. The state legislature hoped that nullification by due process would show that state veto was a peaceable remedy devoid of caprice.

But just in case nullification did not prove peaceable, the legislature passed the Militia Act whereby the governor was authorized to call out the state militia and purchase additional weaponry. Twenty-five thousand men volunteered for military service and companies of soldiers drilled in towns throughout the state. Hayne was sensitive that an overzealous volunteer might be less than careful to avoid a fight with national forces, and he therefore prohibited his growing army from converging on Charleston, the site of several federal forts and custom-houses. In the event that Charleston needed reinforcements, Hayne planned to order 2,500 elite cavalry troops from around the state to converge on the Holy City to hold off the enemy until infantry units arrived.

Outraged at the course of events in South Carolina, President Jackson put on alert federal troops stationed in Charleston. Jackson believed that an "*attempt will be made to surprise the Forts and garrisons by the militia*, and must be guarded against with *vestal vigilance* and any attempt by force repelled with prompt and exemplary punishment."[111] To gain information on South Carolina's troop movements and other preparations, Jackson sent George Breathitt to Charleston ostensibly as a postal official. Breathitt's real assignment was "to ascertain, as far as practicable, to what extremity the nullifyers intend to proceed."[112] The old general relished a good fight, and with South Carolina unionist

Joel Poinsett pressing the President for swift action, the outbreak of hostilities seemed certain.

As early as mid-October 1832, Poinsett urged that Jackson "act decidedly and vigorously" to put down the nullifiers.[113] "[I]f these bad men are put down by the strong arm," Poinsett lectured the President, "the union will be cemented . . . by the vigour of the government, and you will earn imperishable glory of having preserved this great confederacy from destruction."[114] Jackson believed that armed unionists like Poinsett and his followers would be useful in crushing the nullifiers and he ordered federal commanders in Charleston to distribute 5,000 stand of muskets to Poinsett's men. Jackson assured the unionists that they would not be fighting alone. He boasted that he could "have within the limits of So. Carolina fifty thousand men, and in forty days more another fifty thousand."[115] Once federal and unionist forces gained control of the state, Jackson planned to have the leading nullifiers "arrested and arraigned for treason."[116]

So the public and South Carolinians would know his views on the nullification controversy, Jackson drafted a proclamation with the assistance of Secretary of State Edward Livingston. This is the same Livingston who in 1798 declared that the people should rise in rebellion against the Federalists' Alien and Sedition Acts. As the proclamation indicates, Livingston mellowed somewhat with age.

Jackson's proclamation attacked nullification as a panacea for all disenchanted local interests. "[E]very law operating injuriously upon any local interest will perhaps be thought, and certainly represented," Jackson contended, "as unconstitutional."[117] Jackson made clear that he viewed

> the power to annul a law of the United States, assumed by one State, *incompatible with the existence of the Union, contradicted by the letter of the Constitution, unauthorized by its spirit, inconsistent with every principle on which it was founded, and destructive of the great object for which it was formed.*[118]

For Jackson, the union was paramount—majorities in both houses of Congress should rule and state veto threatened this principle. He could not understand how a citizen of the United States could calculate the value of the union. The old general thought of the union as something akin to salvation, something no American would exchange for all the liberty or riches of the earth.

Accordingly, the proclamation adopted a highly nationalistic theory of the union. Jackson believed that the unbreakable bonds of nationhood preceded the Constitution and that never did the separate states "consider [themselves] in any other light than as forming one nation."[119] Rejecting the compact theory, Jackson held that the national government represented the people of the nation, not the states or the people of the several states. This theoretical underpinning of the proclamation was central to Jackson's primary goal: the discrediting of secession. Otherwise, the union would be but "a bag of sand with both ends opened, the moment the least pressure is upon it, the sand flows out at each end."[120] Hence, Jackson argued that secession was not a right that could be inferred from the structure of the Constitution, but rather a revolutionary act. Jackson continued by reminding South Carolinians that revolutionaries gave up the protection of law and "incur[red] the penalties consequent on a failure."[121] Jackson's statements on secession are of great historical significance because, as Robert Remini has observed, Jackson was "the first and only statesman of the early national period to deny publically the right of secession."[122]

Old Hickory's proclamation shocked many across the nation. Throughout his political career, Jackson had been known as a states' rights man. The prenullification Jackson had maintained that "the true glory of the Confederacy is founded on the prosperity and power of several independent sovereignties of which it is composed." In fact, just days before the nullification proclamation issued, Jackson had released his fourth annual message in which he at times sounded like an Old Jeffersonian Republican. Jackson affirmed America's agrarian tradition by describing farmers as "the basis of society and true friends of liberty."[123] In addition, Jackson seemed serious about a change in tariff policy and recommended that it be reduced to a revenue standard.

In the four years before the nullification proclamation, Jackson had vetoed internal improvement legislation that he believed served only local interests. If the American people wanted the national government to build roads and canals, then Jackson suggested an amendment to the Constitution to confer the necessary power. The President was also an enemy of the national bank. Though the Supreme Court had adopted Hamilton's position on the bank, holding that Congress could incorporate such an institution, Jackson still opposed the bank based on his principles of strict construction. Like Jefferson, Jackson believed that all three branches of the national government could interpret the Constitution. The Supreme Court could rule that a bank was within Congress's delegated powers, but the president was not constitutionally required to consider the ruling binding upon him.

The Congress, the Executive, and the Court must each for itself be guided by its own opinion of the Constitution. Each public officer who takes an oath to support the Constitution swears that he will support it as he understands it, and not as it is understood by others . . . The opinion of the judges has no more authority over Congress than the opinion of Congress over the judges, and on that point the President is independent of both. The authority of the Supreme Court must not, therefore, be permitted to control the Congress or the Executive when acting in their legislative capacities, but to have only such influence as the force of their reasoning may deserve.[124]

In light of these sentiments, states' rights advocates were bewildered when Jackson in the nullification proclamation suggested that South Carolina take the tariff question to the Supreme Court for an ultimate determination. Martin Van Buren warned Jackson that the nullification proclamation would "likely bring you in collision with Virginia."[125] As a result, many questioned whether the governor of Virginia would permit Jackson to march national troops through the state if war broke out in South Carolina.

Though his proclamation received much criticism from his friends, Jackson continued to insist that he was truer to the legacy of the Principles of '98 than the South Carolina nullifiers. For this proposition, Old Hickory could point to James Madison's statements regarding nullification. In a letter published in the *North American Review* in 1830, Madison contended "that the proceedings of Virginia [in 1798 and 1799] have been misconceived by those who have appealed to them."[126] Madison denied that the Virginia Resolutions had ever proposed nullification, or that he had ever set up the states as the final arbiters of the Constitution. The Philadelphia Convention, Madison explained, realized "that controversies would arise concerning the boundaries of jurisdiction [between the state and national governments]; and that some provision ought to made for such occurrences."[127] The "provision," of course, was the Supreme Court. Only with the Court as an ultimate arbiter could the nation enjoy uniformity of its national laws. The only action sought by Virginia in 1798, Madison recollected, was the cooperation of the other states in persuading the national legislature to repeal the Alien and Sedition Acts. "Had the resolutions been regarded as avowing & maintaining a right in an individual State, to arrest by force the execution of a law of the United States," Madison concluded, "it must be presumed that it would have been a conspicuous object of their denunciation."[128] As discussed in the previous chapter, the states responding to the Kentucky and Virginia Resolutions did object to nullification and they asserted that the Supreme Court, not the states, was the final arbiter of the Constitution. On this point as with others, Madison was either suffering from advanced age or engaging in deception.

Jefferson had died in 1826 and therefore was unable to challenge Madison's version of events. Early in the South Carolina controversy Madison had claimed that Jefferson had never used the term "nullification" in his draft of the Kentucky Resolutions. However, when a draft turned up in Jefferson's handwriting, Madison was forced to retreat on this point. Madison's Virginia Resolutions were more moderate than Jefferson's Kentucky Resolutions, but this cannot explain his wholesale abandonment of former positions. Perhaps the best conjecture is that Madison, realizing that his years were dwindling, wanted to be remembered as the Father of the Constitution, a creator of the union.[129] Aware that Alexander Hamilton's dreams for America were reaching fruition, Madison jumped on the bandwagon to secure his share of the credit.

Jackson was pleased that an elder statesman like Madison shared his views of the Principles of 1798, but received a shock when his former mentor, Nathaniel Macon of North Carolina, weighed in on the nullification proclamation. Macon agreed with Jackson that nullification was a remedy unknown to the Constitution—a state could not be in the union for some purposes and out for others. However, Macon took issue with the President's views on the union and secession. A sovereign state, in Macon's opinion, could not "commit treason or rebellion or be subject to laws relating to either."[130] After the nullifying Convention adjourned, Macon believed that South Carolina should have been treated as a foreign power, a state out of the union. "The union is a matter of choice and interest," Macon explained, "without these it cannot be lasting."[131] Jackson's opinion on secession seemed to Macon but a variation of "the old British doctrine, once a subject always a subject."[132]

Macon's views on secession were not heterodox nor was the North Carolinian in the minority on this point. For example, General Winfield Scott, a Virginian and the commander of federal forces in Charleston harbor during the nullification crisis, accepted the right of secession even as he prepared for hostilities. Writing to William Campbell Preston in December 1832, Scott lamented the turmoil afflicting the nation. However, he promised his support "to this Union as long as it shall be the duty & interest of Virginia to abide by the family compact. If she withdraws, I hope no longer to be on the scene."[133] South Carolina unionist leader William Drayton adopted a position similar to Macon. He thought nullification was but a brand of constitutional legerdemain, but accepted that a state could "withdraw from the Union" if other forms of redress were unsuccessful.[134]

While soldiers drilled and citizens debated Jackson's nullification proclamation, Congress scrambled to craft a compromise tariff acceptable to all. In early January 1833, the Ways and Means Committee reported the Verplanck tariff bill to the House of Representatives. The bill took its name from the Committee chairman, but Jackson's advisors played key roles in crafting the specifics of the bill. In essence, the Verplanck tariff bill proposed to cut tariff duties by half during a two-year period. This was far from what the nullifiers had demanded, but it did indicate that Congress was serious about a compromise.

Though opposing the Verplanck bill, leading nullifiers met in Charleston and decided that the national government should have more time to reform the tariff laws. Consequently, on January 21, 1833, just days before the scheduled implementation of the nullification ordinance, the Carolina chieftains resolved that they would not make use of the Replevin Act or other statutory mechanisms passed by the legislature to enforce nullification. Things were going South Carolina's way, and the nullifiers wisely sought to avoid any conflict with the national government that could lessen the likelihood of an acceptable adjustment of the tariff laws.

The Verplanck bill was eventually killed in Congress by a strange combination of protectionists, free traders, and general enemies of President Jackson. However, Henry Clay stepped forward in an effort to renew his reputation as the Great Compromiser.[135] Clay had just lost the 1832 presidential election to Jackson and he yearned for revenge. Not only would he be seen as the savior of the union, but Clay also believed that a compromise was the only way to salvage his American System of protection, internal improvements, and a national bank. If one of the three pillars was destroyed completely, Clay knew the other two would crumble as well. Hence, Clay proposed that all duties be reduced to 20 percent over a nine year period. The end result of the rates was identical to the Verplanck bill, but the longer period of adjustment was intended to lessen the blow to manufacturers. Protection would survive in principle, though the rates would be much lower than before.

Clay knew that the success of his proposal depended on one man: John C. Calhoun. If Calhoun and his Southern brethren in the Senate joined with the Clayites, Jacksonian forces would not have the numbers to prevent passage of the compromise tariff. Calhoun longed for a compromise and did not want to see South Carolina move along the road to secession. He also knew that the longer a compromise took, the more likely violence was to occur. On January 21, 1833, the Senate Judiciary Committee had reported the Force Bill which authorized President Jackson to use military power to crush nullification. Calhoun indignantly denied that the national government could rightfully use force against a sovereign state. He further denied that an army turned against its own citizens could save the constitutional republic. "Force may, indeed, hold the parts together," Calhoun admitted, "but such a union would be the bond between master and slave—a union of exaction on one side and of unqualified *obedience* on the other."[136]

Despite Calhoun's objections, the Force Bill was passed by both houses and was sent to President Jackson along with the compromise tariff. Jackson signed both of them on March 2, 1833. The next day, Calhoun began the long journey back to South Carolina. The nullification Convention was scheduled to reassemble on the eleventh. He feared that the compromise tariff would not satisfy the more strident nullifiers and that their response to the Force Bill would be secession. The Convention, however, agreed to rescind the ordinance of nullification. In a report addressing the recent congressional proceeding, the Convention observed that the compromise tariff fell short of the Convention's demands, but that "such an approach has been made towards the true principles on which the duties on imports ought to be adjusted under our system, that the people of South Carolina are willing so far to yield the measure, as to agree that their Ordinance shall henceforth be considered as having no force or effect."[137]

With the ordinance rescinded, there was but one matter left for the Convention to deal with: the Force Bill. The Convention again smelled consolidation in the air. The principles of the Force Bill mocked notions of state sovereignty and promised the ascendancy of the national government. "The alien and sedition laws," the Convention declared, "sink into measures of harmless and insignificant" compared with the Force Bill.[138] Accordingly, the Convention adopted another ordinance nullifying the Force Bill and then adjourned. The union had been preserved, but defiant South Carolina had proved its point.

* * *

In the early national period, the Principles of 1798 gained acceptance throughout the United States. During conflicts between state and national authority, reports and resolutions adopted by state legislatures, messages from state chief executives, opinions of state appellate courts, and speeches of leading citizens all ring with the words of the Kentucky and Virginia Resolutions. The Resolutions, of course, were not the first American statement of the compact theory, the locus of ultimate sovereignty, or the division of legislative sovereignty. But the Resolutions were perhaps the most lucid and succinct statements of first principles ever penned. Though originally condemned by nine states in the late 1790s, the Resolutions' cogent reasoning won acceptance in the marketplace of ideas. So powerful were the Resolutions that Andrew Jackson, even when adopting an ultra nationalistic theory of the union, felt compelled to try to square his new doctrine with the sacred texts of 1798.

Against the wishes of Madison, South Carolina added flesh to the skeleton of nullification and interposition. Though the Carolina doctrine caused a cleft in the states' rights camp of American politics, South Carolina's actions were arguably consistent with the Kentucky Resolutions, and to a large extent, the Virginia Resolutions. Taking to heart Madison's distinction between a legislature and convention, South Carolina rejected nullification by statutory enactment, and instead called a special convention, capable of wielding sovereign power, to void the Tariffs of 1828 and 1832. Calhoun was correct that the calling of a convention was no easy task. The nullifiers failed in 1828 and 1830, and succeeded only when the people realized that President Jackson and the national political process offered them no relief. As implemented, nullification did not depend on bayonets and brigands. Eschewing force, the South Carolina legislature sought to use the state court system to carry out nullification. Only after a state judge and jury heard the case would customs officials be ordered to turn over the goods to the merchant who had refused to pay the duty.

Nevertheless, history has been much harsher on the Carolina doctrine than the Kentucky and Virginia Resolutions. The easiest explanation for this is bad facts. Unlike the Sedition Act, which was blatantly unconstitutional, the tariff question presented a much more difficult call. Congress is specifically permitted to lay and collect duties, and the first Congress, replete with Framers and ratifiers of the Constitution, enacted tariffs with protectionist features. Moreover, scholars with a decidedly nationalistic bent have been successful in linking nullification and the South's later efforts at preserving slavery. Though recent scholarship has shown that there was no nexus between the two,[139] the earlier charge has stuck. President Jackson's bellicose actions (not South Carolina's) also did much to paint nullification as a dangerous remedy.

No matter what one thinks of the Carolina doctrine, the nullification controversy highlights the need for a mechanism to settle disputes between the states and national government. The question of who or what institution is the final arbiter has been a topic of debate. Though this question has existed, in some form, since the ratification debates, the discussion did not become fervent until Jefferson and Madison invoked nullification and interposition. From that point on, Americans were bitterly divided over who has final say on the meaning of the Constitution. In recent years, the Supreme Court's claim to this role has been acquiesced in. And while the Court as final arbiter does provide certainty, we must ask ourselves whether such a state of affairs can be squared with the people's position as ultimate sovereigns.

CHAPTER 5

CONSOLIDATION

The contours of the federal system, with its division of legislative sovereignty, are hardly visible as one surveys the modern governmental landscape. If Madison and Jefferson could return today, they would most likely conclude that we had abandoned the Principles of '98 for the British form of government. A look at the U.S. Code or a federal appropriations bill would convince them that Congress, like the British Parliament, has the authority to legislate on all subjects.

The consolidation feared by Anti-Federalists, the Jeffersonian Republicans, and the South Carolina nullifiers has come to pass. In answering the question of "what went wrong?" with the Framers' plan of government, one is tempted to begin with the War Between the States. As discussed in chapter 3, the state governments were intended to be a powerful check on the authority of the national government. In case of national encroachments, the Framers and ratifiers believed that the states would use all methods at their disposal, including the musket and sword, to return the national government to the bounds set by the Constitution. Lee's surrender to Grant dispelled this possibility. With the issue of secession settled by battle and the union held together by force, the states ceased to be a real barrier to the national government's expansion.

Nevertheless, even with a shift in power to the national government because of the Northern victory and the addition of the three Reconstruction Amendments in the postwar years, much of what the Framers created remained in place. As the Supreme Court noted in 1873, "unquestionably [the War] added largely to the number of those who believe in the necessity of a strong National government. But however pervading this sentiment . . . our statesmen have still believed that the existence of the States with powers for domestic and local government . . . was essential to the perfect working of our complex form of government, though they have thought proper to impose additional limitations on the States, and to confer additional powers on that of the Nation."[1] The Constitution of enumerated powers—its edges singed by the fires of war—lived on.

While the effects of the War on the Republic should not be dismissed lightly, trial by arms was never intended to be the primary method to keep the national government within the bounds set by the Constitution. The Framers would have been reckless not to have incorporated some institutional safeguards of federalism into the constitutional design. The Framers, of course, were not reckless, but unforeseen changes, ill-conceived amendments, and questionable constitutional interpretation have all played a role in undermining the states' reserved powers.

The Senate

A discussion of the Constitution's institutional safeguards meant to guard against consolidation must begin with the Senate. Yes, the Senate—not the Supreme Court. Though most Americans today recognize the Court as the final arbiter of the Constitution, the body that determines the extent of both national and state powers, in the early Republic the Court was not considered such a be-all and end-all.[2] As discussed in the previous chapter, even the nationalistic Andrew Jackson averred that he was not bound by Supreme Court's rulings. And, there was a divergence of opinion on whether states were bound by the Court's pronouncements. In sundry sets of resolutions, from both north and south of the Potomac, Americans asserted that the Framers committed a grave flaw by not providing for an impartial constitutional arbiter to settle disputes between the states and national government over the scope of the delegated powers.

However, there was no such confusion about the role of the U.S. Senate. At the time of ratification, the Framers expected the Senate to serve as guardian of the states' reserved powers. In the Philadelphia Convention, George Mason observed that the appointment of senators by state legislatures would provide the states with a "power of self defence."[3] Madison was unequivocal about the matter in *Federalist* No. 62: "the equal vote allotted each state [in the Senate] is at once a recognition of the portion of sovereignty remaining in the individual states, and an instrument for preserving that residuary sovereignty." No law could be passed, Madison continued, "without the concurrence of first a majority of the people [in the House of Representatives], and then a majority of the States [in the Senate]."[4] Importantly, the state conventions expressed a similar understanding. James Iredell of North

Carolina, for example, described the Senate as the body charged with ensuring that the state governments "be preserved."[5] In commenting on the composition of the Senate, Pierce of Massachusetts echoed Madison and identified senators as "representatives of the sovereignty."[6] The state conventions also expected the state legislatures to exercise much control over the senators. If a state legislature disagreed with the actions of its senators, Rufus King of Massachusetts believed that the legislature would admonish and "instruct them" on the correct course of action.[7] Appointment and control of senators by the state legislatures was seen by all as key to protecting the states' residuary sovereignty.

As Larry Kramer has observed,[8] though the Senate seems like a perfect vehicle for protecting the states, the Framers failed to anticipate a major development in the electoral process: the rise of political parties. The idea of political parties was anathema to the Framers and they associated parties with unruly and dangerous factions. By faction the Framers meant a group formed to achieve a common goal that was "adverse to the rights of other citizens, or to the permanent and aggregate interests of the community."[9] Factions were an evil to be avoided and the Framers never dreamed that "factions" would become central to the operation of our government.

In 1787, the Framers assumed that state officials would be jealous of their reserved powers just as federal officials would be jealous of their delegated powers. The Framers never contemplated that the competing sets of officials would combine to accomplish ultimate goals based on a common ideology or party affiliation.[10] For the federal system to work, the two groups were supposed to clash and thus keep each other in check.[11] Operation in concert was not in the equation.

Political parties turned the world of the Framers upside down as an interstate network developed whereby like-minded politicians pursued common agendas. Though in the early years of the union this network was rather loose, parties eventually became very effective political machines. State legislators identified themselves with a party interest rather than a state interest, and, in turn, so did senators. The end result is a system in which members of political parties battle over the efficacy or wisdom of policies and for the most part ignore concerns of dual sovereignty.

While common ideology is important in explaining the operation of political parties and why parties have undermined the federal system, the mighty dollar is also to blame. Political parties and political action committees (PACs) are the major players in world of campaign finance. Politicians look for funds not from their constituents, but their party's national headquarters or a PAC that embraces the politicians' agenda. Based on the flow of dollars, members of Congress represent not a state or district but a set of donors who might or might not have anything in common with the constituency the member is supposed to represent. Under such a finance system, it is no surprise that the protection of a state's reserved powers has been lost in the flood of greenbacks.

The rise of political parties aside, other forces, such as a blind faith in democracy, were at work to undermine the role of the Senate. By the late 1800s, the Constitution's design for choosing senators appeared to many to be an anachronism. Progressives denounced the Senate as an oligarchic rich man's club and argued that democracy was the cure for ills wrought by industrialization and powerful business combinations.[12] In response to pressure from Progressives, 33 states eventually adopted a system of direct primaries for electing senators. The primaries operated much like Constitution's electoral college, with the state legislators promising to abide by the results of the primary in appointing senators. Going further than primaries, 12 states opted for the "Oregon system" for choosing senators. Under this system, candidates for the state legislature promised in their platforms either (1) to abide by the people's choice of senators in a general election, or (2) to use their own judgment in appointing senators. Choice of the second option was political suicide, and therefore as a practical matter senators were elected by the people in states using the Oregon system.[13]

By 1912, the demand for popular election of senators was so strong that Congress submitted the Seventeenth Amendment to the states for ratification. Within 11 months the requisite three-fourths of the state legislatures approved the amendment and officially disenfranchised themselves. Unfortunately, the debates surrounding the adoption of the Seventeenth Amendment evince little concern for the Senate's role as protector of the states' reserved powers.[14] In light of the outcome of the War Between the States and the growing role of political parties, the people were forgetting the importance of federalism in the American system of government.

Though the role of the Senate was on the decline before the ratification of the Seventeenth Amendment, it was no coincidence that the size of the national government expanded rapidly after 1913. Without the Seventeenth Amendment, one must wonder whether the Wilson administration would have succeeded in establishing the Federal Reserve, the Federal Trade Commission, and the "war socialism" used to control production and other facets of the economy during

World War I. And the same question must be asked when considering the government programs and agencies established during the New Deal.[15] But for the Seventeenth Amendment, the national government likely would be much smaller than it is today.

Every Problem a National Problem

Not only were political parties instrumental in undermining the Senate's role, but they have also blurred distinctions between *intra*state activities, meant to be regulated by local officials, and national concerns falling within Congress's delegated powers. Every problem is now seen as a national problem requiring a national solution. The expansion of federal criminal law is a prime example. At the time of ratification, most Americans recognized that the national government's role in protecting citizens from crime was minuscule. In *Federalist* No. 17, Alexander Hamilton was clear that "the ordinary administration of civil and criminal justice" was "the province of the State governments."[16] Under the Constitution, Congress has the express power to punish a handful of acts such as piracy, crimes committed on the high seas, treason, and counterfeiting. Until the War Between the States, Congress was, on the whole, true to the Constitution and limited federal criminal laws so that there was little overlap between offenses punished by the states and national government. The number of crimes punishable by the federal government increased after Appomattox, but the number of federal offenses did not skyrocket until recent years. According to the American Bar Association's Task Force on the Federalization of Criminal Law, "of all federal crimes enacted since 1865, over forty percent have been created since 1970."[17] In light of this expanding role, the Task Force also notes that "[t]he number of federal justice system personnel increased by 96% from 1982 to 1993, while state personnel increased at a significantly lesser rate, 42%."[18]

The reasons for the increase in federal crimes are manifold, but arguably a chief reason for the expansion of federal authority is political. Specifically, senators and congressmen have found that law-and-order platforms win votes. Though federal criminal laws usually duplicate state laws, national politicians can pontificate that they have taken action to make the streets safer and therefore they should be returned to office. And state officials, members of national political parties who long to be national officials, offer no resistance to the law-and-order platforms put forth by senators and congressmen. In the scramble for reelection, politicians simply ignore the data indicating that federalization of crime has little or no effect on public safety or the fact that crime is a local concern.[19]

In the same vein, the public and politicians often have knee-jerk reactions to high profile local crimes. The recent popularity of the proposed Hate Crimes Prevention Act (HCPA) is emblematic of the problem. The HCPA received much media attention in the wake of two highly publicized incidents: The dragging death of James Byrd (a black man) in Jasper, Texas, and the robbery-turned-murder of Matthew Shepard (a homosexual) in Laramie, Wyoming.

Almost every supporter of the HCPA explicitly referred to the incidents when pushing for its passage. Bill Clinton, in office at the time of the murders, described the incidents as teaching "us how easily prejudice can erupt into violence."[20] Janet Reno remarked that the events "show once again that we [the federal government] must do more to fight hate crimes in America."[21] Byrd's daughter, while participating in a news conference with Senator Edward Kennedy, applauded the HCPA because under the legislation perpetrators of hate crimes "will pay the price."[22] Though these supporters of the HCPA were quick to condemn the acts of violence as they called for federal legislation, they completely ignored the fact that the primary actors involved in the deaths of Byrd and Shepard were rapidly brought to justice by *state* law enforcement officials. Byrd's killer was sentenced to death and Shepard's killer received two consecutive life terms. How federal law will extract a higher price or deter crime is unclear. Though the HCPA has yet to become law, it is only a matter of time before it works its way into the U.S. Code. Tough-on-crime conservative politicians along with their liberal colleagues will likely find common ground, that is, the desire for reelection, and the HCPA will be passed with little opposition.

The federalization of crime, like other enlargements of the national government's powers, raises an interesting question: from where does Congress derive such power? The people of the several states delegated no "law and order power" to the general government. Never one to be tied down by such constitutional niceties, Congress has interpreted its delegated powers to such an extent that the Framers, and even the Anti-Federalists, could never have imagined. So broad is Congress's interpretation of the commerce power that the remainder of the enumerated powers are rendered superfluous. The regulation of interstate commerce has become the equivalent of a general police power.

Revolution by Constitutional Interpretation

A. *The Commerce Power*

If an activity affects or could affect the national economy, Congress claims the power to regulate it. For example, congressional findings in the HCPA aver that hate crimes affect interstate commerce "by impeding the movement of members of targeted groups and forcing such members to move across state lines to escape . . . violence," and "by preventing members of targeted groups from purchasing goods and services, obtaining or sustaining employment or participating in other commercial activity."[23]

The Commerce Clause, in pertinent part, provides that Congress has the power "[t]o regulate commerce with foreign nations, and among the several States, and with the Indian Tribes."[24] At the time of the Framing, commerce was understood as "[i]ntercourse, exchange of one thing for another, interchange of anything; trade; traffick."[25] It was not a synonym for "gainful activity" or "economic activity" or "agriculture" or "manufacturing."

By permitting Congress to regulate commerce with foreign nations, the Framers sought to marshal the strength of the whole when dealing with powerful commercial nations. In the words of Alexander Hamilton, "[b]y prohibitory regulations, extending at the same time throughout the States, we may oblige foreign countries to bid against each other, for the privileges of our markets." In the case of Great Britain, Hamilton postulated that commercial regulations prohibiting entry of British ships into American ports would "enable us to negotiate with the fairest prospect of success for commercial privileges of the most valuable and extensive kind."[26]

By permitting Congress to regulate *inter*state commerce, the Framers sought to create a great free-trade zone. Hamilton predicted that a "unrestrained intercourse between the States themselves will advance the trade of each, by an interchange of their respective productions, not only for the supply of reciprocal wants at home, but for exportation to foreign markets."[27] Madison noted that "[a] very material object [of the power to regulate interstate commerce] was the relief of the States which import and export through other States, from the improper contributions levied on them by the latter."[28] In other words, Madison believed that one of the main purposes of the clause was the removal of internal trade barriers. A nationwide free-trade zone, almost all agreed, would permit the states to take advantage of division of labor and lessen internal tensions as goods freely crossed borders.

As for the power to regulate trade with the Indians, the Framers included this in the Commerce Clause because of a troublesome provision in the Articles of Confederation. Under the Articles, Congress was charged with "regulating the trade, and managing all affairs with Indians, not members of any of the states, providing that the legislative right of any state within its own limits be not infringed or violated."[29] Determining the status of Indian tribes living in the United States proved to be confusing. Were the tribes foreign nations, loose associations of individuals, or domestic dependent nations under the guardianship of the national or state governments? To determine whether an Indian residing within the borders of a state was a "member" of a state only complicated the matter. Add to the mix the prohibition against infringing upon state legislative prerogatives, and Congress's power to regulate trade with the Indians under the Articles was useless. Hence, Indians were specifically included in the Commerce Clause of the Constitution.

But back to interstate commerce. Though the power to regulate commerce among the several states provided Congress with broad authority, the Framers obviously did not intend it as a general power for the regulation of economic activity or matters affecting the economy. Indeed, by the Clause's own language, Congress may only regulate the traffic of goods between or among states. In *Federalist* No. 17, Hamilton stressed that the commerce power would have no effect on "the administration of private justice . . . , the supervision of agriculture and of other concerns of a similar nature."[30] Criminal activity (at least according to the HCPA) and agriculture certainly affect or can affect the national economy, yet even the most nationalistic of the Framers never fathomed that Congress's reach would extend to these matters.

Furthermore, as a textual matter, affairs such as agriculture and manufacturing cannot be read into the Commerce Clause. As Richard Epstein has observed, logic dictates that "commerce" means the same thing in relation to the several states, foreign nations, and Indians.[31] The Clause would make no sense if we substituted manufacturing or agriculture for commerce: Congress shall have the power "[t]o regulate manufacturing [or agriculture] with foreign nations, and among the several states, and with the Indian Tribes." Just how Congress could regulate manufacturing with foreign nations (or among the states) is unclear. Obviously, no nation can regulate the crops grown in another nation or the production of manufactured goods in another nation. Yet if commerce includes manufacturing, agriculture, and gainful activity in general, then the Framers were asserting power over the internal affairs of the states, the Indian tribes, Great Britain, France, and all the countries of the world.

The understanding of commerce as trade or traffic is also borne out by another mention of commerce in Article I. Under Section Nine, "[n]o Preference shall be given by any Regulation of Commerce or Revenue to the Ports of one State over those of another."[32] The provision obviously prohibits Congress from favoring, for example, the port of New York over the port of Charleston. Regulations and duties are not to be fashioned in a way that will make one port more attractive than another. In the same vein, the mention of "commerce" in connection with ports seems to indicate that the Framers had in mind the traffic of goods. And again, it would make no sense to substitute the words agriculture or manufacturing for commerce: "No Preference shall be given by any Regulation of Manufacture [or Agriculture] or Revenue to the Ports of one State over those of another."

Though common sense indicates that the term "commerce" should be construed narrowly, common sense is often superceded by judicial decisions. To understand how the regulation of interstate commerce went from the creation of a great free-trade zone to the modern notion that Congress can regulate all gainful activity, a brief survey of the Supreme Court's Commerce Clause jurisprudence is in order.[33] The Supreme Court's foray into the realm of interstate commerce began in 1824 with the case of *Gibbons v. Ogden* (1824).[34] *Gibbons* dealt with the New York legislature's grant of a monopoly to Robert Fulton and Robert Livingston to operate steamboats in New York waters. Thomas Gibbons, who had a federal license to engage in the coasting trade, began operating a steamboat service between New York and Elizabethtown, New Jersey. Livingston's licensee, pointing to the grant of monopoly, petitioned and was granted an order enjoining Gibbons from ferrying passengers into New York. The decision was affirmed by a state appellate court, but reversed by the U.S. Supreme Court. Writing for the High Court, Chief Justice John Marshall began by noting that "commerce" certainly included navigation. Though defining commerce broadly as "intercourse," Marshall admitted that Congress could not regulate "that commerce . . . which is completely internal" to a state. Using state inspection laws as an example, Marshall observed that the object of such laws "is to improve the quality of articles produced by the labour of a country; to fit them for exportation or, it may be, for domestic use. They act upon a subject before it becomes an article of foreign commerce, or of commerce among the States, and prepare it for that purpose."[35] To Marshall, intercourse or commerce did not include events occurring before goods were shipped across state lines. In other words, the manufacturing process or the cultivation of crops was outside the Congress's authority. In the end, Marshall found New York's grant of monopoly to be in conflict with the federal coasting statute and dismissed the suit for injunction.

Marshall's reasonable interpretation of the Commerce Clause continued long after he left the bench. For example, in *United States v. Dewitt* (1869),[36] the Court struck down a federal law criminalizing the sale of illuminating oils that burned at temperatures less than 110 degrees Fahrenheit. The sale of illuminating oils, the Court concluded, was a matter internal to the states and thus outside of Congress's commerce power. Similarly, in *United States v. E.C. Knight Co.* (1895),[37] the Court gave the national government a black eye in the first case brought under the Sherman Antitrust Act. In *E.C. Knight*, the national government sought the dissolution of the American Sugar Refining Company, an entity through which several firms garnered more than 90 percent of the U.S. sugar refining capacity. The Court observed that the purpose of the Sherman Antitrust Act was to prevent monopolies and restraints on commerce. In light of this purpose, the Court reasoned, the government needed to prove that the activities of the defendants were a restraint or monopoly of interstate commerce. The Court then distinguished the regulation of manufacturing and the regulation of commerce by declaring that "[c]ommerce succeeds to manufacture, and is not a part of it."[38] "It is vital," the Court continued, "that the independence of the commercial power [delegated to Congress] and of the police power [remaining with the states], and the delimitation between them . . . should always be recognized and observed, for while the one furnishes the strongest bond of union, the other is essential to the preservation of the autonomy of the States as by our dual form of government."[39] Because the regulation of the manufacture of sugar was outside Congress's reach, the Court held that the government's case against the monopolists could not move forward.

Until 1937, for the most part, the Court interpreted the Commerce Clause as permitting Congress to regulate the exchange or trading of goods between people in different states. However, the case law did not permit Congress to regulate manufacturing or agriculture. Such a view of the Commerce Clause was consistent with the Framers' intent to create a free-trade zone. This state of affairs changed with the Court's decision in *NLRB v. Jones & Laughlin Steel Corporation* (1937).[40] In this seminal case, the Court sustained the National Labor Relations Act (NLRA), which prohibited unfair labor practices affecting interstate commerce, as a proper exercise of Congress's delegated powers. Jones had terminated 12 employees for allegedly engaging in union activity. The National Labor Relations Board ordered Jones to reinstate the employees and to cease and desist from discouraging the organization of its workers. Relying on cases such as *E.C. Knight*, Jones argued that the relations between an employer and employees were not commerce and therefore could not be reached by Congress. The Supreme Court disagreed. The Court explained that purely local operations could be reached by Congress "if they have such a close and substantial relation to interstate commerce that their control is essential or appropriate to protect commerce from burdens and obstructions."[41] Because the manufacture of steel, according to the Court, had a close relationship with interstate commerce, it upheld the NLRA.

Five years later the Court demonstrated just how far Congress's commerce power could reach when it considered provisions of the Agricultural Adjustment Act. In *Wickard v. Filburn* (1942),[42] the Court was presented with the question of whether Congress could regulate a farmer's growing of wheat intended solely for consumption on his farm. A local activity, lectured the Court, can "be reached by Congress if it exerts a substantial economic effect on interstate commerce." Though the 11.9 acres of wheat in question did not seem to affect interstate commerce, the Court reasoned that the farmer's 11.9 acres, "taken together with that of many others similarly situated, is far from trivial."[43] In other words, because the growing of wheat for home consumption by hundreds or thousands of farmers could affect the demand and price of wheat, the acts of a solitary bucolic soul fall under Congress's power to regulate interstate commerce.

Based on the logic of *Jones* and *Filburn*, Congress enacted a bevy of laws having little relation to the original meaning of the Commerce Clause. For example, criminal laws issued on the basis that criminal activity affects interstate commerce.[44] Congress even used the commerce power to pass sweeping civil rights legislation.[45] The end result was that the Commerce Clause became an unlimited grant of legislative power— so long as an activity tangentially affected the national economy or could affect the economy if large numbers of people engaged in the activity, Congress could reach it via legislation.

B. *The Spending Power*

While the Commerce Clause has been central in the story of Congress's expansion of power, one must not give short shrift to the so-called "spending power," which Congress claims is part of the General Welfare

Clause, and is used to reach objectives falling outside the delegated powers. The spending power is typically used as follows: Congress taxes state citizens, offers the state governments these "federal funds," and then attaches strings to receipt of the money. A highly publicized use of the spending power occurred in October 2000 when President Clinton signed into law a $58 billion transportation bill.[46] Tucked away between election-year, pork-barrel spending was a provision which, in effect, set a nationwide drunk driving standard. Under Section 351 of the bill, state receipt of federal highway funds was made contingent upon adoption of a blood alcohol content level intoxication standard of 0.08. States that refuse to tailor their laws to Washington's liking will lose a portion of their federal highway funds—2 percent in 2004, 4 percent in 2005, 6 percent in 2006, and 8 percent in 2007. At the time the transportation bill was passed, 19 states and the District of Columbia already had 0.08 laws, and in Massachusetts 0.08 was considered evidence but not proof of impairment. The other 31 states used 0.10 to define drunken driving.

Unfortunately, prevailing Supreme Court precedent permits Congress to attach myriad strings to federal spending. In *South Dakota v. Dole* (1987),[47] the Court upheld a congressional enactment directing the secretary of transportation to withhold highway funds from states with drinking ages under 21. Relying on cases from the New Deal, the *Dole* Court reaffirmed that "the power of Congress to authorize expenditure of public moneys for public purposes is not limited by the direct grants of legislative power found in the Constitution."[48] Congressional exercise of the spending power, continued the Court, is valid so long as it is for the general welfare, the conditions imposed are unambiguous, the conditions relate to national concerns, and the conditional grant does not run afoul of other constitutional provisions. In other words, there are no real limits on Congress's spending. Vague concepts like "general welfare" and "national concerns" are hardly restrictive.

Of course, the structure and history of the Constitution, absent the Supreme Court's exegesis, do impose limits on congressional spending. Section One of Article VIII permits Congress to tax and "to pay the Debts and provide for the common Defence and general Welfare of the United States." As pointed out by Madison and discussed in chapter 3, following this declaration is an enumeration of specific powers that would be rendered superfluous if "general welfare" was the standard. In his Virginia Resolutions, Madison stated that the general welfare language was "copied from the very limited grant of powers in the former articles of confederation" to ensure against misconstruction.

"[I]t will scarcely be said," Madison continued in his Report of 1799, that this language found in the Articles of Confederation was "ever understood to be either a general grant of power" or to permit the Confederation Congress to escape the Articles' enumeration of powers.[49] Hence, the text and history of the Constitution belie any assertion of a spending power unconnected to the enumerated powers.

C. The Court's Usurpations

Just as Congress uses the Commerce and Spending Clauses to trample on the reserved powers of the states, so too does the Supreme Court use the Fourteenth Amendment to restrict the exercise of the states' reserved powers. In pertinent part, the Fourteenth Amendment declares that "[n]o State shall . . . deprive any person of life, liberty, or property, without due process of law; nor deny to any person within its jurisdiction the equal protection of the laws."[50] Enacted after the War Between the States, the Fourteenth Amendment was designed to ameliorate the condition of newly freed slaves by protecting their basic civil rights such as their right to own property, to sell their labor, and to have access to state courts on the same basis as white men.[51] Over time judicial interpretation transformed the amendment into a mechanism for aggrandizing the power of the federal courts. In so doing, the justices lost sight of the amendment's original purpose—improving the lot of former slaves—and instead used the terms "due process" and "equal protection" to impose their personal views on the nation.

1. Due Process

The guarantee of due process is found both in the Fifth and Fourteenth Amendments and can be traced back to Magna Carta.[52] Due process had always been thought of in terms of procedure, that is, what procedures the government had to take before it could deprive an individual of life, liberty, or property.[53] At the time of the framing, Hamilton was unequivocal about the matter: "The words 'due process' have a precise technical import, and are only applicable to the process and proceeding of the courts of justice; they can never be referred to an act of the legislature."[54] But under the doctrine of "substantive due process," the Court looks beyond procedure and claims the power to judge the reasonableness or wisdom of laws—the substance of a law.

The doctrine of substantive due process entered the judicial scene in the late 1800s as the Supreme Court dealt with state laws enacted to protect the health and safety of workers from the darker side of industrialization.[55] Appealing to the Fourteenth Amendment, business attacked these state laws as arbitrary and violative of substantive due process. Perhaps the case that embodies substantive due process like no other is *Lochner v. New York* (1905).[56] *Lochner* dealt with a New York statute setting a maximum number of hours—60 per week and 10 per day—that bakers could work. The state defended the statute as a simple exercise of its police power—the reserved power to pass laws beneficial for health, safety, and welfare of the people. The Court, however, held that the statute deprived bakers of liberty without due process of law under the Fourteenth Amendment. Reasoning that bakers were not "wards of the state," the Court averred that there was "no reasonable ground for interfering with the liberty of person or the right of free contract, by determining the hours of labor, in the occupation of a baker."[57] The Court simply ignored that a reasonable legislature could conclude that laboring long hours in the proximity of ovens was unhealthy and therefore there should be some restrictions. In other words, the Court substituted its judgment for that of New York's legislature.

In 1937, the Court got out of the business of stringently judging the wisdom of economic regulations,[58] but the doctrine of substantive due process did not die. The Court began to apply the doctrine to state laws affecting "personal" rather than "economic" liberties. Part and parcel of this new use of the Due Process Clause was "incorporation" of the Bill of Rights into the Clause so the first eight amendments would apply to states as well as the national government.[59] Incorporation, according to Stephen B. Presser, "must be ranked as one of the boldest and most astonishing acts of judicial usurpation in the history of the United States Supreme Court."[60] As discussed in chapter 3, the Bill of Rights was meant to place limits on the national government to prevent it from usurping state power and threatening individuals. Even John Marshall recognized as much in the landmark case of *Barron v. Baltimore* (1833)[61] when he observed that the Bill of Rights was "not applicable to the legislation of the states."[62] With incorporation, the Court brushed aside this understanding and, in effect, rewrote history as well as the Constitution.

Growing ever bolder with its new found power, the Court not only struck state laws that infringed on specific provisions of the Bill of Rights, but also created new rights out of whole cloth and then overturned state laws infringing on these unenumerated rights. For example, in *Griswold v. Connecticut* (1965),[63] the Court struck down a Connecticut statute banning the distribution and use of contraceptives. In holding that this was an inappropriate use of the police power, the Court found a nebulous "right to privacy" arising from "specific guarantees in the Bill of Rights hav[ing] penumbras, formed by emanations from those guarantees that help give them life and substance."[64] Appealing to the "penumbras"[65] of the First, Third, Fourth, Fifth, and Ninth Amendments, the Court concluded that married couples surely had a right to make personal choices about their intimate relations and struck down the statute. In dissent, Justice Stewart conceded that Connecticut's statute was "an uncommonly silly law."[66] But he reminded his colleagues that their job was not to judge "whether we think this law is unwise, or even asinine." Rather, the job of the Court, he continued, is to judge whether the law "violates [the] Constitution."[67] Justice Stewart recognized that high-flown use of terms like penumbra cannot mask the reality of the judicial usurpation.

2. Equal Protection

The Supreme Court also uses the Equal Protection Clause to strike numerous state laws. On its face, the Equal Protection Clause requires that state laws treat everyone the same. But as a general rule, almost every law creates classifications and imposes burdens and benefits on different groups. For example, based on age classifications we permit some citizens to vote but not others. Age classifications also operate to regulate the consumption of alcohol and the operation of motor vehicles. Of course, no one questions the constitutionality of a minimum age for voting, drinking, or driving even though the classifications appear to deny some citizens equal protection of the laws. In light of the reality of classification and legislation, the Supreme Court has crafted a three-tiered standard of review for classifications. For economic and social legislation, the Supreme Court examines the classification to determine whether it is rationally related to a legitimate government interest. This is the most deferential standard of equal protection analysis and very few state laws fail this test. For gender classifications, the Court exercises intermediate scrutiny, examining whether the classification is substantially related to the achievement of an important government interest. For racial and ethnic classifications, the Court uses strict scrutiny. To pass muster under this highest form of scrutiny, the classification must be narrowly tailored to achieve a compelling state interest.[68]

The Court's equal protection methodology has no basis in the Constitution and is adroitly used by judges to uphold laws they fancy by applying a low level of scrutiny and to strike laws they object to by applying a higher standard. A prime example of the Court's equal protection jurisprudence is *United States v. Virginia* (1996),[69] in which the Court struck down the Virginia Military Institute's (VMI) all-male admissions policy. VMI is a state-supported college founded in 1839. For over 150 years, the operation of VMI as a single-gender, state-supported school raised no constitutional questions. Education had always been viewed as falling within reserved powers of the states, and thus VMI's policies were never questioned by the national government. This changed in 1990 when the Bush Justice Department brought suit challenging VMI's admissions policy. The case eventually made its way the Supreme Court where seven justices ruled in favor of the national government.

In defending the school, Virginia put forward two important government interests which it believed permitted the exclusion of women. First, Virginia contended that the benefits of single-gender education and its contribution to diversity in educational approaches militated in favor of the admissions policy. Second, the state claimed that the adversative method, which is a vigorous system focused on the development of the "whole man," would have to be altered in such a way as to forever change the college. The Court dismissed Virginia's diversity argument because the founders of VMI did not establish the college with their hearts and minds set on diversity—the mantra of our modern times. Next, the Court swept aside concerns about developing the "whole man" by stating that "[n]either the goal of producing citizen-soldiers nor VMI's implementing methodology is inherently unsuitable to women."[70] The Court cited as evidence women's entry into the federal military academies and their service in the armed forces.

Tellingly, the Court's analysis of the interests put forward by Virginia rings of public policy, a field normally associated with an elected body. Without question, the policy argument that women should be admitted to a state-supported college on the same terms as men is inherently reasonable. In fact, intelligent policy arguments can be made on behalf of state-supported single-gender education as well as coeducational opportunities. However, these policy arguments belong on the floor of a legislature—it is for Virginians and their representatives to debate such matters, not a federal court. As Justice Scalia pointed out in dissent, "[t]he virtue of a democratic system with a First Amendment is that it readily enables the people, over time, to be persuaded that what they took for granted is not so, and to change their laws accordingly." If a person believes that an all-male admissions program is inequitable, then he is free to present his argument to his fellow citizens and urge that they alter the old way of doing things. This marketplace of ideas "is destroyed if the smug assurances of each age are removed from the democratic process and written into the Constitution."[71] Notwithstanding Justice Scalia's reasoning and his attempts to pull the Court away from policy and back to the law, the Court found a constitutional violation and further held that it could not be remedied by a leadership program for women established at another Virginia college. Without even a nod to the people of Virginia, the Supreme Court, via a sliding scale of scrutiny, found just the right standard of review to permit it to strike a policy with which it disagreed.

As the *Griswold* and *United States v. Virginia* holdings demonstrate, the Court's use of substantive due process and the Equal Protection Clause is tantamount to the abandonment of the so-called judicial mask, which permits a judge to decide a case based on law rather than personal beliefs. The Court's Fourteenth Amendment jurisprudence marks the ascendancy of an unelected superlegislature, the coming of Plato's elite Guardians to check the will of the people when the people's choice is incongruous with the values held by the judges.[72] Such a use of the law cannot be squared with the democratic elements of a federal republic and should give every citizen pause. When our legislators make policy choices with which we disagree, we can boot them out of office. When the Supreme Court makes policy choices with which we disagree, we can only grumble and hope the Court will one day reconsider the matter.

* * *

State power, once meant to be a powerful check on the national government, has never recovered from the rise of political parties and the ratification of the Seventeenth Amendment. Today, state officials seldom clash with national officials over matters of substance, and the states have no voice in our national councils. No longer recognized as equals by Congress, state governments have been reduced to administrative subdivisions of the national government. Via the Spending Clause and other tricks, Congress uses the states to carry out its will.

"A conveyance of part does not entitle the grantee to take more," John Taylor of Caroline observed of the delegated powers, "or the whole residue if he pleases."[73] Though the Constitution has been amended 28 times since it was ratified, and some of the amendments have granted to Congress additional powers (such as enforcing the Thirteenth Amendment's prohibition against slavery, enforcing the Fourteenth Amendment's civil rights guarantees, and taxing incomes), no one amendment or combination of amendments can explain the increase in national power. Desirous of the power to regulate the national economy, for example, Congress has not asked for an amendment pursuant to Article V, but instead has, with the help of the Supreme Court, amended the Constitution via construction. Like a thief, Congress has simply taken something that does not rightfully belong to it.

The warnings from the early national period about consolidation have come to pass. The promises made by the friends of the Constitution in 1787 concerning the limited nature of the national government have been undermined. The only question remaining is whether the beauty and purity of the federal system given to us so long ago can and should be recovered.

CHAPTER 6

LESSONS FOR TODAY

"[T]he preservation of liberty," wrote John Taylor of Caroline, "must depend on the division of power between the state and federal governments."[1] With an eye to securing and maintaining the most cherished liberty of all, the right to self-government, Jefferson and Madison made the proper division of legislative sovereignty the cornerstone of the Kentucky and Virginia Resolutions. By nullification and interposition, Jefferson and Madison sought to give the states a weapon to thwart the national government's encroachments. Though we are over two centuries removed from the Revolution of 1800, concern for the proper division of legislative sovereignty is just as relevant today as when Jefferson and Madison feared for the future of republicanism in America. Considering that our puissant national government scarcely resembles the government of "few and defined" powers that Madison described in the *Federalist*, an appreciation of federalism is perhaps more vital today than ever before.

Though taking no corrective action, Congress is aware that our system of government is not functioning as intended. The Advisory Commission on Intergovernmental Relations, created by Congress to monitor the federal system, has made clear to the senators and representatives that "contemporary federalism is in serious disarray."[2] However, the Commission's recommendations for protecting the autonomy of state and local governments have been largely ignored. Congress either lacks the will to change its ways, or has been so thoroughly corrupted by the exercise of broad powers that it refuses to part with them.

While the early 1990s, in the wake of the so-called "Republican Revolution," featured many calls for returning power to the states, we must not confuse such efforts with federalism. For example, the much vaunted welfare reform in 1996 had little to do with federalism and is better characterized as decentralization.[3] In essence, decentralization "is a management decision that is intended to implement the policies selected by the central government as effectively as possible."[4] Decentralization in no way questions the power of the national government to take action. In the context of welfare reform, the national government has not recognized that the relief of the poor falls under the reserved powers of the states. Though the states were given some room to experiment in the provision of welfare, they are still required to meet standards set by Washington. Among other things, the states must maintain a certain level of spending, deny benefits to drug felons, and limit "lifetime" benefits to five years. Had Congress recognized the sovereignty of the states, it would not and could not have attached these strings. With welfare, as with other decentralized programs, the national government is still in charge.

This is not to say that decentralization is not a positive. In some cases it is, and many of the rationales for decentralization overlap with the rationales for federalism. However, the significant difference between the two concepts is that decentralization is a management decision, whereas federalism—the division of legislative sovereignty—is mandated by our fundamental law, the Constitution. Federalism represents a decision made by the ultimate sovereigns, the people of the several states, to vest different powers in the states and national government. This was no management decision, but an act of constitutional significance that should be respected and adhered to. That it has not been respected and honored by our national councils is evidenced by the level of consolidation existing in Washington today.

Despite this melancholy reality, reform is possible. But a prerequisite to reform is a renewed appreciation for the principles of the Kentucky and Virginia Resolutions. Only when Americans realize that our national government, with its limited powers, is not like the central governments of other countries can we correct the present situation.[5] Of course, with this understanding must also come a renewed desire for a truly federal system. A federal republic would be much different from our current system, and Americans must be desirous of such a change.

Dual Sovereignty Essential

Federalism is a venerable institution. Some scholars trace it back to the Old Testament and the Israelite commonwealth with its federation of tribes and governing covenants.[6] Considering these Biblical roots, it is not surprising that one of the earliest works on the subject arose from the Protestant Reformation. Writing in the early 1600s, Johannes Althusius urged the Europeans to eschew centralized states and to instead concentrate on building a society based on small, self-governing bodies.[7] Such small units of government, Althusius believed, were more conducive to piety and a gainful human existence. Unfortunately, Althusius's prescription was rejected in favor of centralized states that even today predominate in Europe and the world.

The American experience with the Articles of Confederation and the Constitution of 1787 marked rebirth of federalist principles. Just as Althusius in the early seventeenth century offered mankind an alternative to consolidated states, so too did our Framers. Our forefathers demonstrated to the world that small political units could join together in the furtherance of common goals such as defense and free trade, yet retain the power to govern their internal affairs as the habits and circumstances of their peoples dictated.

Of course, many academics and politicians give short shrift to the work of our forefathers, arguing that federalism was suited to the horse-and-buggy days of the eighteenth and early nineteenth centuries but is incompatible with modern life.[8] Such a contention, however, is erroneous inasmuch as it ignores the timelessness of federalist principles. Though much has changed in the last 200 years, federalism remains relevant today for four practical reasons: (1) divergent local circumstances, (2) the need for experimentation and competition in policymaking, (3) the need to monitor those entrusted with power, and (4) the need to ensure that power is properly diffused.[9]

First, in a nation that spans a continent there is a great divergence in local circumstances. For example, in some states there are dense populations, in others sparse; in some states people must spend a substantial amount of income to heat their homes during winter, in others the people see nary a snowflake; in some states agriculture remains an integral part of the economy, in others manufacturing or information technologies predominate; in some states people are very heterogeneous, in others homogeneous; in some states the tax burden is high, in others low; in some states there is much foreign investment, in others little; and in some states the people tend to be conservative, in others progressive. Obviously, this list could go on and on. The point being, of course, that in a nation as diverse as ours, national one-size-fits-all enactments cannot take into account these many differences.

A national speed limit, such as the mandatory 55 mile-per-hour speed limit that existed between 1973 and 1995, provides an excellent example.[10] Never one to learn from past mistakes, Congress might decree that, in the interests of highway safety, no automobile on any road or highway in the United States shall travel at more that 55 miles per hour. Perhaps in areas with much traffic congestion or poor roads such a speed limit would make sense. However, in sparsely populated states with excellent highways and flat terrain, a national speed limit is illogical. One speed limit cannot take into account the conditions of the FDR expressway in New York City and the open roads of a state like Montana. State officials, aware of conditions in their states, are much better qualified to govern the speed of motor vehicles than officials in Washington.[11]

On the other hand, one could argue that local circumstances are taken into account via congressional representation. If a senator or congressman believes that a bill ignores the conditions in his state or district, he can propose amendments to the legislation or vote against it. While this argument seems reasonable on its face, it ignores that states and congressional districts are so large that a senator or congressman cannot be aware of myriad local concerns. State legislators, however, represent much smaller subdivisions and therefore are more likely to understand the needs and circumstances of their constituents. Even if we ignore this reality and assume that national legislators do adequately represent local concerns, we must acknowledge that most of the rules and regulations governing us today are not crafted by Congress, but by bureaucrats in alphabet-soup agencies like the EPA, FCC, FTC, FMC, IRS, and the like. These bureaucrats do not represent anyone and were not hired because of their knowledge of local circumstances.

Assuming that the knowledge problem could be solved—that via technology national officials could gather and assimilate the relevant information—we must not forget that local interests are often outvoted or ignored in national bodies. The fact that King Numbers dictates a policy does not mean that the policy is suitable to the local interests affected. Hence, the knowledge factor aside, the principle of subsidiarity counsels that power should rest with a subunit unless a central unit is the most effective locus for achieving a goal. When an interest is local, control should be local. Otherwise, bad polices will result when the level of decisionmaking and the interest affected are mismatched.

Second, federalism permits the states to operate as laboratories of democracy—to experiment with various policies and programs.[12] For example, if Tennessee wanted to provide a state-run health system for its citizens, the other 49 states could observe the effects of this venture on Tennessee's economy, the quality of care provided, and the overall cost of health care. If the plan proved to be efficacious other states might choose to emulate it, or adopt a plan taking into account any problems surfacing in Tennessee. If the plan proved to be a disastrous intervention, the other 49 could decide to leave the provision of medical care to the private sector. With national plans and programs, the national officials simply roll the dice for all 284 million people in the United States and hope they get things right.

Experimentation in policymaking also encourages a healthy competition among units of government and allows the people to vote with their feet should they find a law or policy detrimental to their interests. Using again the state-run health system as an example, if a citizen of Tennessee was unhappy with Tennessee's meddling with the provision of health care, the citizen could move to a neighboring state. Relocating to a state like North Carolina, with a similar culture and climate, would not be a dramatic shift and would be a viable option. Moreover, if enough citizens exercised this option, Tennessee would be pressured to abandon its foray into socialized medicine, or else lose much of its tax base. To escape a national health system, a citizen would have to emigrate to a foreign country, an option far less appealing and less likely to be exercised than moving to a neighboring state. Without competition from other units of government, the national government would have much less incentive than Tennessee would to modify the objectionable policy. Clearly, the absence of experimentation and competition hampers the creation of effective programs and makes the modification of failed national programs less likely.

Third, state legislators are more susceptible to monitoring and censure because they are closer to the people. State legislators normally maintain close ties with their communities and pursue their various occupations while in office. The Texas legislature, for example, meets only once every two years for a four-month session. Thus, the state legislators feel the effects of the laws they pass and are close at hand should their constituents choose to remonstrate. Conversely, members of the national legislature are separated from their constituents and give up their occupations when they enter office. They spend most of their time in Washington, do not feel the bite of unwholesome laws in their daily affairs, and are not close at hand to witness the agitation of their constituents. Hence, true accountability can only be maintained at the state and local level.

Finally, the Framers rightly feared the concentration of power would lead to arbitrary government. "The accumulation of all powers . . . in the same hands," wrote Madison, "may justly be pronounced the very definition of tyranny."[13] Instead of placing all of the national government's power in one body, the Framers divided the delegated powers between three branches: executive, legislative, and judicial. Every school child learns that these horizontal checks and balances are designed to prevent abuse of power by our elected officials. But the Framers did not stop there. Our system also contains a vertical check, that is, the state governments, and within these state governments power is distributed between three departments just as in the national government. Accordingly, preservation of state power is integral to ensuring that power remains diffused. In a federal system, the vertical checks and balances are just as important as the horizontal ones for ensuring that no one man or level of government accumulates excessive power.

Slavery, Segregation, and Federalism

Despite these sound reasons for maintaining a proper division of legislative sovereignty, proponents of national supremacy invariably throw the race card, asserting that slavery and segregation are inextricably linked to the tenets of federalism and therefore those who defend the reserved powers of the states are forever tainted.[14] While it is true that supporters of slavery and Jim Crow argued that these institutions were not within the purview of national power,[15] this should not be surprising. As demonstrated in chapter 4, a states' rights defense is the natural defense raised when any "domestic" institution is involved, whether it be the jurisdiction of state courts, the use of state militia, construction or improvement of state infrastructure, or race relations.[16] This is not to say that slavery and segregation were cloaked in righteousness; they most certainly were not. From a moral standpoint both institutions were wrong, but from a legal standpoint both were out of Congress's reach under the Constitution.

In linking federalism and racism, proponents of a strong national government forget that racist arguments were made by nationalists in their duels with the states' rights camp. For example, in the Virginia ratifying convention, Governor Edmund Randolph observed that Virginia's slave population was increasing and that only a strong union could be counted upon to put down a slave revolt and keep the slave race in check.[17] In the debates on the Virginia Resolutions in the house of delegates, opponents of the Resolutions also raised the prospect of slave insurrections if the national government was weakened. George K. Taylor predicted that in a frail union "the ties of nature would be cut asunder," permitting slaves to pillage and destroy property. But this could be prevented, Taylor promised, by "vesting the general government with the [requisite] power."[18] Indeed, in the years before the War Between the States, Henry Hughes, one of the South's foremost philosophers, urged Southerners to abandon their beliefs in federalism if they wanted to perpetuate slavery. Hughes believed, and perhaps in hindsight was correct, that only a massive expansion of national power could preserve the peculiar institution.[19]

Unbeknownst by many, the federalist principles of the Kentucky and Virginia Resolutions appear in various parts of the abolitionist movement. William Lloyd Garrison, editor of the antislavery newspaper, the *Liberator*, and organizer of the American Anti-Slavery Society, advocated Northern secession. "I go . . . for the repeal of the Union between North and South," Garrison wrote. "We must dissolve all connexion with those murders of fathers, and murders of mothers, and murders of liberty and traffickers in human flesh. . . ."[20] The *Liberator's* masthead unabashedly read "No Union with Slave-Holders."

Garrison advocated secession because he recognized that the Constitution protected slavery, especially with regard to runaways. Article IV of the Constitution states that

> A Person charged in any State with Treason, Felony, or other Crime, who shall flee from Justice, and be found in another State, shall on Demand of the executive Authority of the State from which he fled, be delivered up, to be removed to the State having jurisdiction of the Crime.
>
> No Person held to Service or Labour in one State, under the Laws thereof, escaping into another, shall, in Consequence of any Law or Regulation therein, be discharged from such Service or Labour, but shall be delivered up on Claim of the Party to whom such Service or Labour may be due.[21]

To carry out these provisions, Congress enacted the Fugitive Slave Act of 1793. Under this statute, a slaveholder or his agent could seize the runaway and present him to a local magistrate or federal judge. Once the owner established "proof [of ownership] to the satisfaction" of the judge via an affidavit or oral testimony, the owner would be permitted to return home with the slave.[22] Citizens obstructing the owner's efforts could be fined $500.

Garrison saw these constitutional provisions and duly enacted statutes as "a covenant with death and an agreement with hell."[23] He believed that a Northern secession would cause irreparable damage to the institution of slavery.[24] An independent North, under Garrisonian theory, would create a refuge for runaway slaves. A slave escaping to free soil could not be returned to his master, and any slaveholder attempting to kidnap a fugitive slave could face draconian penalties.

Garrison hoped that slaves in the upper South would flee in large numbers, causing diehard slave owners to move further south toward the Gulf Coast. Slavery would thus become impracticable in the upper South and whites in the lower South would be so outnumbered that slave rebellions would destroy the peculiar institution or the social and economic costs of bondage would finally take their toll. Had Garrison's theory been given a chance, we possibly could have avoided the War Between the States, yet achieved freedom for the African bondsmen.

This prospect of an end to slavery, without the death of 620,000 people and a massive expansion of government power under Lincoln and his successors, was not chimerical on the part of Garrison and his followers. As Thomas DiLorenzo has observed, "[b]y 1861 there was a long history of peaceful abolition throughout the world, including the northern United States."[25] From 1813 to 1854, peaceful emancipation occurred in Argentina, Columbia, Chile, Central America, Mexico, Bolivia, Uruguay, the French and Danish colonies, Ecuador, Peru, and Venezuela.[26] In the Western Hemisphere, violence predominated in the abolition of slavery only in the United States and Haiti.[27]

Had Lincoln permitted the states of the lower South to depart in peace, the states of the upper South would not have seceded. Not until Lincoln prepared to use force to hold the union together did Arkansas, North Carolina, Tennessee, and Virginia—in a second wave of secession—cast their lot with the lower South. Had Lincoln eschewed violence, abolition would have been more practicable in the slave states remaining in the union. Slave states would have been a distinct minority in Congress and unable to block a constitutional amendment emancipating the slaves. Moreover, the Gulf Coast slave states would have been isolated and the costs of preventing runaways would have posed a tremendous burden on these states just as Garrison envisioned. Such was the case in Brazil, where the state of Ceará abolished slavery and thus caused a massive exodus of slaves from neighboring states. As Jeffrey Rogers Hummel has pointed out, the value of Brazilian slaves plummeted, the institution soon self-destructed, and Brazilian slavery ended shortly thereafter.[28]

Peaceful emancipation was not the course taken by Lincoln. And on top of the death and suffering brought by the War, Lincoln created a centralized government that involved itself in multiple facets of American life. In essence, Lincoln instituted Henry Clay's American System of protection, internal improvements, and fiat money. In so doing, he expanded the power of the federal government to an extent that Clay could not have imagined. With Southern free traders out of the Congress, tariff rates increased to 47 percent of the value of imported goods. Considering that the federal government needed funds for the War, high tariff rates were illogical because they discourage imports and consequently decrease revenue. Federal tariff policy during the War demonstrates to what extent Lincoln's Republicans were wedded to protection. The Tariff of Abominations, so reviled by the nullifiers of the 1830s, had returned.

Republican internal improvements launched a system of corporate welfare that exists to this day. For example, Congress chartered the Union Pacific (UP) and Central Pacific (CP) corporations to build a railroad linking the East with the Pacific Ocean. These corporations received low-interest loans from the federal government and were given ten square miles of public land for every mile of track put down. In an effort to obtain free land and government subsidies, the companies often chose circuitous routes to earn more for mileage. In the race across the continent, speed and not workmanship earned the UP and CP their government checks. Thus, the transcontinental railroad was always in need of some repairs or more government largess.[29] Railroads constructed with private funds during the same time period proved more efficient and safer for travel.[30]

Of course, the federal government did not stop with subsidies for improvements. In an early episode of "war socialism," the federal government owned and operated numerous business ventures. This list of businesses includes drug laboratories, meatpacking plants, and clothing factories. The government also entered into close partnerships with private industry. Large and lucrative contracts, along with a new tax structure, encouraged capitalists to concentrate their wealth in massive, integrated companies. Lincoln rewarded these barons of industry for their loyalty by providing federal troops to oppose various labor movements aimed at garnering a living wage or better working conditions.

National banking was the third prong of the American System. In 1863, Congress enacted the National Currency Act (amended in 1864). Under this legislation, Congress created a web of nationally chartered banks required to hold a certain amount of war bonds. Importantly, the national banks were vested with the power to issue bank notes—promises to pay the bearer out of reserves (specie) on demand. Congress then taxed state bank notes at high rates to ensure that the national banks enjoyed a currency monopoly. In effect, state-chartered banks were driven out of the business of issuing paper money.

In a more imposing display of national power, the Legal Tender Act of 1862 gave the Treasury Department the authority to issue Greenbacks. Unlike the bank notes, this was fiat money in the classic sense. The Greenbacks were not backed by specie and were made legal tender only via the federal government's decree. The government printed approximately $431 million in Greenbacks during the War, and inflation was the natural result of such a printing spree. By 1864, a gold dollar could be exchanged for almost three Greenback dollars.

Not surprisingly, the basic tenets of constitutional government and civil liberty also suffered under Lincoln's wartime measures. Shortly after the Confederates fired on Fort Sumter, Lincoln called for 75,000 volunteers to serve a three-month stint. In so doing, he conveniently forgot that the Constitution vests Congress, and only Congress, with the power "[t]o raise and support Armies."[31] While preparing for hostilities, Lincoln "appropriated" $2 million to personal associates to pay for supplies for the military. Again, Lincoln ignored that appropriations of public money fall under Congress's powers as enumerated in Article I, Section 8. Lincoln never recognized the Confederate States of America (CSA), but he blockaded Southern ports. Here, Lincoln failed to comply with international law, which provided that blockades could only be enforced against sovereign powers.[32]

Lincoln endangered civil liberty when he unilaterally suspended the writ of habeas corpus, which permits a citizen to challenge unlawful deprivations of freedom.[33] Under the Constitution, the Great Writ may be suspended "when in Cases of Rebellion or Invasion the public Safety may require it,"[34] but this power is lodged in Congress, not the executive. With habeas corpus suspended, federal troops began to round up suspected Confederate sympathizers and other individuals seen as unsavory by the Lincoln administration.

A classic example of these police-state tactics occurred on May 25, 1861. Federal soldiers entered the Baltimore home of John Merryman, took him into custody, and confined him in Fort McHenry.[35] The military suspected that Merryman was a Confederate sympathizer preparing to depart to the CSA with a company of volunteers. Friends and family promptly filed an application for a writ of habeas corpus with Chief Justice Taney. The writ issued, but the military ignored the Chief Justice on the grounds that Lincoln had suspended it. "The people of the United States," wrote Taney, "are no longer living under a government of laws, but every citizen holds life, liberty and property at the will and pleasure of an army officer in whose military district he may happen to be found."[36]

Taney's assessment proved accurate. Lincoln closed down over 300 Northern newspapers that dared to criticize his administration.[37] Dozens of editors found themselves in the federal gaol for failing to temper their words. Citizens of Indiana, like many Northerners, were faced with General Order Number Nine, which prohibited the press and public speakers from attempting "to bring the war policy of the Administration into disrepute."[38] In other words, if anyone spoke about the War, they had better be praising the Lincoln administration for a job well done. Federal officials also encouraged troops to destroy the printing presses of the offending newspapers. Not satisfied with suppressing newspapers, Lincoln censored Northern telegraph communications in his war against free speech.

Free elections were not immune from Lincoln's dictatorial measures. Ballot boxes in the border states were stuffed to ensure that Lincoln's party remained in control of Congress. In some cases, Lincoln had opposition politicians arrested. One of the most egregious examples of Lincoln's conduct occurred in Ohio where Clement L. Vallandigham, a former congressman, was running for governor.

Military authorities arrested Vallandigham after he gave a speech in which he, inter alia, described the War as "not being waged for the preservation of the Union" and asserted "that if the Administration had so wished, the war could have been honorably terminated months ago."[39] Unfortunately for Democratic politicians, General Ambrose Burnside, the officer in charge of the district containing Ohio, was an opponent of such political speech. According to Burnside: "That freedom of discussion and criticism which is proper in the politician and the journalist in time of peace, becomes rank treason when it tends to weaken the confidence of the soldier in his officers and his Government."[40]

When interrogated by authorities, Vallandigham asserted that he had not urged a violent overthrow of the government, but merely had issued "an appeal to the people to change [war] policy, not by force, but by free elections and the ballot box."[41] The military court brushed aside Vallandigham's explanation and sentenced him to confinement for the duration of the conflict. Faced with much criticism over the handling of Vallandigham, Lincoln changed the punishment to banishment to the Confederate States of America.[42]

The great historian Clinton Rossiter has observed that "[t]he principle and institutions of constitutional dictatorship played a decisive role in the North's successful effort to maintain the Union by force of arms."[43] The reign of John Adams and the Federalists appears harmless when compared with Lincoln's dictatorship. The Adams Federalists merely threatened civil liberties, whereas Lincoln abrogated the basic principles of republican government. Free speech, free elections, and due process of law—all essential to any republican government—were sacrificed even in the Northern states facing no danger from Confederate forces.

Historians have accepted and praised the Lincoln dictatorship because it resulted in emancipation. Were war and dictatorship the only methods available to end slavery, then Lincoln's measures would deserve the highest encomium. But history teaches that peaceful emancipation is the rule, not the exception. Moreover, the Garrisonian abolitionists provided an alternative course based on the Principles of 1798. Unfortunately, Lincoln never gave Garrison's theory serious consideration. The result was an American dictatorship, the adverse effects of which are still felt today.

The principles of the Resolves in the fight against slavery are also evident outside the secessionist context. Many Northern states preferred the tactics akin to nullification. The "personal liberty laws" enacted by a number of Northern states are a prime example. These laws made it difficult, and in some cases impossible, for a slave owner to regain dominion over his property. The personal liberty laws ran afoul of the pro-slavery provisions of Article IV and amounted to a nullification of the Fugitive Slave Act.

Pennsylvania's personal liberty law is instructive. Under this 1826 Act, a person using force, violence, fraud, or false pretenses to return a runaway to bondage was guilty of a felony and subject to fines and imprisonment.[44] In contradiction of the federal Fugitive Slave Act, the oral testimony of the slaveholder was insufficient to support a certificate of removal of the slave and the slave was permitted to present evidence to defeat the owner's claim.

A controversy arose between Pennsylvania and Maryland when Margaret Morgan, a slave belonging to a Maryland woman, escaped to southern Pennsylvania. After five years of searching, the slave owner's agent, Edward Prigg, found Morgan and instituted proceedings in state court to return her to Maryland. The Pennsylvania court refused to cooperate, causing Prigg to slip out of the state with Morgan.

Prigg was later tried and convicted in a Pennsylvania court for violating the 1826 personal liberty law. On review by the United States Supreme Court in *Prigg v. Pennsylvania* (1842),[45] the conviction was overturned. Writing for the Court, Justice Joseph Story held that "any state law or state regulation, which interrupts, limits, delays, or postpones the right of the owner to immediate possession of the slave, and the immediate command of his service and labour, operates, protanto, as a discharge therefrom" in contravention of the Constitution.[46] Story further observed that the national government's power to legislate on the return of fugitive slaves was "exclusive."[47] Accordingly, the Court struck down Pennsylvania's 1826 personal liberty law. Not impressed by Story's ruling, Pennsylvania passed a similar personal liberty law a few years later.

State nullification of Supreme Court precedent on slavery went far beyond the *Prigg* case. In 1857, the Supreme Court handed down the infamous *Dred Scott* decision.[48] Chief Justice Taney, inter alia, concluded that descendants of slaves could never become citizens of the United States and that Congress could not prohibit slavery in the territories. The opinion could have been kept simple, with the Court ruling on the issue of whether the slave petitioning for his freedom was a citizen of the United States. If he was not a citizen, the Court should have stopped there. Instead, the Court gratuitously picked up the political hot potato of slavery in the territories. With regard to the territories, over which the Constitution gives Congress plenary power, Taney waltzed with substantive due process when he stated that

> an act of Congress which deprives a citizen of the United States of his liberty or property, merely because he came himself or brought his property into a particular Territory of the United States, and who had committed no offense against the laws, could hardly be dignified with the name of due process of law.[49]

Taney thus held that the Missouri Compromise was unconstitutional and that any future attempts to limit slavery in the territories would be void.

The Northern response was prompt and virulent. Vermont's legislature resolved that the Court's opinions "upon questions not contained in the record in the Dred Scott Case, are extra judicial and political, possessing no color of authority or binding force, and that such views and opinions are wholly repudiated by the people of Vermont."[50] Similarly, Massachusetts resolved "that no part of the decision of the Supreme Court of the United States, in the case of *Scott v. Sandford*, is binding, which was not necessary to the determination of that case."[51]

The High Court again earned Northern rebuke over a slave question when it decided *Ableman v. Booth* (1859).[52] Joshua Glover, a fugitive slave in federal custody, was freed from prison by a mob led by abolitionist Sherman M. Booth. Federal authorities arrested Booth for violating the Fugitive Slave Act of 1850. A state court released Booth, but he was arrested again and convicted in federal district court. The Supreme Court of Wisconsin stepped in, held that the Fugitive Slave Act of 1850 was unconstitutional, and released Booth on a writ of habeas corpus.

The U.S. Supreme Court issued a writ demanding that the record of the *Booth* case be sent up for review. The Wisconsin Supreme Court refused, but the federal Supreme Court eventually obtained a clerk's copy of the record. Writing for the Court, Chief Justice Taney held that the state court had no authority to exercise jurisdiction over the proceedings of a federal district court and that a state court could not free a federal prisoner via a writ of habeas corpus. Such action, according to Taney, could not be squared with the Supremacy Clause of the Constitution. Taney also opined that the fugitive slave law was a constitutional exercise of Congress's powers.

The Wisconsin legislature was outraged at the Court's decision. In a set of resolutions, it described the *Booth* decision as "unauthorized by the Constitution . . . without authority, void, and of no force." It denied that "the general government is the exclusive judge of the extent of the powers delegated to it" because "the *discretion* of those who administer the government, and not the *Constitution*, would be the measure of their powers." As for the rightful remedy, Wisconsin called for "a *positive defiance* . . . of all unauthorized acts done or attempted to be done under color of" the Constitution.[53] Without question, Wisconsin used the Principles of 1798 in its fight against the institution of human bondage.

In light of this historical record, the race card has no place in the debate over federalism. Federalist principles, as explained in the Kentucky and Virginia Resolutions, appear in the political theory of pro-slavery and abolitionist forces. Moreover, advocates of federalism and national power both have made racist arguments with one side contending that a strong national government was needed to subjugate blacks and other side warning that the Congress would free slaves and force mixing of the races. Slavery and segregation are an unfortunate legacy in our nation, but memories of these unjust institutions should not cause us to lose sight of the importance of federalism to our system of government.

Shift in the Balance

Though the current state of the federal system is disheartening, recent Supreme Court decisions offer some hope. In a break from past practice, the Court has developed a renewed respect for state sovereignty, especially when examining congressional legislation passed pursuant to the commerce power. As discussed in the previous chapter, the Supreme Court's Commerce Clause decisions in the late 1930s and early 1940s granted Congress carte blanche when legislating pursuant to the commerce power. Now, to the shock of congressional leaders, the Court is more closely scrutinizing legislation that claims to be a regulation of interstate commerce. Though it is too early to judge the long-term consequences of the Court's most recent cases, the Commerce Clause landscape has indeed changed.

In *United States v. Lopez* (1995),[54] the Court began the process of imposing restraints on congressional power when it considered Congress's claim that the Commerce Clause authorized it to ban the possession of firearms near school premises. In defending the Gun-Free School Zones Act, the United States argued that possession of guns in school zones could affect the functioning of the national economy by hampering the education of students, which in turn could affect interstate commerce by resulting in an unproductive workforce. Fortunately, the Court rejected the government's argument, fearing that such a line of reasoning would permit Congress to "regulate any activity that it found was related to the economic productivity of individual citizens,"[55] including areas of traditional state concern such as divorce and marriage.

The Court employed a substantial effects test in reaching its result. In essence, the Court asked whether the activity in question had such a substantial effect on interstate commerce that Congress should be permitted to regulate it. With guns near schools, the Court answered in the negative. Though reaching the right result in *Lopez*, this test still leaves Congress with much power. Concurring in *Lopez*, Justice Clarence Thomas criticized the majority's reasoning as giving Congress a general " 'police power' over all aspects of American life" and suggested a return to the jurisprudence of *E.C. Knight*.[56]

More recently, in *United States v. Morrison* (2000),[57] the Court reaffirmed the limits of the Commerce Clause when it struck down provisions of the Violence Against Women Act (VAWA). The VAWA, in part, declared that all persons in the United States have the right to be free from crimes of violence motivated by gender, and created a private cause of action against individuals committing such a crime. In defending the VAWA, the government argued that gender-motivated violence substantially affects interstate commerce by deterring women from traveling and transacting business. Recognizing that the prohibition and punishment of violent crimes are powers reserved to the states, the Court again lectured the national government that its view of the Commerce Clause would "completely obliterate the Constitution's distinction between national and local authority."[58]

Outside the commerce arena, the Court has also struck unfunded federal mandates. For example, in *Printz v. United States* (1997)[59] the Court struck interim provisions of the Brady Handgun Violence

Prevention Act requiring chief law enforcement officers of local jurisdictions to conduct background checks on prospective handgun purchasers. Writing for the Court, Justice Scalia began by examining early national laws to determine whether they compelled state officials to manage federal programs. Concluding that they did not, Justice Scalia then turned to first principles. "Residual state sovereignty was also implicit, of course, in the Constitution's conferral upon Congress of not all governmental powers," Justice Scalia observed, "but only discrete, enumerated ones . . . , which implication was rendered express by the Tenth Amendment . . . ."[60] In the end, the Court made clear that Congress could not require local officials to regulate or administer federal regulations.

In addition to striking unfunded federal mandates, the Court has also rediscovered the doctrine of sovereign immunity, which prohibits a sovereign state from being haled into court without its consent. In essence, Congress cannot abrogate the states' immunity from suit unless it unequivocally expresses such an intent and acts pursuant to a valid delegated power. In *Seminole Tribe of Florida v. Florida* (1996),[61] a landmark sovereign immunity decision, the Supreme Court considered provisions of the Indian Gaming Regulatory Act requiring states to enter into negotiations with tribes residing within the state's borders that wanted to open casinos. States were required to negotiate in good faith with the tribes and could be haled into federal court by the tribes if they failed to so act. Though the statute expressed an intent to abrogate immunity from suit, the Court held that the Commerce Clause did not permit Congress to stretch the jurisdiction of the federal courts beyond the confines delimited in Article III. Therefore, a suit brought by the Seminole Indians against Florida under the Act had to be dismissed for lack of jurisdiction. Though seemingly a technical legal matter, the Court's sovereign immunity jurisprudence goes to the heart of federalism and the residuary sovereignty remaining with the state governments.

The Need for Additional Safeguards

The Court's recent decisions indicate that its jurisprudence is moving in the right direction. *Lopez, Printz,* and *Seminole Tribe* do curb Congress's powers and mark a departure from the precedents of the New Deal. However, while showing some willingness to cut back on Congress's powers, the Court has refused to divest itself of its own ill-gotten gains. The Court's most egregious substantive due process and equal protection decisions remain the law of the land. Though perhaps slowing the process of consolidation, the Court has shown no tendency to stop the process.

Of course, the Court is but one branch of the national government and Americans should not expect it to work miracles. Besides, as a practical matter, the Court is a poor vehicle for returning the national government to the chains of the Constitution. Before the Court can review a legislative enactment, a number of procedural matters must be satisfied. For instance, the parties claiming injury must have standing to sue[62] and an actual case of controversy must exist.[63] An American wanting to challenge, for example, something like the Gun-Free School Zones Act cannot simply petition the Supreme Court to strike the legislation. The citizen must first violate the law, be arrested, and then begin the challenge in the lower federal courts. The judicial process moves slowly, with years elapsing between a conviction and Supreme Court review. To make matters worse, the Court does not have to review anything and decides which cases it wants to hear. Hence, the citizen who faces arrest so he can challenge a law has no guarantee that the test case will ever be heard by the High Court. The result of his efforts would likely be limited to serving time in a federal correctional facility.

The cumbersomeness of the judicial process aside, should a change in the composition of the Court reverse what has been gained in *Lopez*, *Printz*, and *Seminole Tribe*, there is little the states or the people can do. In Jefferson's words, justices disposed to aggrandize the national government can treat the Constitution as "a mere thing of wax . . . which they may twist and shape into any form they please."[64] Once appointed by the president and confirmed by the Senate, a justice of the Supreme Court holds his office during "good behavior," which typically means for life. At present, the Court's decisions can be overturned only by constitutional amendment.

With the Court acting as the final arbiter of the Constitution, it appears that the Court, rather than the people of the several states, is the ultimate sovereign in our system of government. John Taylor of Caroline foresaw this result in 1807 when he observed that "the judicial power has been made independent of the sovereignty" and recommended that the Constitution be amended "by making the judges removable by the joint vote of the two houses [of Congress] with the assent of the president."[65] Whether the Framers intended the Court to exercise such immense power, or the Court's power evolved to its present level, is immaterial. Either way, the problem exists and requires correction. Otherwise, we will have reverted to the English view of sovereignty whereby ultimate sovereignty resides in an artificial body rather than with the people of the several states. This would be nothing less but the repudiation of the first principles of the Republic.

Without question, our system of dual legislative sovereignty needs additional safeguards if it is to function properly. Jefferson and Madison realized this in 1798 when they put forth state nullification and interposition as mechanisms to preserve the balance of power between the states and national government. Calhoun and the South Carolinians sought to translate the general principles of the Kentucky and Virginia Resolutions into a workable framework, yet the Carolina doctrine raised concerns about a state being in the union for some purposes and out of the union for others. Staunch Jeffersonian Nathaniel Macon, for example, thought nullification was untenable, but he never questioned the validity of secession inasmuch as he correctly understood that ultimate sovereignty resides in the people of the several states.

As peerless statements of the fundamentals of the Constitution, the Principles of 1798 must serve as our guideposts if we try to return the constitutional compact to its original purity. One method of correcting the existing structural damage would be to permit the states to propose constitutional amendments. Currently, amendments are proposed in two ways: two-thirds of both houses of Congress may propose amendments to the states, or two-thirds of the states may petition Congress for a constitutional convention. Under either method no amendment is ratified unless three-fourths of the state legislatures or conventions approve the amendment. Article V of the Constitution as originally drafted by Madison eschewed the dangers of a constitutional convention and forced Congress to submit amendments "on the application of two thirds of the Legislatures of the several States."[66] As the Philadelphia convention prepared to adjourn, Gouverneur Morris suggested the never used and dangerous convention method that we now have. Though Madison noted that the convention method might cause difficulties, he did not put up much of a fight and thus the national government became the de facto agent of constitutional change.

Under a Madisonian amendment process, the states could confer amongst themselves and offer amendments to the Constitution to curb the Court as well as the other branches of the national government. Such an amendment procedure would obviate the need for more radical measures inasmuch as the states would have some voice in revising the Constitution in order to defend the exercise of the reserved powers and the liberties of the people. Thus, Article V should be amended to correspond to Madison's original draft.

But considering how out of kilter our federal system is, a Madisonian amendment process might not be a sufficient check on the national government's powers. Besides, even if a Madisonian amendment process were adopted, the Court via construction could render new amend-ments nugatory. Accordingly, it is perhaps time for Americans to consider a major structural change in the federal system: the creation of an institution, accountable to the state legislative sovereigns and the people, to serve as final arbiter of the Constitution. I propose the follow-ing amendment, crafted in the spirit of the Kentucky and Virginia Resolutions, as a remedy for the defects plaguing our system.

Section 1. The Constitutional Commission shall settle questions presented by the several states concerning the constitutionality of measures or actions taken by the government of the United States.

Section 2. The Constitutional Commission shall be composed of one Commissioner from each state, elected every second year by the people thereof from two candidates chosen by the state legislature, and the elec-tors in each state shall have the qualifications requisite for the electors of the most numerous branch of the state legislature; each Commissioner shall have one vote.

Section 3. No person except a natural born citizen shall be eligible for the office of Commissioner; nor shall any person be eligible for that office who shall not have attained the age of 35 years, and been 14 years a resi-dent within the United States, and been nine years a resident of that state for which he shall be chosen. No person shall be elected to the office of Commissioner more than four times.

Section 4. When vacancies happen by resignation, or otherwise, during the recess of the legislature of any state, the executive thereof may make temporary appointments until the next meeting of the legislature, which shall choose two candidates to present to the people to fill the vacancy.

Section 5. The Constitutional Commission shall assemble at least once in every year, and such meeting shall begin at noon on the 3rd day of January, unless it shall appoint a different day. The Constitutional Commission shall choose its Chairman and other officers. The Commission shall be the judge of the election returns and qualifications of its own members, and three-fourths of the Commissioners shall constitute a quorum to do business. The Commission may determine the rules of its proceedings. The Commission shall keep a journal of the proceedings, and from time to time publish the same.

Section 6. No Commissioner shall receive compensation for his services paid out of the Treasury of the United States. No Commissioner shall, during his time for which he was elected, be appointed to any civil office under the authority of the United States.

Section 7. Whenever the Chairman of the Constitutional Commission shall receive petitions from one-fifth of the legislatures of the several states requesting a ruling on the constitutionality of a specific measure or action of the government of the United States, the Commission shall convene. The act or measure of the national government shall be void and of no force if three-fourths of the Commissioners present vote against its constitutionality.

Section 8. The Constitutional Commission shall not sit as a Convention as prescribed in Article V of the Constitution of the United States.

The operation of the amendment is straightforward. A state legislature chooses two candidates who meet the age and residency requirements of Section 3. The candidates are presented to the people, an election ensues, and the candidate who receives the most votes serves for two years as the state's Commissioner. The Commission does not act as council of revision for federal laws, but rather considers the constitutionality of national acts only if one-fifth of the state legislatures so request. For the questioned measure to be struck, three-fourths of the Commissioners must agree that it violates the Constitution. The term "measures or actions" used in Section 1 is intended to be broad so that the Commission can review the activities of the legislative, executive, and judicial branches of the national government. For example, the Commission could overturn court decisions, executive orders, statutes, and regulations.

A Commissioner who displeases the members of the legislature will not receive a nomination to serve a second term. And inasmuch as a Commissioner's compensation is a matter of state law, this gives the legislature an additional check on the Commissioner. Of course, even if a Commissioner does receive a vote of confidence from the legislature, he must still meet with the people's approval before he will be returned to office. With this mode of election, both the legislative sovereign of the state and the people of the state have a say in who will serve as Commissioner.

The role of the state legislatures in choosing candidates for Commissioner is meant to restore to the legislatures much of what was taken away by the Seventeenth Amendment. For almost a century, the state legislatures have had no representation in the national government. By nominating Commissioners and controlling a Commissioner's compensation, the amendment attempts to restore the legislatures' voices in national affairs. By permitting the people of the several states to choose between candidates presented by the legislature, the amendment recognizes that people of the several states retain ultimate sovereignty. No longer will the ultimate arbiter of the Constitution, in the words of John Taylor, be independent of the sovereignty.

Of course, the Constitutional Commission does nothing to remedy the effect of political parties on our federal system. Parties arose naturally, and will disappear, if ever, in the same manner. Efforts to ban political parties would infringe upon the right of freedom of association, and in the end would cause more damage to our system of government than parties ever have.

However, before any amendments are added to the Constitution, the spirit of 1776 must be rekindled in the people. Congress will never proffer amendments surrendering the discretion of the national government to interpret the Constitution or giving the states a role in suggesting amendments unless there is a tremendous grassroots effort. A revival of this spirit led to the Revolution of 1800, the ascendancy of the Jeffersonians, and is needed again today. Writing to Thomas Lomax during the crisis of the Alien and Sedition Acts, Jefferson optimistically observed that

> [t]he spirit of 1776 is not dead. It has only been slumbering. The body of the American people is substantially republican. But their virtuous feelings have been played on by some fact with more fiction; they have been the dupes of artful maneuvers, and made for a moment to be willing instruments in forging chains for themselves.[67]

Like the Americans who supported the unconstitutional Acts of the Federalists, modern Americans have been "dupes" in forging their own chains. This has been most recently evidenced in the "War on Terrorism." Few voices of opposition were heard in the aftermath of September 11 when Congress passed the USA PATRIOT Act of 2001.[68] The Senate approved the measure by a vote of 98-1, while the House passed the Act by a vote of 356-66.

Without much thought, Congress has consolidated law enforcement powers in the Department of Justice. In essence, Justice now has the power to investigate all violent acts taken against federal property and officials. Formerly, this authority was divided among numerous government agencies and therefore was less likely to be abused. Americans should be concerned that Justice has such power considering Attorney General John Ashcroft's remarks to those championing civil liberties during the War on Terror. "To those who scare peace-loving people with phantoms of lost liberty," the Attorney General warned, "my message is this: Your tactics only aid terrorists—for they erode our national unity and diminish our resolve."[69] Ashcroft's emphasis on national unity rather than liberty reminds one of the Federalists' efforts to unify America by the force of the Alien and Sedition Acts.

At least Americans can take some solace that they have elected representatives in Congress to monitor "anti-terrorism" efforts of the Attorney General and others. Well, not quite. Under the PATRIOT Act, required intelligence reports may be postponed if they could impede the work of antiterrorism operatives. Congress will be kept in the dark about antiterrorism efforts and can only hope that Ashcroft and his minions do not abuse power.

Of course, the Justice Department is not the only government entity to be given some central authority. Congress has given the Central Intelligence Agency (CIA) the power and responsibility to collect and utilize information from domestic sources. CIA abuses when spying on various New Left organizations during the Vietnam conflict earned its banishment from the arena of domestic intelligence gathering. But, with the hysteria existing after September 11, Congress has forgotten lessons learned and has empowered the CIA to spy on ordinary Americans.

Groups opposing the Bush administration's policy should be concerned about CIA activities, especially since Congress has broaden the definition of "domestic terrorism." Essentially, "domestic terrorism" encompasses acts dangerous to human life that have the effect of coercing the civilian population.[70] So broad is this definition that it could cover various heterodox, domestic political groups seeking to influence public policy (e.g., militant abortion protestors).

Some of the most disturbing aspects of the PATRIOT Act deal with amendments to the Foreign Intelligence Surveillance Act (FISA). FISA allows electronic surveillance for foreign intelligence purposes if there is probable cause to believe that "the target of the electronic surveillance is a foreign power or an agent of a foreign power."[71] Under Section 218 of the PATRIOT Act, foreign intelligence must no longer be the purpose of the surveillance, but rather "a significant purpose."[72] The PATRIOT Act also amends FISA to permit the federal government (absent probable cause or reasonable suspicion) to monitor Internet sites visited by the person under surveillance.

Abridgment of rights goes far beyond the PATRIOT Act. Less than two months after September 11, the Justice Department issued a rule for federal correctional facilities that permits monitoring of communications between an attorney and his client. Monitoring is permitted when "there has been a specific determination that such actions are reasonably necessary in order to deter future acts of violence or terrorism, and upon a specific notification to the inmate and the attorneys involved."[73] Confidential communications are essential if an attorney is to prepare a defense for his inmate-client. By decree the Justice Department has placed yet another hurdle in the way of an accused seeking to win his freedom. Without question, this is an abridgement of the accused's right to counsel under the Sixth Amendment.

Reminiscent of the Alien Acts of 1798, chains are also being forged for aliens residing in the United States. President Bush has signed an executive order providing for secret military tribunals to try suspected foreign terrorists.[74] An individual is subject to the executive order if "there is reason to believe" he is a member of al Qaida, has aided or abetted terrorism, or has harbored terrorists.[75] These military tribunals will not apply the principles of law and rules of evidence that are used in the trial of criminal cases in federal district courts. The tribunals may, on a two-thirds vote, hand out the sentences of life imprisonment or death.

In addition, the Immigration and Naturalization Service, via the USA PATRIOT Act, may detain immigrants suspected of terrorism for lengthy, and in some cases, an indefinite periods of time. The curtailing of rights and indefinite detention, however, are not limited to the hapless alien. American citizens may suffer the same fate if they are deemed "enemy combatants."[76] Enemy combatant are defined as "[u]nlawful combatants [who] are likewise subject to capture and detention, but in addition they are subject to trial and punishment by military tribunals for acts which render their belligerency unlawful."[77] So long as the undeclared War on Terrorism continues, enemy combatants may be held indefinitely and denied access to an attorney—all without formal charges being filed against them. Fundamental constitutional protections are lost based on an arbitrary label.

The War on Terrorism aside, Americans forge chains for themselves when they support programs concocted by Congress such as Social Security, Medicare, and Medicaid, which render the recipients dependent on the national government. Rather than looking to local leaders for solutions or assistance, Americans have been conditioned to turn to Washington. For example, in the 2000 presidential election the condition of public education was an oft debated issue. George W. Bush promised to be the "education president" and both candidates proposed programs to improve academic performance. However, neither candidate bothered to point to a provision in the Constitution giving the national government the authority to meddle in education, an inherently local concern. The people, so used to Washington governing the minute aspects of their lives, were oblivious to this lack of authority. Instead of looking to local school boards to improve education, the crowds cheered the candidates' education proposals. Sadly, the Framers' careful division of legislative sovereignty is unknown to modern Americans. This, rather than low test scores, is the real education crisis.

For true change to take place, Americans must rediscover their proud history. Like the Republicans of 1798 and the Carolinians of 1832, modern Americans must reacquaint themselves with the fundamental principle of our Revolution: the right of self-government. If self-government encompassed only equal representation and voting rights for all, then our current system would be a nonpareil of our revolutionary tradition. But self-government, if it is to have any value or meaning, must be much more than that. We must remember that our revolutionary forefathers fought not for representation in the British Parliament, but for the right to govern themselves via state and local assemblies. They understood that true self-governance must be carried on in bodies close to the people. Small units of government permit the people to know their representatives and the representatives to know the circumstances and habits of the people. In these bodies the community's voice is heard and laws are crafted to conform to the character of the citizenry. In a national assembly, such careful craftsmanship is not possible.

Once reacquainted with our first principles, Americans must then decide whether they want a federal republic or whether they prefer a system, such as we have, that more closely resembles the central governments of Europe. A true federal republic would be far different from our current system and would likely be opposed by voices on the Right as well as the Left. With our nationalized political discourse,[78] the people are used to debating and choosing programs based on the positions of the two major parties—we forget that there could be 50 different ways of handling a problem based on local circumstances and predilections in each state.

Take the medicinal use of marijuana as an example. Eight states have laws permitting the infirm to receive, grow, possess, or smoke marijuana. However, the federal Controlled Substances Act, which was enacted pursuant to Congress's commerce power, prohibits the manufacture and distribution of certain drugs, including marijuana. Recently, federal authorities sought to shut down a California medical cannabis dispensary, a lawful organization under California's Compassionate Use Act, as violative of federal law. The case, styled as *United States v. Oakland Cannabis Buyers' Cooperative* (2001),[79] made its way to the U.S. Supreme Court, which based its decision on narrow statutory grounds. Writing for the Court, Justice Thomas held that "medical necessity is not a defense to the manufacturing and distribution of marijuana."[80] The Court recognized that the federal law raises serious constitutional questions, but sidestepped these issues. After the Supreme Court remanded the case, Ed Rosenthal, an agent of Oakland's marijuana program, was convicted on three counts of conspiracy and marijuana cultivation. At sentencing, Rosenthal faces up to 85 years in prison.

Rosenthal was prohibited from introducing evidence that he was grow-ing medical marijuana, and the government portrayed him as a typical drug dealer.

Quite obviously, growing a marijuana plant at home for personal consumption is an intrastate activity and should be beyond the reach of Congress. Even with *Lopez* and *Morrison* as precedent, the Supreme Court would be unlikely to strike down the Controlled Substances Act. For one thing, the Court can always fall back on the reasoning of *Wickard v. Filburn* to uphold the Act. If the federal government can prevent a farmer from growing wheat for personal consumption, then surely it can do the same with marijuana. Though the reasoning of *Filburn* has obviously been called into doubt by *Lopez*, tough-on-crime conservatives in the judiciary and elsewhere, though often paying lip service to the principles of strict construction, would rather write their puritanical views on drugs into the Constitution than permit the states to legalize marijuana for medicinal or recreational use. To them the ends, that is, the criminalization of drug use, justify the means, that is, expansion of national power beyond the bounds of the Constitution.

The right of the states, as a matter of constitutional law, to legalize certain drugs for medicinal use will most likely soon be before the courts. And this time there will be no narrow statutory ground to save the judges from passing on the constitutionality of the federal drug laws. Despite the Supreme Court's holding that medical necessity is not a defense to the manufacturing and distribution of marijuana, states continue to pass laws permitting their citizens to possess marijuana for medicinal purposes. Before the Supreme Court decision in *Oakland Cannabis*, the people of Nevada via a ballot initiative instructed their legislature to legalize marijuana for medicinal use. Though aware of the Supreme Court's decision in *Oakland Cannabis*, the legislature passed such a law. In the preamble, the legislature declared that

> the State of Nevada as a *sovereign state* has the duty to carry out the will of the people of this state and to regulate the health, medical practices and well-being of those people in a manner that respects their personal deci-sions concerning the relief of suffering through medical use of marijuana.[81]

In language reminiscent of the Kentucky and Virginia Resolutions, Nevada has issued a challenge to the national government. In effect, Nevada has interposed between its citizens and the federal government. Though the legislature should be applauded for this act, so long as a branch of the national government serves as the arbiter of state and federal power, Nevada's chances of success are not good.

The possibility that drugs like marijuana could be legalized is but one example of how different life would be in a federal republic. Under the true principles of the Constitution, the states could legalize or criminalize marijuana; prohibit or regulate abortions; offer or decline to offer single-gender educational programs in state-supported schools; permit or ban prayer in public schools; and deal with many other matters falling under the states' general police power. Currently, Americans view such issues as an all-or-nothing matter. They debate whether marijuana should be legalized in the United States, not whether a state should be permitted to chart its own course. So often we look only at the substance of an issue and ignore the procedural question of who is to decide. But in a federal system the question of who decides (the states or the national government) is often more important than the ultimate decision. The United States would not crumble if California or Nevada chose to legalize marijuana. But can we say the same for liberty if all power is lodged with a consolidated government far removed from the governed?[82]

* * *

While the modern world is much different from that of the late 1700s, the march of years has in no way rendered federalism obsolete. If anything, the diversity that is modern America highlights the need for local self-governance and decentralized decision-making. The more heterogeneous we become, the more we need a pure federalist system. Only in a federalist system can we continue to work together toward great national objectives while at the same time we govern ourselves in light of our myriad differences.

Unfortunately, our modern federal system is in disarray and functioning nothing like the system designed by the Framers. In the words of Edward S. Corwin, "our system has lost resiliency and what was once vaunted as a Constitution of Rights, both state and private, has been replaced by a Constitution of Powers."[83] However, if we have the will, our system of government can be reformed.

The first step in this process is the rediscovery of our revolutionary tradition and its lessons about self-government. Integral parts to this understanding are the Kentucky and Virginia Resolutions. The Resolutions articulate the basics of our government in an eloquent, yet logical, manner; they are second only to the Constitution in their import and merit inclusion in the Pantheon of American charters. Along with documents such as the Declaration of Independence,

Articles of Confederation, and Constitution, the Resolves tell the story of the birth and growth of republican government in North America. If Americans embrace the Resolves' lessons about ultimate sovereignty and divided legislative sovereignty, then a renewal of federalism and a restoration of our Constitution is possible.

Appendices

The Kentucky Resolutions of 1798[1]

November 10th, 1798.

I. Resolved, that the several States composing the United States of America, are not united on the principles of unlimited submission to their General Government; but that by compact under the style and title of a Constitution for the United States and of amendments thereto, they constituted a General Government for special purposes, delegated to that Government certain definite powers, reserving each State to itself, the residuary mass of right to their own self Government; and that whensoever the General Government assumes undelegated powers, its acts are unauthoritative, void, and of no force: That to this compact each State acceded as a State, and is an integral party, its co-States forming as to itself, the other party: That the Government created by this compact was not made the exclusive or final *judge* of the extent of the powers delegated to itself; since that would have made its discretion, and not the Constitution, the measure of its powers; but that as in all other cases of compact among parties having no common Judge, each party has an equal right to judge for itself, as well of infractions as of the mode and measure of redress.

II. Resolved, that the Constitution of the United States having delegated to Congress a power to punish treason, counterfeiting the securities and current coin of the United States, piracies and felonies committed on the High Seas, and offenses against the laws of nations, and no other crimes whatever, and it being true as a general principle, and one of the amendments to the Constitution having also declared, "that the powers not delegated to the United States by the Constitution, nor prohibited by it to the States, are reserved to the States respectively, or to the people," therefore also the same act of Congress passed on the 14th day of July, 1798, and entitled "An act in addition to the act entitled an act for the punishment of certain crimes against the United States," as also the act passed by them on the 27th day of June, 1798, entitled "An act to punish frauds committed on the Bank of the United States" (and all their other acts which assume to create, define, or punish crimes other than those enumerated in the Constitution) are altogether void and of no force, and that the power to create, define, and punish such other crimes is reserved, and of right appertains solely and exclusively to the respective States, each within its own Territory.

III. Resolved, that it is true as a general principle, and is also expressly declared by one of the amendments to the Constitution that "the powers not delegated to the United States by the Constitution, nor prohibited by it to the States, are reserved to the States respectively or to the people"; and that no power over the freedom of religion, freedom of speech, or freedom of the press being delegated to the United States by the Constitution, nor prohibited by it to the States, all lawful powers respecting the same did of right remain, and were reserved to the States, or to the people: That thus was manifested their determination to retain to themselves the right of judging how far the licentiousness of speech and of the press may be abridged without lessening their useful freedom, and how far those abuses which cannot be separated from their use, should be tolerated rather than the use be destroyed; and thus also they guarded against all abridgement by the United States of the freedom of religious opinions and exercises, and retained to themselves the right of protecting the same, as this state by a Law passed on the general demand of its Citizens, had already protected them from all human restraint or interference: And that in addition to this general principle and express declaration, another and more special provision has been made by one of the amendments to the Constitution which expressly declares, that "Congress shall make no law respecting an Establishment of religion, or prohibiting the free exercise thereof, or abridging the freedom of speech, or the press," thereby guarding in the same sentence, and under the same words, the freedom of religion, of speech, and of the press, insomuch, that whatever violates either, throws down the sanctuary which covers the others, and that libels, falsehoods, and defamation, equally with heresy and false religion, are withheld from the cognizance of federal tribunals. That therefore the act of the Congress of the United States passed on the 14th day of July 1798, entitled "An act in addition to the act for the punishment of certain crimes against the United States," which does abridge the freedom of the press, is not law, but is altogether void and of no effect.

IV. Resolved, that alien friends are under the jurisdiction and protection of the laws of the State wherein they are; that no power over them has been delegated to the United States, nor prohibited to the individual States distinct from their power over citizens; and it being true as a general principle, and one of the amendments to the Constitution having also declared, that "the powers not delegated to the United States by the Constitution nor prohibited by it to the States are reserved to the States respectively or to the people," the act of the Congress of the United States passed on the 22d day of June, 1798, entitled "An act concerning aliens," which assumes power over alien friends not delegated by the Constitution, is not law, but is altogether void and of no force.

V. Resolved, that in addition to the general principle as well as the express declaration, that powers not delegated are reserved, another and more special provision inserted in the Constitution from abundant caution has declared, "that the *migration* or importation of such persons as any of the States now existing shall think proper to admit, shall not be prohibited by the Congress prior to the year 1808." That this Commonwealth does admit the migration of alien friends described as the subject of the said act concerning aliens; that a provision against prohibiting their migration, is a provision against all acts equivalent thereto, or it would be nugatory; that to remove them when migrated is equivalent to a prohibition of their migration, and is therefore contrary to the said provision of the Constitution and void.

VI. Resolved, that the imprisonment of a person under the protection of the Laws of this Commonwealth on his failure to obey the simple *order* of the President to depart out of the United States, as is undertaken by the said act entitled "An act concerning Aliens," is contrary to the Constitution, one amendment to which has provided, that "no person shall be deprived of liberty without due process of law," and that another having provided "that in all criminal prosecutions, the accused shall enjoy the right to a public trial by an impartial jury, to be informed of the nature and cause of the accusation, to be confronted with the witnesses against him, to have compulsory process for obtaining witnesses in his favour, and to have the assistance of counsel for his defence," the same act undertaking to authorize the President to remove a person out of the United States who is under the protection of the Law, on his own suspicion, without accusation, without jury, without public trial, without confrontation of the witnesses against him, without having witnesses in his favour, without defence, without counsel, is contrary to these provisions also of the Constitution, is therefore not law but utterly void and of no force.

That transferring the power of judging any person who is under the protection of the laws, from the Courts to the President of the United States, as is undertaken by the same act concerning Aliens, is against the article of the Constitution which provides, that "the judicial power of the United States shall be vested in Courts, the Judges of which shall hold their offices during good behaviour," and that the said act is void for that reason also; and it is further to be noted, that this transfer of Judiciary power is to that magistrate of the General Government who already possesses all the Executive, and a qualified negative in all the Legislative powers.

VII. Resolved, that the construction applied by the General Government (as is evinced by sundry of their proceedings) to those parts of the Constitution of the United States which delegate to Congress a power to lay and collect taxes, duties, imposts, and excises; to pay the debts, and provide for the common defence, and general welfare of the United States, and to make all laws which shall be necessary and proper for carrying into execution the powers vested by the Constitution in the Government of the United States, or any department thereof, goes to the destruction of all the limits prescribed to their power by the Constitution—That words meant by that instrument to be subsiduary only to the execution of the limited powers, ought not to be so construed as themselves to give unlimited powers, nor a part so to be taken, as to destroy the whole residue of the instrument: That the proceedings of the General Government under colour of these articles, will be a fit and necessary subject for revisal and correction at a time of greater tranquility, while those specified in the preceding resolutions call for immediate redress.

VIII. Resolved, that the preceeding Resolutions be transmitted to the Senators and Representatives in Congress from this Commonwealth, who are hereby enjoined to present the same to their respective Houses, and to use their best endeavours to procure at the next session of Congress, a repeal of the aforesaid unconstitutional and obnoxious acts.

IX. Resolved lastly, that the Governor of this Commonwealth be, and is hereby authorised and requested to communicate the preceding Resolutions to the Legislatures of the several States, to assure them that this Commonwealth considers Union for specified National purposes, and particularly for those specified in their late Federal Compact, to be friendly to the peace, happiness, and prosperity of all the States: that faithful to that compact, according to the plain intent and meaning in which it was understood and acceded to by the several parties, it is sincerely anxious for its preservation: that it does also believe, that to take from the States all the powers of self government, and transfer them to a general and consolidated Government, without regard to the special delegations and reservations solemnly agreed to in that compact, is not for the peace, happiness, or prosperity of these States: And that therefore, this Commonwealth is determined, as it doubts not its co-States are, tamely to submit to undelegated & consequently unlimited powers in no man or body of men on earth: that if the acts before specified should stand, these conclusions would flow from them; that the General Government may place any act they think proper on the list of crimes & punish it themselves, whether enumerated or not enumerated by the Constitution as cognizable by them: that they may transfer its cognizance to the President or any other person, who may himself be the accuser, counsel, judge, and jury, whose *suspicions* may be the evidence, his order the sentence, his officer the executioner, and his breast the sole record of the transaction: that a very numerous and valuable description of the inhabitants of these States, being by this precedent reduced as outlaws to the absolute dominion of one man and the barrier of the Constitution thus swept away from us all, no rampart now remains against the passions and the power of a majority of Congress, to protect from a like exportation or other more grievous punishment the minority of the same body, the Legislatures, Judges, Governors, & Counsellors of the States, nor their other peaceable inhabitants who may venture to reclaim the constitutional rights & liberties of the States & people, or who for other causes, good or bad, may be obnoxious to the views or marked by the suspicions of the President, or be thought dangerous to his or their elections or other interests public or personal: that the friendless alien has indeed been selected as the safest subject of a first experiment: but the citizen will soon follow, or rather has already followed; for, already has a Sedition Act marked him as its prey: that these and successive acts of the same character, unless arrested on the threshold, may tend to drive these States into revolution and blood, and will furnish new calumnies against Republican Governments, and new pretexts for those who wish it to be believed, that man cannot be governed but by a rod of iron: that it would be a dangerous delusion were a confidence in the men of our choice to silence our fears for the safety of our rights: that confidence is every where the parent of despotism: free government is founded in jealousy and not in confidence; it is jealousy and not confidence which prescribes limited Constitutions to bind down those whom we are obliged to trust with power: that our Constitution has accordingly fixed the limits to which and no further our confidence may go; and let the honest advocate of confidence read the Alien and Sedition Acts, and say if the Constitution has not been wise in fixing limits to the Government it created, and whether we should be wise in destroying those limits? Let him say what the Government is if it be not a tyranny, which the men of our choice have conferred on the President, and the President of our choice has assented to and accepted over the friendly strangers, to whom the mild spirit of our Country and its laws had pledged hospitality and protection: that the men of our choice have more respected the bare suspicions of the President than the solid rights of inno-cence, the claims of justification, the sacred force of truth, and the forms & substance of law and justice. In questions of power then let no more be heard of confidence in man, but bind him down from mischief by the chains of the Constitution. That this Commonwealth does therefore call on its co-States for an expression of their sentiments on the acts concerning Aliens, and for the punishment of certain crimes herein before specified, plainly declaring whether these acts are or are not authorized by the Federal Compact? And it doubts not that their sense will be so announced as to prove their attachment unaltered to limited Government, whether general or particular, and that the rights and liberties of their co-States will be exposed to no dangers by remaining embarked on a common bottom with their own: That they will concur with this Commonwealth in considering the said acts as so palpably against the Constitution as to amount to an undisguised declaration, that the Compact is not meant to be the measure of the powers of the General Government, but that it will proceed in the exercise over these States of all powers whatsoever: That they will view this as seizing the rights of the States and consolidating them in the hands of the General Government with a power assumed to bind the States (not merely in cases made federal) but in all cases whatsoever, by laws made, not with their consent, but by others against their consent: That this would be to surrender the form of Government we have chosen, and to live under one deriving its powers from its own will, and not from our authority; and that the co-States recurring to their natural right in cases not made federal, will concur in declaring these acts void and of no force, and will each unite with this Commonwealth in requesting their repeal at the next session of Congress.

EDMUND BULLOCK, S. H. R.
JOHN CAMPBELL, S. S. P. T.

Passed the House of Representatives, Nov. 10th, 1798.
   Attest,

THOMAS TODD, C. H. R

In SENATE, *November 13th, 1798, unanimously*
   concurred in,
   Attest,

B. THRUSTON, *Clk. Sen.*

Approved November 16th, 1798.

JAMES GARRARD, G. K.

By THE GOVERNOR,

HARRY TOULMIN,
Secretary of State.

The Virginia Resolutions of 1798[2]

Friday, December 21, 1798.

Resolved, That the General Assembly of Virginia, doth unequivocally express a firm resolution to maintain and defend the Constitution of the United States, and the Constitution of this State, against every aggression either foreign or domestic, and that they will support the government of the United States in all measures warranted by the former.

That this Assembly most solemnly declares a warm attachment to the Union of the States, to maintain which it pledges all its powers; and that for this end, it is their duty to watch over and oppose every infraction of those principles which constitute the only basis of that Union, because a faithful observance of them, can alone secure its existence and the public happiness.

That this Assembly doth explicitly and peremptorily declare, that it views the powers of the federal government, as resulting from the compact, to which the States are parties; as limited by the plain sense and intention of the instrument constituting that compact; as no further valid than they are authorized by the grants enumerated in that compact; and that in case of a deliberate, palpable, and dangerous exercise of other powers, not granted by the said compact, the States who are parties thereto, have the right, and are in duty bound, to interpose for arresting the progress of the evil, and for maintaining within their respective limits, the authorities, rights, and liberties appertaining to them.

That the General Assembly doth also express its deep regret, that a spirit has in sundry instances, been manifested by the federal government, to enlarge its powers by forced constructions of the constitutional charter which defines them; and that indications have appeared of a design to expound certain general phrases (which having been copied from the very limited grant of powers in the former articles of confederation were the less liable to be misconstrued) so as to destroy the meaning and effect, of the particular enumeration which necessarily explains and limits the general phrases; and so as to consolidate the States by degrees, into one sovereignty, the obvious tendency and inevitable consequences of which would be, to transform the present republican system of the United States, into an absolute, or at best a mixed monarchy.

That the General Assembly doth particularly protest against the palpable and alarming infractions of the Constitution, in the two late cases of the "Alien and

Sedition Acts" passed at the last session of Congress; the first of which exercises a power nowhere delegated to the federal government, and which by uniting legislative and judicial powers to those of executive, subverts the general principles of free government, as well as the particular organization, and positive provisions of the federal Constitution; and the other of which acts, exercises in like manner, a power not delegated by the Constitution, but on the contrary, expressly and positively forbidden by one of the amendments thereto;—a power, which more than any other, ought to produce universal alarm, because it is leveled against that right of freely examining public characters and measures, and of free communication among the people thereon, which has ever been justly deemed, the only effectual guardian of every other right.

That this State having by its Convention, which ratified the Federal Constitution, expressly declared, that among other essential rights, "the Liberty of Conscience and of the Press cannot be cancelled, abridged, restrained, or modified by any authority of the United States," and from its extreme anxiety to guard these rights from every possible attack of sophistry or ambition, having with other States, recommended an amendment for that purpose, which amendment was, in due time, annexed to the Constitution; it would mark a reproachful inconsistency, and criminal degeneracy, if an indifference were now shewn, to the most palpable violation of one of the Rights, thus declared and secured; and to the establishment of a precedent which may be fatal to the other.

That the good people of this Commonwealth, having ever felt, and continuing to feel, the most sincere affection for their brethren of the other States; the truest anxiety for establishing and perpetuating the union of all; and the most scrupulous fidelity to that Constitution, which is the pledge of mutual friendship, and the instrument of mutual happiness, the General Assembly doth solemnly appeal to the like disposition of the other States, in confidence that they will concur with this Commonwealth in declaring, as it does hereby declare, that the acts aforesaid, are unconstitutional; and that the necessary and proper measures will be taken by each, for cooperating with this State, in maintaining the Authorities, Rights, and Liberties, reserved to the States respectively, or to the People.

That the Governor be desired, to transmit a copy of the foregoing Resolutions to the executive authority of each of the other States, with a request that the same may be communicated to the Legislature thereof; and that a copy be furnished to each of the Senators and Representatives representing this State in the Congress of the United States.

Agreed to by the Senate, December 24, 1798.

Kentucky Resolutions of 1799[3]

November 14th, 1799.

Resolved, That this Commonwealth considers the federal Union, upon the terms and for the purposes specified in the late compact, conducive to the liberty and happiness of the several States: That it does now unequivocally declare its attachment to the Union, and to that compact, agreeably to its obvious and real intention, and will be among the last to seek its dissolution: That, if those who administer the General Government be permitted to transgress the limits fixed by that compact, by a total disregard to the special delegations of power therein contained, an annihilation of the State Governments, and the creation upon their ruins, of a General Consolidated Government, will be the inevitable consequence: That the principle and construction contended for by sundry of the State legislatures, that the General Government is the exclusive judge of the extent of the powers delegated to it, stop nothing short of *despotism*—since the discretion of those who administer the government, and not the *Constitution*, would be the measure of their powers: That the several States who formed that instrument being sovereign and independent, have the unquestionable right to judge of the infraction; and *That a Nullification by those sovereignties, of all unauthorized acts done under color of that instrument is the rightful remedy*: That this Commonwealth does, under the most deliberate reconsideration, declare, that the said Alien and Sedition Laws are, in their opinion, palpable violations of the said Constitution: and, however cheerfully it may be disposed to surrender its opinion to a majority of its sister States, in matters of ordinary or doubtful policy, yet, in momentous regulations like the present, which so vitally wound the best rights of the citizen, it would consider a silent acquiescence as highly criminal: That, although this Commonwealth, as a party to the federal compact, will bow to the laws of the Union, yet, it does, at the same time declare, that it will not now, or ever hereafter, cease to oppose in constitutional manner, every attempt at what quarter soever offered, to violate that compact. And, finally, in order that no pretext or arguments may be drawn from a supposed acquiescence, on the part of this Commonwealth in the constitutionality of these laws, and be thereby used as precedents for similar future violations of the federal compact—this Commonwealth does now enter against them its solemn PROTEST.

Attest,

THOMAS TODD, C. H. R.

In SENATE, *Nov. 22, 1799.*
Attest,

B. THRUSTON, C. S.

Jefferson's Draft of the Kentucky Resolutions of 1798[4]

[Sept.? 1798]

1. *Resolved,* That the several States composing the US. of America are not united on the principle of unlimited submission to their general government; but that by a compact under the style and title of a Constitution for the US. and of amendments thereto, they constituted a general government for special purposes, delegated to that government certain definite powers, reserving, each state to itself, the residuary mass of right to their own self-government; and that

whensoever the General government assumes undelegated powers, it's acts are unauthoritative, void, and of no force: that to this compact each state acceded as a state, and is an integral party, it's co-states forming, as to itself, the other party: that the government created by this compact was not made the exclusive or final judge of the extent of the powers delegated to itself; since that would have made it's discretion, and not the constitution, the measure of its powers; but that, as in all other cases of compact among powers having no common judge, each party has an equal right to judge for itself, as well of infractions as of the mode and measure of redress.

2. *Resolved*, That the constitution of the US. having delegated to Congress a power to punish treason, counterfeiting the securities and current coin of the US. piracies and felonies committed on the high seas, and offences against the law of Nations, and no other crimes whatsoever, and it being true as a general principle, and one of the Amendments to the constitution having also declared, that "the powers not delegated to the US. by the constitution, nor prohibited by it to the states, are reserved to the states respectively, or to the people," therefore the act of Congress, passed on the 14th day of July, 1798, and intituled "An Act in addition to the act intituled An Act for the punishment of certain crimes against the U.S." as also the act passed by them on the [27th] day of June, 1798, intituled "An Act to punish frauds committed on the bank of the US." (and all their other acts which assume to create, define or punish crimes, other than those so enumerated in the Constitution,) are altogether void, and of no force; and that the power to create, define and punish such other crimes is reserved, and of right appurtains solely and exclusively to the respective states, each within its own territory.

3. *Resolved*, that it is true as a general principle, and is also expressly declared by one of the Amendments to the Constitution, that "the powers not delegated to the US. by the constitution, nor prohibited by it to the states, are reserved to the states respectively, or to the people"; and that no power over the freedom of religion, freedom of speech, or freedom of the press being delegated to the US. by the constitution, nor prohibited by it to the states, all lawful powers respecting the same did of right remain, and were reserved, to the states or the people: that thus was manifested their determination to retain to themselves the right of judging how far the licentiousness of speech and of the press may be abridged without lessening their useful freedom, and how far those abuses which cannot be separated from their use should be tolerated, rather than the use be destroyed; and thus also they guarded against all abridgment by the U.S. of the freedom of religious opinions and exercises, and retained to themselves the right of protecting the same, as this state, by a law passed on the general demand of it's citizens, had already protected them from all human restraint or interference: And that in addition to this general principle and express declaration, another and more special provision has been made by one of the amendments to the constitution which expressly declares that "Congress shall make no law respecting an establishment of religion, or prohibiting the free exercise thereof, or abridging the

freedom of speech or of the press": thereby guarding in the same sentence, and under the same words, the freedom of religion, of speech, and of the press: insomuch, that whatever violates either throws down the sanctuary which covers the others, and that libels, falsehood and defamation, equally with heresy and false religion, are withheld from the cognizance of federal tribunals: that, therefore, the act of Congress of the US. passed on the 14th Day of July, 1798, intituled "An Act in addition to the act intituled An Act for the punishment of certain crimes against the US." which does abridge the freedom of the press, is not law, but is altogether void, and of no force.

4. *Resolved*, that alien friends are under the jurisdiction and protection of the laws of the state wherein they are; that no power over them has been delegated to the US. nor prohibited to the individual states distinct from their power over citizens: and it being true as a general principle, and one of the amendments to the constitution having also declared that "the powers not delegated to the US. by the constitution, nor prohibited by it to the states, are reserved to the states respectively, or to the people," the act of the Congress of the US. passed on the—day of July, 1798, intituled "An Act concerning Aliens," which assumes powers over Alien-friends, not delegated by the constitution, is not law, but is altogether void, and of no force.

5. *Resolved*, that in addition to the general principle, as well as the express declaration, that powers not delegated are reserved, another and more special provision, inserted in the constitution from abundant caution, has declared that "the migration or importation of such persons as any of the states now existing shall think proper to admit, shall not be prohibited by the Congress prior to the year 1808"; that this commonwealth does admit the migration of Alien-friends, described as the subject of the said act concerning aliens: that a provision against prohibiting their migration, is a provision against all acts equivalent thereto, or it would be nugatory; that to remove them when migrated, is equivalent to a prohibition of their migration, and is therefore contrary to the said provision of the Constitution, and void.

6. *Resolved*, that the imprisonment of a person under the protection of the laws of this commonwealth on his failure to obey the simple *order* of the President to depart out of the US. as is undertaken by said act intituled "An Act concerning Aliens," is contrary to the constitution, one Amendment to which has provided that "no person shall be deprived of liberty without due process of law." And that another having provided that "in all criminal prosecutions the accused shall enjoy the right to public trial, by an impartial jury, to be informed of the nature and cause of the accusation, to be confronted with the witnesses against him, to have compulsory process for obtaining witnesses in his favor, and to have the assistance of counsel for his defence," the same act, undertaking to authorize the President to remove a person out of the US. who is under the protection of the law, on his own suspicion, without accusation, without jury, without public

trial, without confrontation of the witnesses against him, without hearing witnesses in his favor, without defence, without counsel, is contrary to the provision also of the constitution, is therefore not law, but utterly void, and of no force. That transferring the power of judging any person, who is under the protection of the laws, from the courts to the President of the US. as is undertaken by the same act concerning Aliens, is against the article of the constitution which provides that "the judicial power of the United States shall be vested in courts, the judges of which shall hold their offices during good behavior" and that the said act is void for that reason also. And it is further to be noted that this transfer of judiciary power is to that magistrate of the general government who already possesses all the Executive, and a negative on all Legislative powers.

7. *Resolved*, That the construction applied by the General government (as is evidenced by sundry of their proceedings) to those parts of the constitution of the US. which delegate to Congress a power "to lay and collect taxes, duties, imposts and excises, to pay the debts and provide for the common defence and general welfare of the US." and "to make all laws which shall be necessary and proper for carrying into execution the powers vested by the constitution in the government of the US. or in any department or officer thereof," goes to the destruction of all limits prescribed to their power by the constitution: that words meant by the instrument to be subsidiary only to the execution of limited powers, ought not to be so construed as themselves to give unlimited powers, nor a part to be so taken as to destroy the whole residue of that instrument: that the proceedings of the General government under color of these articles, will be a fit and necessary subject of revisal and correction, at a time of greater tranquility, while those specified in the proceding resolutions, call for immediate redress.

8th. *Resolved*, that a committee of conference and correspondence be appointed, who shall have in charge to communicate the preceding resolutions to the legislatures of the several states, to assure them that this commonwealth continues in the same esteem for their friendship and union which it has manifested from the moment at which a common danger first suggested a common union: that it considers union, for specified national purposes, and particularly for those specified in the late federal compact, to be friendly to the peace, happiness and prosperity of all the states; that faithful to that compact, according to the plain intent and meaning in which it was understood and acceded to by the several parties, it is sincerely anxious for it's preservation: that it does also believe, that to take from the states all the powers of self-government, and transfer them to a general and consolidated government, without regard to the special delegations and reservations solemnly agreed to in that compact, is not for the peace, happiness or prosperity of these states; and that therefore this commonwealth is determined, as it doubts not its co-states are, to submit to undelegated, and consequently unlimited powers in no man, or body of men, on earth: that in cases of an abuse of the delegated powers, the members of the general government being chosen by the people, a change by the people would be the constitutional remedy; but, where powers are assumed which have not been delegated, a nullification of the act is the rightful remedy: that every state has a natural right in cases not within the compact (casus non foederis) to nullify of their own authority all assumptions of power by others within their limits: that, without this right, they would be under the dominion, absolute and unlimited, of whosoever might exercise this right of judgment for them: that nevertheless this commonwealth, from motives of regard and respect for its co-states, has wished to communicate with them on the subject; that with them alone it is proper to communicate, they alone being parties to the compact, and solely authorized to judge in the last resort of the powers exercised under it, Congress being not a party, but merely the creature of the compact, and subject, as to it's assumptions of power, to the final judgment of those by whom, and for whose use, itself, and it's powers were all created and modified: that if the acts before specified should stand, these conclusions would flow from them; that the General government may place any act they think proper on the list of crimes, and punish it themselves whether enumerated or not enumerated by the constitution as cognizable by them; that they may transfer it's cognizance to the President, or any other person, who may himself be the accuser, counsel, judge and jury, whose *suspicions* may be the evidence, his *order* the sentence, his *officer* the executioner, and his breast the sole record of the transaction: that a very numerous and valuable description of the inhabitants of these states being, by this precedent, reduced, as Outlaws, to the absolute dominion of one man, and the barrier of the constitution thus swept away for us all, no rampart now remains against the passions and the power of a majority in Congress to protect from a like exportation, or other more grievous punishment the minority of the same body, the legislatures, judges, governors and counsellors of the states, nor their other peaceable inhabitants, who may venture to reclaim the constitutional rights and liberties of the states and people, or who for other causes, good or bad, may be obnoxious to the views, or marked by the suspicions of the President, or be thought dangerous to his or their elections or other interests public or personal: that the friendless alien has indeed been selected as the safest subject of a first experiment; but the citizen will soon follow, or rather, has already followed; for already has a Sedition act marked him as it's prey: that these and successive acts of the same character, unless arrested at the threshold, necessarily drive these states into revolution and blood, and will furnish new calumnies against republican government, and new pretexts for those who wish it to be believed that man cannot be governed but by a rod of iron: that it would be a dangerous delusion, were a confidence in the men of our choice to silence our fears for the safety of our rights; that confidence is everywhere the parent of despotism; free government is founded in jealousy, and not in confidence; it is jealousy and not confidence which prescribes limited constitutions, to bind down those whom we are obliged to trust with power: that our constitution has accordingly fixed the limits to which, and no further, our confidence may go: and let the honest advocate of confidence read the Alien and Sedition acts, and say if the Constitution has not been wise in fixing limits to the government it created, and whether we should be wise in destroying those limits. Let him say

What the government is, if it be not a tyranny, which the men of our choice have conferred on our President, and the President of our choice has assented to, and accepted over the friendly strangers, to whom the mild spirit of our country and it's laws have pledged hospitality and protection: that the men of our choice have more respected the bare *suspicions* of the President than the solid rights of innocence, the claims of justification, the sacred force of truth, and the forms and substance of law and justice: in questions of power, then, let no more be heard of confidence in man, but bind him down from mischief by the chains of the constitution. That this commonwealth does therefore call on its co-states for an expression of their sentiments on the acts concerning aliens, and for the punishment of certain crimes herein before specified, plainly declaring whether these acts are or are not authorized by the federal compact? And it doubts not that their sense will be so enounced as to prove their attachment unaltered to limited government, whether general or particular; and that the rights and liberties of their co-states will be exposed to no dangers by remaining embarked in a common bottom with their own: that they will concur with this commonwealth in considering the said acts as so palpably against the constitution as to amount to an undisguised declaration that that compact is not meant to be the measure of the powers of the General government, but that it will proceed in the exercise, over these states, of all powers whatsoever; that they will view this as seizing the rights of the states, and consolidating them in the hands of the General government, with a power assumed to bind the States (not merely in the cases made federal [casus foederis] but) in all cases whatsoever, by laws made, not with their consent, but by others against their consent; that this would be to surrender the form of government we have chosen, and to live under one deriving it's powers from its own will, and not from our authority, and that the co-states, recurring to their natural right in cases not made federal, will concur in declaring these acts void and of no force, and will each take measures of its own for providing that neither these acts, nor any others of the general government, not plainly and intentionally authorized by the constitution, shall be exercised within their respective territories.

9th. *Resolved*, that the said committee be authorized to communicate, by writing or personal conferences, at any times or places whatever, with any person or persons who may be appointed by any one or more of the co-states to correspond or confer with them; and that they lay their proceedings before the next session of assembly.

NOTES

Foreword

1. John Locke, *Second Treatise of Civil Government* (1690), Chap. XIX, § 225.
2. King James I, Speech Before Parliament, March 21, 1609.
3. *An Act Declaring the Rights and Liberties of the Subject and Settling the Succession of the Crown* [the English Bill of Rights] (1689).
4. Thomas Hobbes, *Leviathan* . . . (London 1651), Pt. I, Chap. XVIII.
5. Locke, op. cit., Chap. IX, §§ 123, 124.
6. Polybius, *Histories*, trans. W.R. Paton, 6 vols. (Cambridge, Mass.: Harvard University Press [Loeb Classical Library], 1922–27), Bk. VI, 6.3–6.10).
7. William Blackstone, *Commentaries on the Laws of England*, 4 vols. (Oxford: Clarendon Press, 1765–69), Bk. I, Pt. 1, § 2.
8. James Burgh, *Political Disquisitions* . . . 3 vols. (London: E. and C. Dilly, 1774–75), III, 278.
9. Thomas Paine, *Common Sense* (1776) in Philip S. Foner, ed., *The Complete Writings of Thomas Paine*, 2 vols. (New York: Citadel Press, 1969), I, 4, 7, 38.
10. See J. Paul Selsam, *The Pennsylvania Constitution of 1776* (Philadelphia: University of Pennsylvania Press, 1936), 186–96.
11. For the views of French *américanistes* and *anglomanes*, see Joyce Appleby, "The Jefferson–Adams Rupture, and The First Translation of John Adams' *Defence*," *American Historical Review*, Vol. LXXIII, No. 14 (April, 1968).
12. Lyman H. Butterfield, ed., *The Adams Papers: Diary and Autobiography of John Adams*. 4 vols. (Cambridge, Mass.: Belknap Press of Harvard University Press, 1961–62), III, 333.
13. *Thoughts on Government: Applicable to the Present State of the American Colonies in a Letter from a Gentleman to his Friend* (Boston, 1776) in Robert J. Taylor, ed., *The Adams Papers: Papers of John Adams*, 10 vols. (Cambridge, Mass.: Belknap Press of Harvard University Press, 1977–), IV, 88–9.
14. "A Constitution or Form of Government for the Commonwealth of Massachusetts," ibid., VIII, 237–61.
15. See fn. 11.
16. John Adams, *A Defence of The Constitutions of Government of the United States of America* in Charles Francis Adams, ed., *The Works of John Adams* . . . 10 vols. (Boston: C.C. Little Brown, 1850–56), IV, 272, 299–302.
17. Ibid., IV, 435–45.

18. Ibid., IV, 359.
19. Ibid., IV, 468. For the development of John Adams's view of balanced government, see Joyce Appleby, "The New Republican Synthesis and the Changing Political Ideas of John Adams," *American Quarterly*, Vol. 25, No. 5 (December, 1973), 578–95.
20. TJ to William Short, Monticello, January 8, 1825, Paul Leicester Ford, ed., *The Works of Thomas Jefferson*. Federal Edition, 12 vols. (New York: London: G.P. Putnam's Sons, 1904–05), XII, 388, 394–5.
21. JM to TJ, New York, May 12, 1791, James Morton Smith, ed., *The Republic of Letters: The Correspondence Between Jefferson and Madison 1776–1826*, 3 vols. (New York: W.W. Norton, 1995), II, 688.
22. For a general discussion of the tripartite balance in the U.S. Constitution (including Adams's views), see Gilbert Chinard, "Polybius and the American Constitution," *Journal of the History of Ideas*, Vol. I, Issue 1 (January, 1940), 38–58.
23. JA to John Taylor, Quincy, April 15, 1814, Adams, op. cit., VI, 470–2.
24. "Benjamin Franklin's Speech at the Conclusion of the Constitutional Convention" in Bernard Bailyn, ed., *The Debate on the Constitution*, 2 vols. (New York: Literary Classics of the United States, 1993), I, 3–4.
25. Jonathan Elliot, *The Debates, Resolutions, and other Proceedings, in Convention, on the Adoption of the Federal Constitution* . . . 4 vols. (Washington, 1827–30), III, 53.
26. Federalist 46 (Madison) in *The Federalist Papers* (New York: New American Library, 1961), 294.
27. For a thoughtful analysis of American sovereignty in the people, see Gordon Wood, *Creation of the American Republic, 1776–1787* (Chapel Hill, 1969), 372–83.
28. TJ to JM, Paris, March 15, 1789, Smith, op. cit., I, 586, 588.
29. Gaillard Hunt and James Brown Scott, eds., *The Debates in the Federal Convention of 1787 Which Framed the Constitution* . . . *Reported by James Madison* . . . 2 vols. (Buffalo, New York: Prometheus Books, 1987), I, 115–16 (June 18).
30. JM to TJ, New York, May 23, 1789, Smith, op. cit., I, 612.
31. Benjamin Rush to JA, Phil, June 4, 1789, L.H. Butterfield, ed., *Letters of Benjamin Rush*, 2 vols. (Princeton, N.J.: Princeton University Press, 1951), I, 513, 514.
32. JA to Benjamin Rush, N.Y., June 19, 1789, *Old Family Letters: Copied from the Originals for Alexander Biddle, Series A-B* (Philadelphia: J.B. Lippincott, 1892), 39–40.
33. John Adams authored 32 "Discourses on Davila" that appeared in the *Gazette of the United States* (Philadelphia) from April 28, 1790 through April 27, 1791.
34. "Discourses on Davila. No. 32," *Gazette of the United States* (Philadelphia), April 27, 1791.
35. TJ to JM, Philadelphia, May 9, 1791, Smith, op. cit., II, 687, 688.
36. TJ to JM, New York, May 12, 1791, ibid., II, 688.

37. TJ to George Washington, Philadelphia, May 8, 1791, Merrill D. Peterson, ed., *Thomas Jefferson Writings* (New York: Library Classics of the U.S., 1984), 977–9.
38. TJ to GW, Philadelphia, May 23, 1792, ibid., 985, 986–7.
39. TJ to GW, Monticello, September 9, 1792, ibid., 992, 994.
40. JM to TJ, Orange, June 13, 1793, Smith, op. cit., II, 782, 783.
41. TJ to JM, Monticello, September 21, 1795, Smith, op. cit., II, 897, 898.
42. TJ To Philip Mazzei, Monticello, April 24, 1796, Peterson, op. cit., 1035, 1036–7.
43. "Speech to Both Houses of Congress," May 16, 1797, Adams, op. cit., IX, 111, 114.
44. TJ to Edward Rutledge, Philadelphia, June 24, 1797, Ford, op. cit., VIII, 316, 318–19
45. TJ to John Taylor, Philadelphia, June 4, 1798, Peterson, op. cit., 1048, 1050.
46. TJ to JM, Philadelphia, March 21 and 22, 1798, Smith, op. cit., II, 1028, 1029.
47. TJ to Benjamin Rush, Monticello, September 23, 1800, Peterson, op. cit., 1080, 1081–2.
48. Richard N. Rosenfeld, *American Aurora: A Democratic-Republican Returns: The Suppressed History of Our Nation's Beginnings and The Heroic Newspaper That Tried to Report It* (New York: St. Martin's Press, 1997), 168–70.
49. Ibid., 184, 193, 204, 526–7.
50. TJ to Stevens T. Mason, Monticello, October 11, 1798, Ford, op. cit., VIII, 449–50.

1   Monocrats and Jacobins

1. As used throughout the book, "Federalist" and "Federalism" refer to the party and its tenets, while "federalist" and "federalism" refer to the division of legislative sovereignty between the national and state governments.
2. What I describe as a "party" in no way resembles the modern version of a political party. As Dumas Malone has observed, "[t]he term 'party' was something of a misnomer at a time when the affiliations of members of Congress were not a matter of record, and the organization was rudimentary from our point of view. Parties were loose groupings without legal sanction or formal leadership." Dumas Malone, *Jefferson the President: Second Term 1805–9* (Boston, Mass.: Little, Brown and Company, 1974) p. xiii. For lack of a better term, I will describe the opposing groups as the Federalist party and the Republican party.
3. The Court/Country distinction originates from English political struggles of the seventeenth and eighteenth centuries. English Whigs saw the Court party as ever struggling to increase the influence of the executive by bribing members of Parliament with places and pensions in exchange for their support of programs meant to increase the size and power of government.

Hence, the Country party saw the Court politicians as poor protectors of the people's liberties. See John M. Murrin, The Great Inversion, or Court versus Country: A Comparison of the Revolution Settlement in England (1688–721) and America (1776–816), in J.G.A. Pocock, ed., *Three British Revolutions: 1641, 1688, 1776* (Princeton, N.J.: Princeton University Press, 1980) pp. 368–430; Lance Banning, *The Jeffersonian Persuasion: Evolution of a Party Ideology* (Ithaca, N.Y.: Cornell University Press, 1978) pp. 126–60; Bernard Bailyn, *The Ideological Origins of the American Revolution* (Cambridge, Mass.: Harvard University Press, 1967) pp. 22–54.

4. Thomas Jefferson, *The Anas of Thomas Jefferson*, Franklin B. Sawvel, ed. (New York: Da Capo Press, 1970) p. 27. Though Jefferson's fear of monarchy was real, "not even in his wildest moments did he describe the monarchial-aristocratic faction as anything but small." Dumas Malone, *Jefferson and the Ordeal of Liberty* (Boston, Mass.: Little, Brown and Company, 1962) p. 365.

5. For an example of American objections to hereditary rule, see Thomas Paine, Common Sense, in Lloyd S. Kramer, ed., *Paine and Jefferson on Liberty* (New York: Continuum Publishing Company, 1988) pp. 34–43.

6. Some High Federalists so missed the rule of George III that they freely conveyed information and government confidences to British secret agents. See Julian P. Boyd, *Number 7: Alexander Hamilton's Secret Attempts to Control American Foreign Policy* (Princeton, N.J.: Princeton University Press, 1964) p. 8.

7. Speech of Alexander Hamilton in the Federal Convention (June 18, 1797), in James Madison, *Notes of Debates in the Federal Convention of 1787* (New York: W.W. Norton & Company, 1987) p. 134.

8. Ibid., p. 135.

9. See Peter Shaw, *The Character of John Adams* (Chapel Hill, N.C.: University of North Carolina Press, 1976) p. 231. According to Shaw, "some time after he became vice-president, Adams concluded that the United States would have to adopt a hereditary legislature and a monarch." Ibid.

10. James H. Hutson, "John Adams's Title Campaign," 41 *New England Quarterly* 30, 30 (1968). For a discussion of Adams's belief in a strong executive, see David McCullough, *John Adams* (New York: Simon & Schuster, 2001) pp. 375–9.

11. JM, "Who Are the Best Keepers of the People's Liberties?," December 20, 1792, *PJM* 14:426.

12. Ibid., p. 427.

13. AH, Report on Public Credit, January 9, 1790, *PAH* 6:69.

14. Ibid., p. 68.

15. Ibid., p. 78.

16. Ibid., p. 80.

17. Ibid., p. 70.

18. Some scholars take issue with the suggestion that Hamilton wished for a permanent national debt. In fact, Swanson and Trout argue that under Hamilton's plan the debt could have been paid off in 24 years. See Donald F.

Swanson and Andrew P. Trout, "Alexander Hamilton's Hidden Sinking Fund," 49 *William and Mary Quarterly* 108 (1992).

19. An excise tax is defined as "[a] tax on the manufacture, sale, or use of goods or on the carrying on of an occupation or activity." *Black's Law Dictionary* 390 (6th ed. 1991).

20. *Federalist* No. 51, p. 57 (Alexander Hamilton) (Bantam Books ed., 1982).

21. Thomas P. Slaughter, *The Whiskey Rebellion: Frontier Epilogue to the American Revolution* (New York: Oxford University Press, 1986) p. 199.

22. JM to TJ, November 30, 1794, *PJM* 15:396.

23. *Black's Law Dictionary* 719 (6th ed. 1991).

24. AH, Report on Public Credit, January 9, 1790, *PAH* 6:73.

25. Jefferson, *Anas*, supra note 4, at 31.

26. AH, Report on a National Bank, December 13, 1790, *PAH* 7:305.

27. Ibid., pp. 306–7.

28. Murray N. Rothbard, *The Case Against the Fed* (Auburn, Ala: Ludwig von Mises Institute, 1994) p. 40. For an excellent critique of fractional reserve banking see pp. 33–70.

29. For a discussion of the Framers' experience with paper money see Clarence B. Carson, The Constitution and Paper Money, in *The Foundation of American Constitutional Government* (Irvington-on-Hudson, N.Y.: Foundation for Economic Education, 1996) pp. 166–75.

30. Jefferson, *Anas*, supra note 4, p. 54. For one of the more interesting Republican critiques of Hamilton's bank, see John Taylor, *An Enquiry into the Principles and Tendency of Certain Public Measures* (Philadelphia, Penn.: Thomas Dobson, 1794).

31. See Rothbard, supra note 28, pp. 27–9; Mark Skousen, *Economics of a Pure Gold Standard* (Irvington-on-Hudson, N.Y.: Foundation for Economic Education, 1996) pp. 1–10.

32. AH, Report on Manufactures, December 5, 1791, *PAH* 10:291.

33. Thomas Jefferson, *Notes on the State of Virginia*, William Peden, ed. (Chapel Hill, N.C.: University of North Carolina Press, 1955) pp. 164–5. Though Jefferson remained a firm believer in the agrarian social system, his objections to industrialism grew less virulent in his later years.

34. TJ to JM, December 20, 1787, *PTJ* 12:442.

35. Benjamin Franklin, *The Political Thought of Benjamin Franklin*, Ralph Ketcham, ed. (Indianapolis, Ind.: MacMillan Publishing Co., Inc., 1965) p. 229.

36. For an excellent statement of agrarian principles see Frank Lawrence Owsley, The Irrepressible Conflict, in *I'll Take My Stand* (Baton Rouge, La.: Louisiana State University Press, 1977). For a thorough discussion of Jefferson's agrarian views, see Richard K. Matthews, *The Radical Politics of Thomas Jefferson: A Revisionist View* (Lawrence, Kan.: University of Kansas Press, 1984) pp. 31–52. But see Joyce Appleby, *Capitalism and the New Social Order: The Republican Vision of the 1790s* (New York: New York University Press, 1984) (arguing that Republicans were modernists and actually saw agriculture as a parent of commerce, rather than the enemy of a modern capitalist order); Joyce Appleby, "Republicanism in Old and

New Contexts," 43 *William and Mary Quarterly* 20, 33 (1986). ("Nor can Jeffersonians be distinguished from Federalists on the basis of their enthusiasm for economic development. It was the economy's ordering of society with minimal compulsion that stirred the Jeffersonian imagination, not its capacity to produce wealth.")

37. Lance Gilbert Banning, *The Quarrel with Federalism: A Study in the Origins and Character of Republican Thought* (St. Louis, Mo.: Washington University, 1972) p. 317.

38. Jefferson, *Anas*, supra note 4, p. 60.

39. A.V. Dicey, *Introduction to the Study of the Laws of the Constitution* (Indianapolis, Ind: Liberty Fund, 1982) (1885) p. 3.

40. Speech of Alexander Hamilton in the Federal Convention (June 18, 1797), in Madison, supra note 7, p. 138.

41. For a general history of the French Revolution, see Simon Schama, *Citizens: A Chronicle of the French Revolution* (New York: Alfred A. Knopf, 1989).

42. John Cartwright to the President of the Committee of the Constitution of the Estates General (August 18, 1789), in Alfred Cobban, ed., *The Debate on the French Revolution 1789–800* (London: Adam & Charles Black, 1960) p. 41.

43. TJ to George Washington, December 4, 1788, *PTJ* 14:330.

44. Celebration of the Fourth of July, in Philip S. Foner, ed., *The Democratic-Republican Societies, 1790–800: A Documentary Sourcebooks of Constitutions, Addresses, Resolutions, and Toasts* (Westport, Conn.: Greenwood Press, 1976) p. 338.

45. Civic Festival on ye 1st of May 1794, in Foner, supra note 44, p. 103.

46. Merrill D. Peterson, *Adams and Jefferson: A Revolutionary Dialogue* (Athens, Ga.: The University of Georgia Press, 1976) p. 57.

47. TJ, Opinion on the Treaties with France, April 28, 1793, *PTJ* 25:609.

48. See, e.g., TJ to James Monroe, July 14, 1793, *PTJ* 26:501.

49. See, e.g., JM to TJ, April 2, 1798, *PJM* 17:104.

50. *Federalist* No. 69, p. 350 (Alexander Hamilton) (Bantam Books ed., 1982). But see *Federalist* No. 6 in which Hamilton also observes that the people can drag a nation into war just as easily as a monarch.

51. JM to TJ, June 13, 1793, *PJM* 15:29.

52. Though Jefferson did not believe the president had the authority to issue the proclamation, he nonetheless believed that "a fair neutrality" was required "to keep us out of the calamities of a war." TJ to JM, April 28, 1793, *PTJ* 23:619.

53. 1 James D. Richardson, ed., *A Compilation of the Messages and Papers of the Presidents* (New York: National Bureau of Literature, 1897) p. 148.

54. JM to TJ, May 8, 1793, *PJM* 15:33.

55. TJ, Opinion on the Treaties with France, April 28, 1793, *PTJ* 25:612.

56. U.S. Const. art. II., § 2, cl. 3.

57. Some scholars question whether this was an error or a deliberate attempt by the revolutionaries to go over Washington's head and appeal directly to the representatives of the people. See, e.g., Conor Cruise O'Brien, *The Long Affair: Thomas Jefferson and the French Revolution, 1785–800* (Chicago, Ill.: University of Chicago Press, 1996) pp. 156–7.

58. See TJ to Edmund Charles Genet, June 17, 1793, *PTJ* 26:298.
59. TJ to JM, May 19, 1793, *PTJ* 26:62.
60. TJ to JM, May 7, 1793, *PTJ* 26:444.
61. TJ to Edmund Charles Genet, July 16, 1793, *PTJ* 26:513.
62. Jefferson, *Anas,* supra note 4, p. 141.
63. Ibid., pp. 133–5.
64. JM to TJ, September 2, 1793, *PJM* 15:92.
65. In fact, the Jacobins were so paranoid that they believed Genet was a counterrevolutionary. See Eugene R. Sheridan, "The Recall of Edmond Charles Genet: A Study in Transatlantic Politics and Diplomacy," 18 *Diplomatic History* 463, 482–7 (1994).
66. Harry Ammon, *The Genet Mission* (New York: W.W. Norton & Company, Inc., 1973) p. 146.
67. Samuel Flagg Bemis, *Jay's Treaty: A Study in Commerce and Diplomacy* (New York: Macmillan Company, 1923) p. 6.
68. Annals of Congress, 3rd Congress, 1st sess., pp. 156–7, January 3, 1794.
69. Quoted in Bemis, supra note 67, p. 158.
70. Ibid., p. 207.
71. Boyd, supra note 6, p. 12; see also, Albert H. Bowman, "Jefferson, Hamilton and American Foreign Policy," 71 *Political Science Quarterly* 18, 20 (1956) (describing Hamilton's sharing of information with the English). Viewing Hamilton as somewhat of a British agent, Jefferson wrote that Hamilton was "almost panick struck if we refuse our breach to every kick which Great Britain may chose to give it." TJ to James Monroe, May 5, 1793, *PTJ* 25:66; see also Richard E. Ellis, *The Jeffersonian Crisis: Courts and Politics in the Young Republic* (New York: W.W. Norton & Company, 1971) p. 271 (observing that Hamilton and the High Federalists "believed that nothing should be done to disrupt or jeopardize America's relations with England, even if it meant compromising America's political independence and allowing economic domination by Great Britain"). Upon Hamilton's death in 1804 at the hands of Aaron Burr, the British consul general in New York sent the following eulogy to the Foreign Office: "I consider him even as a loss to His Majesty and our Government, from the prudence of his measures, his conciliatory disposition, his abhorrence of the French Revolution and all republican principles and doctrines, and his great attachment to the British Government." Quoted in W.E. Woodward, *A New American History* (New York: Garden City Publishing Co., Inc., 1938) p. 309.
72. Quoted in James Roger Sharp, *American Politics in the Early Republic: The New Nation in Crisis* (New Haven, Conn.: Yale University Press, 1993) p. 119.
73. Ibid.
74. JM to TJ, February 12, 1798, *PJM* 17:78.
75. Bemis, supra note 67, p. 271.
76. For an excellent account of the election see John Ferling, "1796: The First Real Election," *American History*, March 1996, p. 24.
77. Jefferson, *Anas*, supra note 4, p. 185.
78. Annals of Congress, 5th Congress, 1st sess., p. 56, May 15, 1797.
79. Ibid., p. 57.

80. Ibid., p. 59.

81. Annals of Congress, 5th Congress, 1st sess., p. 72, May 22, 1797.

82. James McHenry quoted in Stanley Elikins & Eric McKitrick, *The Age of Federalism* (New York: Oxford University Press, 1993) p. 556.

83. Annals of Congress, 5th Congress, 1st sess., p. 64, May 19, 1797.

84. Pro-French factions in the United States were not convinced that X, Y, and Z were indeed acting on behalf of the French government or officials. Jefferson in his letter of January 29, 1799, to Edmund Pendleton described the event as "cooked up" with "the swindlers . . . made to appear as the French Government." *WTJ* 9:27.

85. TJ to Peregrine Fitzhugh, February 23, 1798, *WTJ* 8:376.

86. Quoted in Alexander DeConde, *The Quasi War: The Politics and Diplomacy of the Undeclared War with France 1797–801* (New York: Charles Scribner's Sons, 1966) p. 72.

87. Jefferson described the public as "in a state of astonishment." TJ to JM April, 12 1798, *WTJ* 8:404.

88. TJ to JM, April 6, 1798, *WTJ* 8:401.

89. TJ to Peter Carr, April 12, 1798, *WTJ* 8:406.

90. TJ to Edmund Pendleton, January 29, 1799, *WTJ* 9:27.

91. See Bernard A. Weisberger, *America Afire: Jefferson, Adams, and the Revolutionary Election of 1800* (New York: HarperCollins, 2000) p. 222 (noting that "General Hamilton would have liked nothing better than an excuse to use his army to threaten Jefferson's home state").

92. JM to TJ, May 13, 1798, *PJM* 17:130.

93. See generally, Robert Higgs, *Crisis and Leviathan: Critical Episodes in the Growth of American Government* (New York: Oxford University Press, 1987).

2   Legislation and Persecution

1. For a comparison of the British and American laws, see Manning J. Dauer, *The Adams Federalists* (Westport, Conn.: Greenwood Press, 1953) pp. 157–9.

2. For a discussion of the influence of these emigres, see Michael Durey, "Thomas Paine's Apostles: Radical Emigres and the Triumph of Jeffersonian Republicanism," 44 *William and Mary Quarterly* 661 (1987).

3. See 1 Stat. 566 (1798). The Naturalization Act as well as the other three Acts discussed in this chapter are reprinted in full in James Morton Smith, *Freedom's Fetters: The Alien and Sedition Laws and American Civil Liberties* (New York: Cornell University Press, 1956) pp. 435–42.

4. This reaction to the sudden rise in immigration supports the conclusion that the American tradition has not been immigration, but intermittent immigration. See Peter Brimelow, *Alien Nation: Common Sense About America's Immigration Disaster* (New York: Random House, 1995) pp. 30–1.

5. TJ to JM, April 26, 1798, *WTJ* 8:412. Though much of this book focuses on the efforts of Jefferson and Madison, "the survival of Republicanism at the seat of government" was in large part due to the efforts of Gallatin in

the House of Representatives. See Dumas Malone, *Jefferson and the Ordeal of Liberty* (Boston, Mass.: Little, Brown and Company, 1962) p. 359.

6. Annals of Congress, 5th Congress, 2nd sess., p. 1567, May 2, 1798.

7. Annals of Congress, 5th Congress, 2nd sess., p. 1570, May 3, 1798.

8. U.S. Const. art. I, § 2., cl. 1.

9. Annals of Congress, 5th Congress, 2nd sess., p. 1780, May 22, 1798.

10. Annals of Congress, 5th Congress, 2nd sess., p. 1577, May 21, 1798.

11. Annals of Congress, 5th Congress, 2nd sess., p. 1792, May 22, 1798.

12. Annals of Congress, 5th Congress, 2nd sess., p. 1793, May 23, 1798.

13. Annals of Congress, 5th Congress, 2nd sess., p. 1791, May 22, 1798.

14. U.S. Const. art. I, § 1.

15. 1 Stat. 577, 577 (1798).

16. The Senate's bill is not reprinted in the Annals of Congress, but is fully discussed in *Freedom's Fetters*. See Smith, supra note 3, pp. 50–5.

17. Quoted in Richard N. Rosenfeld, ed., *American Aurora: A Democratic-Republican Returns* (New York: St. Martin's Press, 1997) p. 112.

18. TJ to JM, May 31, 1798, *WTJ* 8:428.

19. AH to Timothy Pickering, June 7, 1798, *PAH* 21:495.

20. TJ to JM, June 7, 1798, *WTJ* 8:434.

21. For a general account of Bache's life, see James Tagg, *Benjamin Franklin Bache and the Philadelphia Aurora* (Philadelphia, Penn.: University of Pennsylvania Press, 1991).

22. GW to Benjamin Walker, January 12, 1797, *WGW* 35:364.

23. Abigail Adams to Mary Cranch, April 21, 1798, *NLAA* p. 159.

24. Annals of Congress, 5th Congress, 2nd sess., pp. 1972–3, June 18, 1798.

25. Benjamin Franklin Bache, *Truth Will Out!* (Philadelphia, 1798) p. 1.

26. Ibid., p. 3.

27. Annals of Congress, 5th Congress, 2nd sess., p. 1955, June 16, 1798.

28. U.S. Const. art. I, § 9, cl. 1.

29. Annals of Congress, 5th Congress, 2nd sess., p. 1960, June 16, 1798.

30. Ibid., p. 1962.

31. Annals of Congress, 5th Congress, 2nd sess., p. 1974, June 19, 1798.

32. U.S. Const. art. I, § 8, cl. 1.

33. Annals of Congress, 5th Congress, 2nd sess., p. 1975, June 19, 1798.

34. Annals of Congress, 5th Congress, 2nd sess., p. 1968, June 16, 1798.

35. Annals of Congress, 5th Congress, 2nd sess., p. 1990, June 19, 1798.

36. Annals of Congress, 5th Congress, 2nd sess., p. 2008, June 21, 1798.

37. Ibid., pp. 2010–11.

38. Ibid., p. 2013.

39. Ibid., p. 2014.

40. Annals of Congress, 5th Congress, 2nd sess., p. 1382, June 19, 1798.

41. Annals of Congress, 5th Congress, 2nd sess., p. 2111, July 5, 1798.

42. Annals of Congress, 5th Congress, 2nd sess., p. 2018, June 19, 1798.

43. 1 Stat. 570, 571 (1798).

44. Ibid.

45. Ibid.

46. Ibid.

47. Ibid., p. 572.

48. Ibid.

49. Ibid.

50. Abigail Adams to Mary Cranch, May 26, 1798, *NLAA* p. 179.

51. TJ to JM, April 26, 1798, *WTJ* 8:412.

52. Ibid.

53. Fisher Ames, Laocoon II, *WFA* 1:209.

54. John Thayer, A Discourse Delivered at the Roman Catholic Church in Boston, in Ellis Sandoz, ed., *Political Sermons of the American Founding Era, 1730–1805* (Indianapolis, Ind.: Liberty Press, 1991) p. 1358.

55. JA to the grand jury for the County of Plymouth, Massachusetts, May 28, 1798, *WJA* 9:195.

56. See James P. Martin, "When Repression is Democratic and Constitutional: The Federalist Theory of Representation and the Sedition Act of 1798," 66 *University of Chicago Law Review* 117 (1999).

57. Fisher Ames, Laocoon I, *WFA* 1:194.

58. John Thayer, *Sermons*, supra note 54, p. 1344 (emphasis added).

59. Annals of Congress, 5th Congress, 2nd sess., p. 2093, July 5, 1798.

60. Ibid., p. 2097.

61. Ibid., p. 2102.

62. Ibid., p. 2110.

63. Annals of Congress, 5th Congress, 2nd sess., p. 2139, July 10, 1798.

64. U.S. Const. amend. I.

65. *Federalist* No. 84, p. 437 (Alexander Hamilton) (Bantam Books ed., 1982).

66. Annals of Congress, 5th Congress, 2nd sess., p. 2146, July 10, 1798.

67. U.S. Const. art. I, § 8, cl. 18.

68. 1 Stat. 596, 596 (1798).

69. Ibid.

70. For a general discussion of the development of the law of seditious libel, see Philip Hamburger, "The Development of the Law of Seditious Libel and the Control of the Press," 37 *Stanford Law Review* 661 (1985).

71. Leonard W. Levy, *Emergence of Free Press* (New York: Oxford University Press, 1985) p. 287.

72. Clyde N. Wilson, Foreword to St. George Tucker, *View of the Constitution of the United States* (Indianapolis, Ind.: Liberty Fund, 1999) p. ix.

73. Ibid.

74. Tucker, supra note 72, p. 382.

75. Ibid., p. 393.

76. TJ to JM, May 3, 1798, *WTJ* 8:415.

77. 2 U.S. (2 Dall.) 384 (1798).

78. At this time, justices of the Supreme Court rode circuit. Chase, though a member of the Supreme Court, often sat as a circuit judge.

79. For an excellent discussion of federal common law in the 1790s, see Stewart Jay, "Origins of Federal Common Law: Part One", 133 *University of Pennsylvania Law Review* 1003 (1985).

80. See, e.g., Trial of Gideon Henfield, in Francis Wharton, ed., *State Trials of the United States During the Administrations of Washington and Adams* (Philadelphia, Penn.: Carey and Hart, 1849) p. 49.

81. See *United States v. Hudson*, 11 U.S. (7 Cranch) 32 (1812).
82. Bache, supra note 25, p. 11.
83. Trial of Matthew Lyon, *State Trials*, supra note 80, p. 333.
84. Ibid., p. 334.
85. Ibid.
86. Ibid.
87. Ibid.
88. Ibid., p. 335.
89. Ibid.
90. Ibid., p. 336.
91. Ibid., p. 341.
92. Ibid.
93. Adams quoted in TJ to JM, January 3, 1799, *WTJ* 9:5.
94. Dumas Malone, *The Public Life of Thomas Cooper* (New Haven, Conn: Yale University Press, 1926) p. xiii.
95. Trial of Thomas Cooper, *State Trials*, supra note 80, p. 659. For an additional account of the trial, see Thomas Cooper, *An Account of the Trial of Thomas Cooper* (Philadelphia, Penn.: John Boiren, 1800).
96. Ibid., p. 662.
97. Ibid., p. 663.
98. Ibid., p. 665.
99. Ibid.
100. Ibid., p. 666.
101. Ibid., p. 670.
102. Ibid.
103. Ibid., pp. 670–1.
104. Ibid., p. 671.
105. Ibid., p. 676.
106. Ibid.
107. Ibid., p. 678.
108. For a general account of Callender's life, see Michael Durey, "*With the Hammer of Truth*": *James Thomson Callender and America's Early National Heroes* (Charlottesville, Va.: University of Virginia Press, 1990).
109. Trial of James Thompson Callender, *State Trials*, supra note 80, pp. 688–9.
110. James Haw et al., *Stormy Patriot: The Life of Samuel Chase* (Baltimore, Md.: Maryland Historical Society, 1980) p. 203.
111. Ibid.
112. Ibid., p. 201.
113. Trial of James Thompson Callender, *State Trials*, supra note 80, p. 695.
114. See *Trial of Samuel Chase* (Washington, D.C., 1805) pp. 4–10.
115. Professor Raoul Berger, after examining the evidence against Chase, has described Chase's acquittal as "a failure of justice." See Raoul Berger, "Justice Chase v. Thomas Jefferson: A Response to Stephen Presser," 1990 *Brigham Young University Law Review* 873, 891 (1990).
116. Callender to JM, April 27, 1801, in Chauncey Ford, ed., *Thomas Jefferson and James Thomson Callender* (Boston, Mass.: Press of David Clapp & Son, 1897) p. 36.

117. See John Trenchard and Thomas Gordon, The Right and Capacity of the People to Judge of Government, in David L. Jacobson, ed., *The English Libertarian Heritage* (San Francisco, Cal.: Fox & Wilkes, 1994) pp. 93–101.

3   The Principles of 1798

1. TJ to Joseph Cabell Breckinridge, December 11, 1821, *WTJ* 8:459.
2. See Adriene Koch and Harry Ammon, "The Virginia and Kentucky Resolutions: An Episode in Jefferson's and Madison's Defense of Civil Liberties," 5 *William and Mary Quarterly* 145, 148–50 (1948); Lowell H. Harrison, *John Breckinridge: Jeffersonian Republican* (Louisville, K.Y.: Filson Club, Inc., 1969) p. 76.
3. TJ to Joseph Cabell Breckinridge, December 11, 1821, *WTJ* 8:460.
4. TJ to A.C.V.C. Destutt de Tracy, January 26, 1811, *WTJ* 11:187. See also *Federalist* No. 26, pp. 128–9 (Alexander Hamilton) (Bantam Books, ed., 1982) (observing that the state legislatures "will always be not only vigilant but suspicious and jealous guardians of the rights of the citizens, against incroachments from the Federal government, will constantly have their attention awake to the conduct of the national rulers and will be ready enough, if any thing improper appears, to sound the alarm to the people and not only to be the VOICE but if necessary the ARM of their discontent").
5. *Federalist* No. 51, p. 264 (James Madison) (Bantam Books, ed., 1982). Hamilton made an almost identical representation to the New York ratifying convention: "This balance between the national and state governments ought to be dwelt on with peculiar attention, as it is of the utmost importance. It forms a double security to the people. If one encroaches on their rights, they will find a powerful protection in the other. Indeed, they will both be prevented from overpassing their constitutional limits, by a certain rivalship, which will ever subsist between them." 2 *Elliot's Debates* pp. 257–8.
6. 3 *Elliot's Debates* p. 18. Though an opponent of ratification, Patrick Henry also recognized the role of the state governments. "If there be a real check intended to be left on Congress," warned Henry, "it must be left in the state governments." 3 *Elliot's Debates* p. 174. See also Roger Sherman, Observations on the New Federal Constitution, in Colleen A. Sheehan and Gary L. McDowell, eds., *Friends of the Constitution: Writings of the "Other" Federalists 1787–8* (Indianapolis, Ind.: Liberty Fund, 1998) p. 269 (observing that the state legislatures would "be a powerful and effective check to [the national government] interfering with [the states'] jurisdiction").
7. *Federalist* No. 28, p. 137 (Alexander Hamilton) (Bantam Books, ed., 1982). Madison expressed the same idea in Federalist No. 46. According to Madison, should the federal government ever exceed its enumerated powers, "[e]very [state] Government would espouse the common cause.

A correspondence would be opened. Plans of resistance would be concerted. One spirit would animate and conduct the whole." *Federalist* No. 46, p. 241 (James Madison) (Bantam Books, ed., 1982). See also Philodemos, Essay, in Sheehan and McDowell, supra note 6, p. 35 (expressing a certainty "of a concert of the state legislatures and executives against encroachments of the federal legislature or executive").

8. TJ, To the Speaker and House of Delegates of the Commonwealth of Virginia . . . , in Saul K. Padover, ed., *The Complete Jefferson* (New York: Duell, Sloan & Pierce, Inc., 1943) pp. 313–18.

9. TJ to James Monroe, September 7, 1797, *WTJ* 8:340.

10. "Resolutions Adopted in Prince Edward County, Virginia," in the *Kentucky Gazette*, November 7, 1798. See also Resolutions of Clark County, Kentucky, in Ethelbert Dudley Warfield, *The Kentucky Resolutions of 1798: An Historical Study* (New York: G.P. Putnam's Sons, 1894) pp. 41–2. The resolves of these two counties are typical of those passed on the local level in Kentucky and Virginia.

11. See James Morton Smith, "The Grass Roots Origins of the Kentucky Resolutions," 27 *William and Mary Quarterly* 221, 229 (1970).

12. TJ, Draft of the Kentucky Resolutions of 1798, *The Republic of Letters* 2:1080.

13. The Virginia Resolutions of 1798, *VCCG* p. 152.

14. A compact is an agreement between persons or states, "which creates obligations and rights capable of being enforced, and contemplated as such between the parties, in their distinct and independent characters." *Black's Law Dictionary* 192–3 (6th ed. 1991). As for the obligations and rights created, Article V provides the best examples. For instance, each state—acting in its highest sovereign capacity—agreed to give full faith and credit to public acts and proceedings of other states, and promised to return fugitives and runaway slaves to the proper authorities. By implication, the states agreed not to exercise powers delegated to the national government, and retained the right to exercise the reserved powers.

15. Declaration and Resolves of the First Continental Congress, in David L. Brooks, ed., *From Magna Carta to the Constitution: Documents in the Struggle for Liberty* (San Francisco, Cal.: Fox &Wilkes, 1993) p. 53.

16. The Mayflower Compact, in Brooks, supra note 15, p. 17. The Mayflower Compact was not known as such until 1793—it was referred to by the inhabitants of the Plymouth colony as the Plymouth Combination. See Donald S. Lutz, Introductory Essay, in Donald S. Lutz, ed., *Colonial Origins of the American Constitution: A Documentary History* (Indianapolis, Ind.: Liberty Fund, 1998) p. xxvi. For a discussion of the role of the compact theory in efforts to protect minority rights, see David L. Smiley, "Revolutionary Origins of the South's Constitutional Defenses," 44 *North Carolina Historical Review* 256, 259–66 (1967).

17. Dumas Malone, *Jefferson and the Ordeal of Liberty* (Boston, Mass.: Little, Brown and Company, 1962) p. 402; see also Forrest McDonald, *States' Rights and the Union: Imperium in Imperio 1776–876* (Lawrence, Kan.: University Press of Kansas, 2000) pp. 7–25; Diane Tipton, *Nullification*

and Interposition in American Political Thought (N.M.: The University of New Mexico, 1969) p. 10 (stating that the compact theory "was not seriously challenged even by extreme nationalists until the 1830's").

18. Samuel Tenny, Alfredus Essay I, in Sheehan and McDowell, supra note 6, p. 252.

19. 2 *Elliot's Debates* p. 497.

20. Ibid., p. 498.

21. James Madison, *Notes of the Debates in the Federal Convention of 1787* (New York: W.W. Norton & Company, 1987) p. 385.

22. Gouverneur Morris did move that the Constitution be submitted "to one general Convention, chosen & authorized by the people," but his motion was never seconded. Madison, supra note 21, p. 353.

23. "Mr. Madison's Report" to the Virginia Assembly, in 4 *Elliot's Debates* p. 547.

24. Long before the Sedition Act crisis, Madison observed "that this assent and ratification is to be given by the people, not as individuals composing one entire nation; but as composing the distinct and independent States to which they respectively belong. It is to be the assent and ratification of the several states, derived from the supreme authority in each State, the authority of the people themselves. The act therefore establishing the Constitution, will not be a *national* but a *federal* act." *Federalist* No. 39, p. 192 (James Madison) (Bantam Books, ed., 1982). Madison made similar assertions in the Virginia ratifying convention: "Who are to parties to it? The people—but not the people as composing one great national body; but the people as composing thirteen sovereignties." 3 *Elliot's Debates* p. 94.

25. Gordon S. Wood, *The Creation of the American Republic 1776–1787* (New York: W.W. Norton & Company, 1969) p. 345; see also McDonald, supra note 17, p. 4 (observing that "what broke apart the empire was an inability to agree on the locus and nature of sovereignty"); Samuel H. Beer, *To Make a Nation: The Rediscovery of American Federalism* (Cambridge, Mass.: The Belknap Press of Harvard University Press, 1993) pp. 146–53 (same). Madison in his Report to the Virginia Assembly eloquently expressed the impetus for the Revolution. "The fundamental principle of the revolution was, that the colonies were coordinate members with each other, and with Great Britain, of an empire united by a common executive sovereign, but not united by any common legislative sovereign. The legislative power was maintained to be as complete in each American Parliament, as in the British Parliament. . . . A denial of these principles by Great Britain, and the assertion of them by America, produced the revolution." "Mr. Madison's Report" to the Virginia Assembly, in 4 *Elliot's Debates* p. 562.

26. For a comparison of the British and American views of sovereignty, see Lord Irvine of Lairg, "Sovereignty in Comparative Perspective: Constitutionalism in Britain and America," 76 *New York University Law Review* 1 (2001).

27. See Lance Banning, *The Sacred Fire of Liberty: James Madison & the Founding of the Federal Republic* (Ithaca, N.Y.: Cornell University Press, 1995) p. 443 n. 30. This difference between ultimate sovereignty and legislative sovereignty is ably expressed in the instruction given by the

people of Mecklenburg, North Carolina, to their delegates to the provincial congress:

1st. Political power is of two kinds, one principal and superior, and the other derived and inferior.

2nd. The principal supreme power is possessed by the people at large, the derived and inferior power by the servants which they employ.

3rd. Whatever persons are delegated, chosen, employed and intrusted by the people are their servants and can possess only derived inferior power.

4th. Whatever is constituted and ordained by the principal supreme power can not be altered, suspended or abrogated by an other power, but the same power that ordained may alter, suspend and abrogate its own ordinances.

5th. The rules whereby the inferior power is to be exercised are to be constituted by the principal supreme power, and can be altered, suspended and abrogated by the same and no other.

Instructions to the Delegates From Mecklenburg, North Carolina, to the Provincial Congress at Halifax, in 1 Philip B. Kurland and Ralph Lerner, eds., *The Founder's Constitution* (Indianapolis, Ind.: Liberty Fund, 1987) p. 56. Of course, some scholars contend that the states were never sovereign and reject the distinction between ultimate and governmental sovereignty. See, e.g., Garry Wills, *A Necessary Evil: A History of American Distrust of Government* (New York: Simon & Schuster, 1999) pp. 59–70.

28. *Federalist* No. 46, p. 237 (James Madison) (Bantam Books, ed., 1982).

29. Even as the union became more consolidated, this division of sovereignty was readily apparent to a perspicacious visitor. Alexis de Tocqueville, touring the United States in the 1830s, observed of the Constitution "that the principal aim [of the Framers] was to divide the sovereign authority into two parts. In the one they placed the control of all general interests of the Union, in the other the control of the special interests of its component states." 1 Alexis de Tocqueville, *Democracy in America* (New York: Vintage Classics, 1990) p. 146.

30. For a discussion of how Madison and the other Framers came to believe legislative sovereignty could be divided, see Banning, supra note 27, pp. 138–64.

31. TJ, Draft of the Kentucky Resolutions of 1798, *The Republic of Letters* 2:1080.

32. The Virginia Resolutions of 1798, *VCCG* p. 152.

33. 3 *Elliot's Debates* p. 46. Serving in Paris at the time, Jefferson was initially shocked that the Philadelphia Convention would propose a new constitution. Like most Americans, he expected amendments to the Articles. Writing to John Adams, Jefferson observed that "three or four new articles . . . added to the good, old, and venerable fabrick" of the Articles of Confederation would have sufficed. TJ to John Adams, November 13, 1787, *PTJ* 12:351. Jefferson later warmed to the idea of the Constitution but pressed for a bill of rights. See TJ to JM, February 6, 1788, *PTJ* 12:568.

34. 3 *Elliot's Debates* p. 45.

35. 2 *Elliot's Debates* p. 250.

36. Letter from Elbridge Gerry Containing the Reasons for Not Signing the Federal Constitution, in 1 *Elliot's Debates* p. 493.

37. See, e.g., Brutus No. 1, in Ralph Ketcham, ed., *The Anti-Federalist Papers and the Constitutional Convention Debates* (New York: Penguin Books USA Inc., 1986) pp. 270–80.

38. 3 *Elliot's Debates* p. 95.

39. 3 *Elliot's Debates* p. 107. Hamilton expressed the same idea in *Federalist* No. 32. "[T]he State Governments would clearly retain all the rights of sovereignty which they before had and which were not by [the Constitution] *exclusively* delegated to the United States." *Federalist* No. 32, p. 152 (Alexander Hamilton) (Bantam Books, ed., 1982). Returning from the Philadelphia Convention, Roger Sherman and Luther Martin made the same representation to the governor of Connecticut. The powers of Congress "extend only to matters respecting the common interests of the Union, and are specially defined, so that the particular states retain their sovereignty in all other matters." Letter from Roger Sherman and Luther Martin to the Governor of Connecticut, in 1 *Elliot's Debates* p. 492.

40. 1 *Elliot's Debates* p. 322.

41. Ibid.

42. South Carolina declared "that no section or paragraph of the said Constitution warrants a construction that the states do not retain every power not expressly relinquished by them, and vested in the general government of the Union." 1 *Elliot's Debates* p. 325. New Hampshire requested an amendment to specifically declare "that all powers not expressly and particularly delegated by the aforesaid Constitution are reserved to the several states." 1 *Elliot's Debates* p. 326. New York averred "that those clauses in the said Constitution, which declare that Congress shall not have or exercise certain powers, do not imply that Congress is entitled to any powers not given by the said Constitution." 1 *Elliot's Debates* p. 327. Rhode Island observed that "every other power, jurisdiction, and right, which is not by the said Constitution clearly delegated to the Congress of the United States, or to the departments of government thereof, remain to the people of the several states, or their respective state governments." 1 *Elliot's Debates* p. 334. In the Virginia convention, Patrick Henry specifically complained that "[i]t was expressly declared in our Confederation that every right was retained by the states, respectively, which was not given up to the government of the United States. But there is no such thing here. You, therefore, by natural and unavoidable implication, give up your rights to the general government." 3 *Elliot's Debates* p. 446. The provision in the Articles of Confederation Henry was referring to was Article II: "Each state retains its sovereignty, freedom and independence, and every power, jurisdiction and right which is not by this Confederation expressly delegated to the United States in Congress assembled."

43. TJ to JM, December 20, 1787, *PTJ* 12:440.

44. JM to TJ, October 17, 1788, *PJM* 11:297. See Jack N. Rakove, *Original Meanings: Politics and Ideas in the Making of the Constitution*

(New York: Vintage Books, 1997) pp. 330–8 (discussing Madison's crafting of the Bill of Rights).

45. 1 *Elliot's Debates* p. 338.

46. U.S. Const. amend. X.

47. TJ, Opinion on the Constitutionality of the Bill for Establishing a National Bank, February 15, 1791, *PTJ* 19:276.

48. Herbert J. Storing, Introduction, in Sheehan and McDowell, supra note 6, p. xxiii.

49. TJ, Draft of the Kentucky Resolutions of 1798, *The Republic of Letters* 2:1082.

50. The Virginia Resolutions of 1798, *VCCG* p. 153.

51. "All charges of war, and all other expenses that shall be incurred for the common defence or general welfare, and allowed by the United States in Congress assembled, shall be defrayed out of a common treasury, which shall be supplied by the several states. . . . " Articles of Confederation art. VIII.

52. "Mr. Madison's Report" to the Virginia Assembly, in 4 *Elliot's Debates* p. 551.

53. In *Federalist* No. 41, Madison confronted Anti-Federalist arguments concerning the General Welfare Clause. "For what purpose could the enumeration of particular powers be inserted, if these and all others were meant to be included in the preceding general power? Nothing is more natural or common than first to use a general phrase, and then to explain and qualify it by a recital of particulars." *Federalist* No. 41, p. 210 (James Madison) (Bantam Books, ed., 1982). Jefferson held an identical view. In his opinion on the constitutionality of the national bank, Jefferson observed that the General Welfare Clause "would reduce the whole instrument to a single phrase, that of instituting a Congress with power to do whatever would be for the good of the United States; and, as they would be the sole judge of good and evil, it would be also a power to do whatever evil they please." TJ, Opinion on the Constitutionality of the Bill for Establishing a National Bank, February 15, 1791, *PTJ* 19:277.

54. Such a generous view of the national government's powers was the hallmark of Hamilton's constitutional philosophy. As Clinton Rossiter has observed: "T[he] rule of Hamiltonian constitutionalism can be reduced, not merely to one phrase, but to one word: *liberality*. To him the Constitution was more properly viewed as a grant of powers than as a catalogue of limitations. He searched in it almost always for encouragement rather than dissuasion, for ways to get things done rather than ways to keep things from being done." Clinton Rossiter, *Alexander Hamilton and the Constitution* (New York: Harcourt, Brace & World, Inc., 1964) p. 189.

55. AH, Opinion on the Constitutionality of an Act to Establish a Bank, February 23, 1791, *PAH* 8:107.

56. TJ, Opinion on the Constitutionality of the Bill for Establishing a National Bank, February 15, 1791, *PTJ* 19:278.

57. Ibid. The Virginia jurist Spencer Roane will a bit more forceful on the subject. "That man must be a deplorable idiot who does not see that there is no earthly difference between an unlimited grant of power, and a grant

limited in its terms, but accompanied with unlimited means of carrying it into execution." Spencer Roane, Hampden No. 1, in Gerald Gunther, ed., *John Marshall's Defense of* McCulloch v. Maryland (Stanford, Cal.: Stanford University Press, 1969) p. 110.

58. Annals of Congress, 1st Congress, 3rd sess., p. 1951, February 3, 1791. This feeling of betrayal is further evident in Madison's Report when he noted that "[i]t is painful to remark how much the arguments now employed in behalf of the Sedition Act, are at variance with the reasoning which then justified the Constitution, and invited its ratification." "Mr. Madison's Report" to the Virginia Assembly, in 4 *Elliot's Debates* p. 572.

59. George Washington, Resolution of Transmittal, in *VCCG* p. 66.

60. Annals of Congress, 1st Congress, 3rd sess., p. 1946, February 3, 1791; see also H. Jefferson Powell, "The Original Understanding of Original Intent," 98 *Harvard Law Review* 885, 887–8 (1985) (observing that "the original intent relevant to the constitutional discourse was not that of the Philadelphia framers, but rather that of the parties to the constitutional compact"). See Rakove, supra note 44, 339–65 (discussing Madison's originalism).

61. TJ to Elbridge Gerry, January 26, 1799, *WTJ* 9:17. John Taylor expressed similar sentiments in the Virginia House of Delegates during the debate on the Virginia Resolutions, arguing that the state ratification debates "ought to be looked upon as a contemporaneous exposition of the . . . constitution." *Debates in the House of Delegates of Virginia, on Certain Resolutions Before the House* (Richmond, Va.: Thomas Nicolson, 1798) p. 8. For the view that original intent should play no part in constitutional interpretation, see Laurence H. Tribe & Michael C. Dorf, *On Reading the Constitution* (Cambridge, Mass.: Harvard University Press, 1991) pp. 8–13.

62. "That useful alterations will be suggested by experience, could not but be foreseen." *Federalist* No. 43, p. 223 (James Madison) (Bantam Books, ed., 1982).

63. Annals of Congress, 1st Congress, 3rd sess., p. 1950, February 3, 1791.

64. "If there be any capital defects in this Constitution, it is most probable that experience alone will discover them. Provision is made for an alteration if on trial it be found necessary." Oliver Ellsworth, "To the Landholders and Farmers No. 5," in Sheehan and McDowell, supra note 6, p. 303. "But after all, if the constitution should, in its future operation, be found defective or inconvenient, two-thirds of both houses of Congress or the application of two-thirds of the legislatures, may open the door for amendments. Such improvements may then be made, as experience shall dictate." Noah Webster, "An Examination into the Leading Principles of the Federal Constitution," in Sheehan and McDowell, supra note 6, p. 405. "Let us give it a trial; and when experience has taught its mistakes, the people, whom it preserves absolutely all powerful, can reform and amend them." Tench Coxe, "An Examination of the Constitution of the United States," in Sheehan and McDowell, supra note 6, p. 476.

65. This definition was given by Edmund Pendleton. See 3 *Elliot's Debates* p. 40. Similarly, Melancton Smith described consolidation as "collect[ing] all powers ultimately, in the United States into one entire government."

Melancton Smith, "Letters from the Federal Farmer No. 1," in Ketcham, supra note 37, p. 264. In the preface to his *Notes*, Madison highlighted that the Philadelphia Convention was "anxious for a system that would avoid the inefficacy of a mere confederacy without passing into the opposite extreme of a consolidated government." Madison, *Notes*, supra note 21, p. 15.

66. In *Federalist* No. 45, Madison made clear that the powers of the national government would "be exercised principally on external objects, as war, peace, negociation, and foreign commerce. . . . The powers reserved to the several States will extend to all the objects, which, in the ordinary course of affairs, concern the lives, liberties and properties of the people; and the internal order, improvement, and prosperity of the State." *Federalist* No. 45, p. 236 (James Madison) (Bantam Books, ed., 1982).

67. Banning, supra note 27, p. 402.

68. TJ, Draft of the Kentucky Resolutions of 1798, *The Republic of Letters* 2:1081.

69. Ibid.

70. David N. Mayer, *The Constitutional Thought of Thomas Jefferson* (Charlottesville, V.A.: University of Virginia Press, 1994) p. 203.

71. TJ, Draft of the Kentucky Resolutions of 1798, *The Republic of Letters* 2:1082.

72. The Virginia Resolutions of 1798, *VCCG* p. 153.

73. TJ, Draft of the Kentucky Resolutions of 1798, *The Republic of Letters* 2:1080.

74. *Federalist* No. 33, p. 158 (Alexander Hamilton) (Bantam Books, ed., 1982).

75. TJ, Draft of the Kentucky Resolutions of 1798, *The Republic of Letters* 2:1082–4.

76. TJ to JM, October 1, 1792, *PTJ* 24:432–3.

77. JM to TJ, October 9, 1792, *PJM* 14:377.

78. The Virginia Resolutions of 1798, *VCCG* pp. 152–3.

79. Ibid., p. 154.

80. Harrison, supra note 2, p. 77.

81. Governor Garrard's message is reprinted in the *Kentucky Gazette*, November 14, 1798.

82. Warfield, supra note 10, p. 94.

83. Ibid.

84. Mayer, supra note 70, p. 207.

85. TJ to Wilson Cary Nicholas, November 29, 1798, *WTJ* 8:483.

86. *Debates in the House of Delegates of Virginia*, supra note 61, pp. 78–9.

87. See e.g., ibid., p. 165.

88. Ibid., p. 123.

89. H. Jefferson Powell, "The Principles of '98: An Essay in Historical Retrieval," 80 *Virginia Law Review* 689, 736 (1994); see also Wayne D. Moore, "Reconceiving Interpretive Autonomy: Insights from the Kentucky and Virginia Resolutions," 11 *Constitutional Commentary* 315, 323 (1994).

90. TJ to JM, November 17, 1798, *WTJ* 8:457.

91. JM to TJ, December 29, 1798, *PJM* 17:191.

92. Ibid., pp. 191–2.

93. In concluding his lengthy Report on the Virginia Resolutions, Madison stated that Virginia was renewing its "PROTEST" against the Alien and Sedition Acts. Madison's use of capital letters indicates his efforts to distinguish Virginia's actions from nullification. See "Mr. Madison's Report" to the Virginia Assembly, in 4 *Elliot's Debates* p. 580.

94. Debates in the House of Delegates of Virginia, supra note 61, p. 28.

95. Ibid., p. 169. Of course, others of Taylor's remarks support a broader reading of the Virginia Resolutions. For example, he declared that if a legislature could not declare a federal law unconstitutional, then "the check mediated against Congress in the existence of the state governments, was demolished." Ibid., p. 122. One could interpret this statement as an avowal of nullification, or as an assertion that state government's have the right to express opinions on the validity of national laws. Opponents of the Virginia Resolutions stressed the former interpretation and accused Taylor and his supporters of "erecting [the legislature] into a court of justice . . . as the resolutions declare those laws null and void, for where is the department of government except the judiciary that can exercise this power." Ibid., p. 67.

96. See, e.g., TJ to William Johnson, June 12, 1823, *WTJ* 12:259.

97. John Taylor to TJ, June 25, 1798, in 2 *John P. Branch Historical Papers* 253, 276 (1908). Evidence of influence is apparent inasmuch as Jefferson made lengthy notes on the letter. See Robert E. Shalhope, *John Taylor of Caroline: Pastoral Republican* (Columbia, S.C.: University of South Carolina Press, 1980) p. 248 n. 116.

98. John Taylor, *An Enquiry into the Principles and Tendency of Certain Public Measures* (Philadelphia, Penn.: Thomas Dobson, 1794) p. 55.

99. Taylor's role in providing the theoretical underpinnings of the Kentucky Resolutions should not be given short shrift. In fact, Garry Wills has described him as the true "father of nullification." Wills, supra note 27, p. 127.

100. John Taylor, *Construction Construed and Constitutions Vindicated* (New York: De Capo Press, 1970) p. 131. As David Mayer has observed, Jefferson's opinion of judicial review "changed most dramatically over time." Mayer, supra note 70, p. 257. In June 1787, Jefferson responded to Madison's ill-conceived proposal for vesting the national government with negative over all state laws by suggesting "an appeal from the state judicatures to a federal court in all cases" involving a national question. TJ to JM, June 20, 1787, *PTJ* 11:481. Though Jefferson recognized that a supreme court might encroach upon the jurisdiction of the state courts, he believed that Congress would "watch and restrain" the federal court. Ibid. The Philadelphia convention apparently opted for a federal court to decide controversies concerning the scope of state and national powers, see *Federalist* No. 39, p. 194 (James Madison) (Bantam Books, ed., 1982), but over time Jefferson became one of the federal judiciary's biggest critics. Jefferson believed a written Constitution provided certainty and security, see TJ to Wilson Cary Nicholas, September 7, 1803, *VCCG* p. 249, and saw liberal interpretation by the federal judiciary turning the document

into "a mere thing of wax ... which they may twist and shape into any form they please." TJ to Spencer Roane, September 6, 1819, *WTJ* 12:237. Toward the end of his life, Jefferson believed the people gathered in convention, rather than the Supreme Court, to be the final arbiter of the Constitution. See TJ to William Johnson, June 12, 1823, *WTJ* 12:259.

101. For both the formal and informal responses from the state legislatures see 4 *Elliot's Debates* pp. 532–9; Frank M. Anderson, "Contemporary Opinion of the Virginia and Kentucky Resolutions II," 5 *American Historical Review* 225, 244–52 (1900).

102. 4 *Elliot's Debates* p. 539.

103. Ibid., p. 533.

104. Ibid., p. 534. See also St. George Tucker, Of the Several Forms of Government, in Clyde N. Wilson, ed., *View of the Constitution of the United States* (Indianapolis, Ind.: 1999) p. 32 (observing that if government "becomes corrupt, the people will probably find the necessity of a resumption of the sovereignty, in order to correct the abuses, and vices of the government").

105. 4 *Elliot's Debates* p. 537.

106. See Annals of Congress, 5th Congress, 3rd sess., pp. 2992–3, February 25, 1799. According to the Annals, thousands of people signed petitions inveighing against the Alien and Sedition Acts. Gallatin, e.g., estimated that over 18,000 Pennsylvanians had signed petitions praying for repeal of the Acts. See Annals of Congress, 5th Congress, 3rd sess., p. 2993, February 25, 1799.

107. AH to Jonathan Dayton, October 1799, *PAH* 23:600.

108. TJ to JM, August 23, 1799, *Republic of Letters* 2:1119.

109. 1 *Elliot's Debates* p. 327. The other two states were New York and Rhode Island. Similar principles were expressed in the state ratifying conventions. For example, Edmund Pendleton declared that if the national government became oppressive "we will assemble in Convention; wholly recall our delegated powers, or reform them so as to prevent such abuse; and punish those servants who have perverted powers, designed for our happiness, to their own emolument." 3 *Elliot's Debates* p. 37. According to Dumas Malone, in the late 1790s "there was nothing particularly startling in the idea that the Union was dissolable, and threats against it were common." Malone, *Ordeal of Liberty*, supra note 17, p. 421.

110. Resolutions Adopted in Prince Edward County, Virginia, in the *Kentucky Gazette*, November 7, 1798.

111. Though the American Revolution is not often described in terms of secession, it was a secession. Secession is generally defined as "[t]he act of withdrawing from membership in a group." *Blacks Law Dictionary* 940 (6th ed. 1991). At its essence, "the American Revolution was a successful attempt by a part of the British Empire ... to secede from that empire." Allen Buchanan, *Secession: The Morality of Political Divorce from Fort Sumter to Lithuania and Quebec* (Boulder, Col.: Westview Press, 1991) p. 69.

112. TJ to John Taylor, June 1, 1798, *WTJ* 8:431–2.

113. TJ to JM, May 3, 1798, *WTJ* 8:415.
114. TJ to Wilson Cary Nicholas, September 5, 1799, *WTJ* 9:80. The "repeated and enormous violations" language bears a resemblance to Madison's "deliberate, palpable, and dangerous" language used in the Virginia Resolutions.
115. Ibid.
116. The Kentucky Resolutions of 1799, *VCCG* pp. 155–6. The emphasis of the term "protest" is consistent with Governor Garrard's original instructions to the Kentucky legislature in November 1798. Moreover, in that address Garrard scoffed at "reports circulated in the Eastern parts of the union" indicating that Kentucky was "in a state of insurrection." *Kentucky Gazette*, November 14, 1798. The governor apparently contemplated nothing but a firm expression of odium toward the Alien and Sedition Acts.
117. "Mr. Madison's Report" to the Virginia Assembly, in 4 *Elliot's Debates* p. 549.
118. George Nicholas, a prominent Kentucky Republican, made similar statements about the Kentucky Resolutions of 1798. "[A]lthough we consider [the Alien and Sedition Acts] as dead letters, and therefore we might legally use force in opposition to any attempts to execute them; yet we contemplate no means of opposition, even to these unconstitutional acts, but appeal to the *real laws* of our country." George Nicholas, *Letter from George Nicholas of Kentucky to His Friend in Virginia* (Lexington, K.Y.: John Bradford, 1798) pp. 33–4.
119. TJ to James Monroe, February 6, 1800, *WTJ* 9:113.
120. AH to Timothy Pickering, May 14, 1800, *PAH* 24:487.
121. AH to John Jay, May 7, 1800, *PAH* 24:465.
122. John Mitchell Mason, The Voice of Warning to Christians on the Ensuing Election of a President, in Ellis Sandoz, ed., *Political Sermons of the American Founding Era 1730–805* (Indianapolis, Ind.: Liberty Press, 1991) p. 1425.
123. TJ to JM, December 19, 1800, *The Republic of Letters* 2:1154.
124. TJ to Spencer Roane, September 6, 1819, *WTJ* 12:136. Some Republicans, however, thought the Revolution of 1800 to be but a change in men, and thus insufficient to remedy the flaws in the Constitution exposed by Federalist rule. See generally Norman K. Risjord, *The Old Republicans: Southern Conservatism in the Age of Jefferson* (New York: Columbia University Press, 1965). For an example of the amendments suggested, see Wilson Cary Nicholas to John Taylor, November 19, 1807, in David N. Mayer, ed., "Of Principles and Men: The Correspondence of John Taylor of Caroline with Wilson Cary Nicholas, 1806–1808," 96 *Virginia Magazine of History and Biography* 370, 370–1 (1988).
125. TJ, A Summary View of the Rights of British America, in Lloyd S. Kramer, ed., *Paine and Jefferson on Liberty* (New York: The Continuum Publishing Company, 1988) pp. 9 and 11.
126. Ibid., p. 22.
127. TJ to Thomas Lomax, March 12, 1799, *WTJ* 9:63.

4   Influence of the Resolutions

1. For a comprehensive discussion of clashes between the national and state governments, see Forrest McDonald's *States' Rights and the Union: Imperium in Imperio 1776–1876* (Lawrence, Kan.: University Press of Kansas, 2000); James Jackson Kilpatrick, *The Sovereign States: Notes of a Citizen of Virginia* (Chicago, Ill.: Henry Regnery Company, 1957).
2. *United States v. Peters*, 9 U.S. (5 Cranch) 115, 132 (1809).
3. Ibid.
4. Ibid., p. 136. For a discussion of the Olmstead affair in the context of the *Peters* decision, see William O. Douglas, "Interposition and the Peters Case, 1778–1809," 9 *Stanford Law Review* 3 (1956).
5. Resolution of the Legislature of Pennsylvania, April 3, 1809, in Herman V. Ames, ed., *State Documents on Federal Relations: The States and the United States* (New York: Da Capo Press, 1970) pp. 46–8.
6. Quoted in 2 George Lee Haskins and Herbert A. Johnson, *History of the Supreme Court of the United States* (New York: McMillan Publishing Co., Inc., 1981) p. 330.
7. TJ to JM, December 17, 1807, *The Republic of Letters* 3:1513.
8. TJ, Embargo Message, in 1 James D. Richardson, ed., *A Compilation of the Messages and Papers of the Presidents* (New York: National Bureau of Literature, 1897) p. 421. For a discussion of the day to day enforcement of the embargo, see Richard Mannix, "Gallatin, Jefferson, and the Embargo of 1808," 3 *Diplomatic History* 151 (1979). Jefferson's support of the embargo and its draconian enforcement apparatus was the greatest failing of his second term. For a critique of Jefferson's actions during the embargo, see Leonard Levy, *Jefferson and Civil Liberties: The Darker Side* (Cambridge, Mass.: Harvard University Press, 1963) pp. 93–141.
9. 2 Stat. 451, 451–2 (1807).
10. 2 Stat. 499, 501 (1808).
11. Ibid.
12. U.S. Const. amend. IV.
13. For a discussion of American defiance and protest during the War of 1812, see Samuel Eliot Morison, Dissent in the War of 1812, in *Dissent in Three American Wars* (Cambridge, Mass.: Harvard University Press, 1970).
14. TJ, Lake Champlain Proclamation, in 1 Richardson, supra note 8, p. 439.
15. *United States v. The William* 28 F. Cas. 614 (D. Mass. 1808). In this case, the national government brought an action for the forfeiture of a vessel that had violated the embargo. Counsel for the defendants argued, inter alia, that Congress's power to regulate interstate and foreign commerce "cannot be understood to give a power to annihilate." Ibid., p. 621. Judge Davis rejected this argument, holding that "the power to regulate commerce is not to be confined to the adoption of measures, exclusively beneficial to commerce itself, or tending to its advancement." Ibid. Appealing to the situation "in all modern sovereignties" Judge Davis described the regulation of commerce as "an instrument for other purposes of general policy and interest." Ibid. Not content to rest his holding on the Commerce Clause

alone, Judge Davis next turned to the nebulous war power. Finding the nation's difficulties with Great Britain and France to be a time of "great impending peril," Judge Davis observed that Congress's power to regulate commerce "must take a still more expanded range." Ibid., p. 622. The end result of Judge Davis's broad reading of the Constitution was the forfeiture of the *William* and continuance of the embargo.

16. Extracts from the Answer of the [Massachusetts] House, in Ames, supra note 5, pp. 30–1.
17. [Massachusetts'] Resolutions of the Enforcement Act, February 15, 1809, in Ames, supra note 5, p. 35.
18. Resolutions of Delaware, in Ames, supra note 5, p. 37.
19. Speech of Governor Trumbull at the Opening of the Special Session of the [Connecticut] Legislature, February 23, 1809, in Ames, supra note 5, p. 40.
20. Resolutions of the [Connecticut] General Assembly, in Ames, supra note 5, p. 41.
21. Report and Resolutions of Rhode Island on the Embargo, in Ames, supra note 5, p. 44.
22. Timothy Pickering to Edward Pennington, July 12, 1812, in Henry Adams, ed., *Documents Relating to New England Federalism 1800–1815* (Boston, Mass.: Little, Brown, and Company, 1905) p. 388.
23. U.S. Const. art. I, § 8, cl. 15.
24. Extract from the Opinion of the Judges of Massachusetts on the Militia Question, 1812, in Ames, supra note 5, p. 58.
25. Ibid.
26. Report and Resolutions of Connecticut on the Militia Question, in Ames, supra note 5, p. 61.
27. Ibid.
28. Ibid.
29. Quoted in Edward Payson Powell, *Nullification and Secession in the United States: A History of the Six Attempts during the First Century of the Republic* (New York: Knickerbocker Press, 1897) p. 213.
30. Quoted in Robert V. Remini, *Daniel Webster and His Time* (New York: W.W. Norton & Company, 1997) pp. 128–9.
31. Connecticut on the Conscription Bill, in Ames, supra note 5, p. 76.
32. See ibid.
33. Extracts from the Report of the Committee of the General Court of Massachusetts, October 15, 1814, in Ames, supra note 5, p. 78.
34. Ibid., p. 79.
35. Roger Griswold to Oliver Wolcott, March 11, 1804, in Adams, supra note 22, p. 356.
36. Timothy Pickering to George Cabot, January 29, 1804, in Adams, supra note 22, p. 339.
37. Timothy Pickering to Theodore Lyman, February 11, 1804, in Adams, supra note 22, p. 345.
38. John Quincy Adams, Reply to the Appeal of the Massachusetts Federalists, in Adams, supra note 22, p. 245.

39. Resolutions Adopted by the Hartford Convention, in Ames, supra note 5, pp. 83–4.
40. Ibid., p. 85.
41. Ibid., p. 84.
42. Samuel Eliot Morison, *Harrison Gray Otis: The Urbane Federalist* (Boston, Mass.: Houghton Mifflin Company, 1969) pp. 366–7.
43. John Lowell to Timothy Pickering, December 3, 1814, in Adams, supra note 22, p. 413.
44. 7 S.C. Stat. 461 (1840). For a thorough account of this episode, see Alan F. January, *The First Nullification: The Negro Seamen Acts Controversy in South Carolina, 1822–1860* (1976) (unpublished Ph.D. thesis, University of Iowa).
45. *Elkison v. Deliesseline*, 8 F. Cas. 493, 496 (1823).
46. Ibid., p. 495.
47. Ibid.
48. Ibid.
49. For a detailed account of the nullification controversy, see William W. Freehling, *Prelude to Civil War: The Nullification Controversy in South Carolina, 1816–1836* (New York: Harper & Row, Publishers, 1968). The book contains valuable factual and background information, but is severely flawed inasmuch as Freehling places an inordinate amount of emphasis on the role of slavery in the nullification controversy. Research published since *Prelude to Civil War* was written indicates that the slavery issue was not tied to South Carolina's embrace of nullification. See, e.g., J.P. Ochenkowski, "The Origins of Nullification in South Carolina," 83 *South Carolina Historical Magazine* 121 (1982).
50. Annals of Congress, 14th Congress, 1st sess., p. 1334, April 4, 1816.
51. Ibid., p. 1333.
52. Ibid. As his view of protection changed, Calhoun would later describe this speech as "impromptu" and "made without having duly reflected on the subject." John C. Calhoun, Speech on the Revenue Collection [Force] Bill, in Ross M. Lence, ed., *Union and Liberty: The Political Philosophy of John C. Calhoun* (Indianapolis, Ind.: Liberty Fund, 1992) p. 413.
53. Annals of Congress, 14th Congress, 1st sess., p. 1316, April 3, 1816.
54. U.S. Const. art. I, § 8, cl. 1.
55. Annals of Congress, 14th Congress, 1st sess., p. 1316, April 3, 1816.
56. 1 Stat. 24, 24 (1789).
57. For a discussion of why Southerners favored the Tariff of 1816, see Norris W. Preyer, "Southern Support of the Tariff of 1816—A Reappraisal," 25 *Journal of Southern History* 306 (1959).
58. South Carolina on Internal Improvements and the Tariff, December 16, 1825, in Ames, supra note 5, p. 140.
59. Resolutions of Virginia, March 4, 1826, in Ames, supra note 5, p. 142.
60. Thomas Cooper, "Value of the Union" Speech, July 2, 1827, in William W. Freehling, ed., *The Nullification Era: A Documentary Record* (New York: Harper & Row, 1967) p. 21.
61. Ibid., p. 25.

62. Dumas Malone, *The Public Life of Thomas Cooper* (Columbia, S.C.: University of South Carolina Press, 1961) p. 310.
63. James Hamilton, Jr., Speech at Walterborough, October 21, 1828, in Freehling, supra note 60, p. 60.
64. Robert Y. Hayne to AJ, September 3, 1828, *WAJ* 3:435.
65. AJ, First Inaugural Address, March 24, 1829, in 2 Richardson, supra note 8, p. 437.
66. AJ, First Annual Message, December 8, 1829, in 2 Richardson, supra note 8, p. 450.
67. John C. Calhoun to Littleton Walker Tazewell, August 25, 1827, *PJCC* 10:301.
68. John C. Calhoun to Micah Sterling, September 1, 1828, *PJCC* 10:415.
69. John C. Calhoun to James Monroe, September 5, 1828, *PJCC* 10:417.
70. George McDuffie, Speech at Charleston, May 19, 1831, in Freehling, supra note 60, p. 110.
71. Clyde N. Wilson, Introduction, *The Essential Calhoun* (New Brunswick, N.J.: Transaction Publishers, 1992) p. xix.
72. John C. Calhoun, Rough Draft of What is Called the South Carolina Exposition, in Lence, supra note 52, pp. 314–15.
73. Ibid., p. 320.
74. Ibid., p. 331.
75. Ibid., p. 343.
76. Ibid., p. 344.
77. Ibid., p. 345.
78. John C. Calhoun to Littleton Walker Tazewell, August 25, 1827, *PJCC* 10:301.
79. John C. Calhoun, Rough Draft of What is Called the South Carolina Exposition, in Lence, supra note 52, p. 348.
80. Ibid., p. 351.
81. Ibid., p. 354.
82. Ibid., p. 353.
83. Ibid.
84. South Carolina States Rights and Free Trade Association, *The Proceedings of the First Meeting of the Charleston State Rights and Free Trade Association of South Carolina* (1831) p. 7.
85. Ibid., p. 5.
86. John C. Calhoun, The Fort Hill Address: On the Relations of the States and Federal Government, in Lence, supra note 52, p. 371.
87. Thomas Cooper, *Consolidation: An Account of Parties in the United States from the Convention of 1787 to the Present Period* (1824) p. 5.
88. Ibid., p. 6
89. South Carolina States Rights and Free Trade Association, *A Catechism on the Tariff for the use of Plain People of Common Sense* (1831) p. 4.
90. Ibid., p. 9.
91. Ibid., p. 32
92. Ibid., p. 33.
93. William Drayton, Noon Oration, in Freehling, supra note 60, p. 129.

94. Daniel E. Huger, *Speech in the House of Representatives of South Carolina* (1831) p. 11.
95. See Pauline Maier, "The Road Not Taken: Nullification, John C. Calhoun, and the Revolutionary Tradition in South Carolina," 82 *South Carolina Historical Magazine* 1, 6 (1981) (discussing trends of the 1820s and South Carolina's renewed interest in the American Revolution); William H. Denny, "South Carolina's Conception of the Union in 1832," 78 *South Carolina Historical Magazine* 171, 171 (1977) (stressing that "[f]or South Carolina in 1832 the issue was the same as 1776—the balance of liberty and authority"); David L. Smiley, "Revolutionary Origins of the South's Constitutional Defenses," 44 *North Carolina Historical Review* 256 (1967).
96. South Carolina States Rights and Free Trade Association, *An Appeal to the People on the Question What Shall We Do Next?* (1832) p. 10.
97. George McDuffie, Speech at Charleston, May 19, 1831, in Freehling, supra note 60, p. 117.
98. Ibid., p. 118.
99. Journal of the Convention of the People of South Carolina, in General Court of Massachusetts, *State Papers on Nullification* (Boston, Mass.: Dutton and Wentworth, 1834) p. 306 [hereinafter Massachusetts *State Papers*].
100. Report of the Committee of Twenty-One, in Massachusetts *State Papers*, supra note 99, p. 23.
101. Address to the People of the United States, in Massachusetts *State Papers*, supra note 99, p. 68.
102. Ibid., p. 68.
103. JM to TJ, October 24 and November 1, 1797, *The Republic of Letters* 1:499.
104. Thomas Cooper, *Hints, Suggestions, and Contributions toward the Labours of a Convention* (1832) p. 6.
105. Address to the People of the United States, in Massachusetts *State Papers*, supra note 99, p. 69.
106. Ibid., pp. 69–70.
107. Ibid., p. 71.
108. Ordinance of Nullification, in Massachusetts *State Papers*, supra note 99, p. 31.
109. Hayne's celebrated debate with Webster in 1830 is not discussed in the text because the central concepts brought out in the debate are dealt with in other contexts. Nevertheless, this was one of the more important dramas in the nullification controversy. For the relevant documents, see Herman Belz, ed., *The Webster–Hayne Debate on the Nature of the Union* (Indianapolis, Ind.: Liberty Fund, 2000).
110. 1 S.C. Stat. 371, 371–6 (1836).
111. AJ to Lewis Cass, October 29, 1832, *CAJ* 4:483. For a discussion of the nullification controversy that concentrates on the role of President Jackson, see Richard E. Ellis, *The Union at Risk: Jacksonian Democracy, States' Rights, and the Nullification Crisis* (New York: Oxford University Press, 1987).

112. AJ to George Breathitt, November 7, 1832, *CAJ* 4:484.

113. Joel Poinsett to AJ, October 16, 1832, *CAJ* 4:481.

114. Joel Poinsett to AJ, November 29, 1832, *CAJ* 4:492.

115. AJ to Joel Poinsett, December 9, 1832, *CAJ* 4:498.

116. Ibid.

117. AJ, Nullification Proclamation, December 8, 1829, in 2 Richardson, supra note 8, p. 643.

118. Ibid., p. 643.

119. Ibid., p. 650.

120. AJ to Martin Van Buren, December 23, 1832, *CAJ* 4:505.

121. AJ, Nullification Proclamation, December 8, 1829, in 2 Richardson, supra note 8, p. 649.

122. 3 Robert V. Remini, *Andrew Jackson and the Course of American Democracy* (New York: Harper & Row, 1984) p. 31.

123. AJ, Fourth Annual Message, December 8, 1829, in 2 Richardson, supra note 8, p. 600.

124. AJ, Veto Message, December 8, 1829, in 2 Richardson, supra note 8, p. 583.

125. Martin Van Buren to AJ, December 27, 1832, *CAJ* 4:507.

126. JM to Edward Everett, August 28, 1832, *WJM* 9:384.

127. JM to Edward Everett, August 28, 1832, *WJM* 9:388–9.

128. JM to Edward Everett, August 28, 1832, *WJM* 9:403. See also Argicola, *The Virginia Doctrines, not Nullification* (1832) p. 19 (interpreting the Virginia Resolutions in order "to rescue from misrepresentation and perversion, opinions and acts, which when properly understood, do not lead to disunion and revolution, but are conservative of the Constitution of the United States as well as the reserved rights of the states and of the people.").

129. For differing views on Madison's adherence to the Principles of '98, compare Drew R. McCoy, *The Last of the Fathers: James Madison and the Republican Legacy* (New York: Cambridge University Press, 1989) (arguing that Madison was better able to interpret his own words than Calhoun and the South Carolinians) with Kevin R. Gutzman, "A Troublesome Legacy: James Madison and 'The Principles of '98," 15 *Journal of the Early Republic* 569 (1995) (arguing that Madison's position on nullification in South Carolina is irreconcilable with his views expressed in 1798).

130. Nathaniel Macon to AJ, August 26, 1833, *CAJ* 5:171.

131. Ibid.

132. Nathaniel Macon to AJ, September 25, 1833, *CAJ* 5:209.

133. Winfield Scott to William Campbell Preston, December 14, 1832, in Freehling, supra note 60, p. 176.

134. William Drayton, Noon Oration, in Freehling, supra note 60, p. 125.

135. For a discussion of the crafting of Clay's compromise tariff, see Merrill D. Peterson, *Olive Branch and Sword: The Compromise of 1833* (Baton Rouge, La.: Louisiana State University Press, 1982). Of Clay's role, a young naval officer stationed in Charleston aptly observed: "[F]ull may a Mother and daughter of Carolina has cause to bless to the name of

Henry Clay. They should teach infancy to lisp it, and tell it as a nursery tale to be remembered, how the generous Kentuckyan buried the bloody hatchet in our land." Levin M. Powell to Garrett J. Pendergast, March 10, 1833, in Howard H. Wehmann, "Noise, Novelties, and Nullifiers: A U.S. Navy Officer's Impressions of the Nullification Controversy," 76 *South Carolina Historical Magazine* 21, 22 (1975).

136. John C. Calhoun, Speech on the Revenue Collection [Force] Bill, in Lence, supra note 52, p. 436. For a discussion of the Force Bill debate, see David F. Ericson, "The Nullification Crisis, American Republicanism, and the Force Bill Debate," 61 *Journal of Southern History* 249 (1995).

137. Journal of the Convention of the People of South Carolina, in Massachusetts *State Papers*, supra note 99, p. 349.

138. Report on the Force Bill, in Massachusetts *State Papers*, supra note 99, p. 370.

139. See Ochenkowski, supra note 49; see also Remini, supra note 122, pp. 14–15.

5   Consolidation

1. *The Slaughter-House Cases*, 83 U.S. (16 Wall.) 36, 82 (1873).

2. For a discussion of the differing views of the Court's role as final arbiter of the Constitution, see William J. Watkins, Jr., "The Federal Judiciary: Friend or Foe of States' Rights, Southern Partisan," Third Quarter 2001, pp. 18–24.

3. James Madison, *Notes of the Debates in the Federal Convention of 1787* (New York: W.W. Norton & Company, 1987) pp. 190–1. See also, Madison, supra, p. 164 (James Wilson of Pennsylvania observing that "[t]he State Legislatures . . . by this participation in the Genl. Govt. would have an opportunity of defending their rights").

4. *Federalist* No. 62, p. 314 (James Madison) (Bantam Books, ed., 1982); see also *Federalist* No. 39, p. 193 (James Madison) (Bantam Books, ed., 1982) (observing that the Senate will represent and protect the states); Roger Sherman to John Adams, in Philip B. Kurland and Ralph Lerner, eds., *The Founders' Constitution* (Indianapolis, Ind.: Liberty Fund, 1987) p. 232 ("It appears to me that the senate is the most important branch in the government . . . for . . . securing the rights of the individual states. . . . The senators being eligible by the legislatures of the several states, and dependent on them for reelection, will be vigilant in supporting their rights against infringement by the legislature or executive of the United States.").

5. 4 *Elliot's Debates* p. 38.

6. 2 *Elliot's Debates* p. 22; see also 2 *Elliot's Debates* p. 26 (Parsons observing that in Congress "the sovereignty of the states is represented in the Senate").

7. 2 *Elliot's Debates* p. 47.

8. See Larry Kramer, "Putting the Politics Back into the Political Safeguards of Federalism," 100 *Columbia Law Review* 215, 268–78 (2000).

9. *Federalist* No. 10, p. 43 (James Madison) (Bantam Books, ed., 1982).

10. See Kramer, supra note 8, pp. 268–78.

11. See John Taylor, *Construction Construed, Constitutions Vindicated* (New York: Da Capo Press, 1970) (1820) p. 171 (stating that collisions between the national and state governments "are natural and certain, and must have been foreseen by the framers of the constitution").

12. See Declaration of Principles of the National Progressive Republican League, January 21, 1911, in 2 Henry Steele Commager, ed., *Documents of American History* (New York: Appleton-Century-Crofts, Inc., 1958) p. 240 (calling for direct election of senators); The Progressive Party Platform, August 5, 1912, in 2 Commager, supra, p. 254 (same).

13. For a discussion of the forces behind direct election of senators, see Ralph A. Rossum, "The Irony of Constitutional Democracy: Federalism, the Supreme Court, and the Seventeenth Amendment," 36 *San Diego Law Review* 671, 704–15 (1999); Jay S. Bybee, "Ulysses at the Mast: Democracy, Federalism, and the Sirens' Song of the Seventeenth Amendment," 91 *Northwestern University Law Review* 500, 538–49 (1997).

14. See Rossum, supra note 13, p. 711 ("What is particularly noteworthy of the lengthy debate over adoption and ratification of the Seventeenth Amendment is the absence of any serious or systematic consideration of its potential impact on federalism.").

15. See Todd J. Zywicki, "Beyond the Shell and Husk of History: The History of the Seventeenth Amendment and Its Implications for Current Reform Proposals," 45 *Cleveland State Law Review* 165, 175 (1997) (questioning whether "a senator during the pre-Seventeenth Amendment era would vote for an 'unfunded federal mandate,' thereby requiring state legislatures to raise taxes and spend money on projects they did not devise and for which they receive no political benefit").

16. *Federalist* No. 17, p. 81 (Alexander Hamilton) (Bantam Books, ed., 1982).

17. ABA Task Force, *The Federalization of Criminal Law* (Washington, D.C.: American Bar Association, 1998) p. 2.

18. Ibid., p. 14.

19. See ibid., p. 18.

20. William J. Clinton, *A Proclamation*, 64 Fed. Reg. 22,777 (1999).

21. http://www.usdoj.gov/opa/pr/1998/October/475ag.htm.

22. Quoted in Rebecca Leung, *Bill Strikes Back at Hate*, July 9, 1999, ABCNEWS.com.

23. 145 Cong. Rec. S2730. See Dan Hasenstab, "Is Hate a Form of Commerce? The Questionable Constitutionality of the Federal 'Hate Crime' Legislation," 45 *St. Louis University Law Journal* 973 (2001).

24. U.S. Const. art. I, § 8, cl. 3.

25. Samuel Johnson, *Dictionary of the English Language* (3rd. ed. 1765).

26. *Federalist* No. 11, p. 50 (Alexander Hamilton) (Bantam Books, ed., 1982); see also Joseph Story, *A Familiar Exposition of the Constitution of the United States* (Lake Bluff, Ill.: Regnery, 1986) pp. 140–1 ("The power 'to regulate foreign commerce,' enabled the government at once to place the whole country upon an equality with foreign nations; to compel them to abandon

their narrow and selfish policy towards us; and to protect our own commercial interests against their injurious competitions.").

27. *Federalist* No. 11, p. 53 (Alexander Hamilton) (Bantam Books, ed., 1982); see also Story, supra note 26, p. 141 ("The power to regulate commerce 'among the several states,' in like manner, annihilated the cause of domestic feuds and rivalries. It compelled every state to regard the interest of each, as the interests of all; and thus diffused over all the blessings of a free, active, and rapid exchange of commodities, upon the footing of perfect equality.").

28. *Federalist* No. 42, p. 214 (James Madison) (Bantam Books, ed., 1982).

29. Articles of Confederation, art. XI.

30. *Federalist* No. 17, p. 80 (Alexander Hamilton) (Bantam Books, ed., 1982). For a comprehensive discussion of the original meaning of the Commerce Clause, see Randy E. Barnett, "The Original Meaning of the Commerce Clause," 68 *University of Chicago Law Review* 101 (2001).

31. Richard A. Epstein, "The Proper Scope of the Commerce Power," 73 *Virginia Law Review* 1387, 1393–4 (1987).

32. U.S. Const. art. I, § 9, cl. 6.

33. See Raoul Berger, "Judicial Manipulation of the Commerce Clause," 74 *Texas Law Review* 695 (1996).

34. 22 U.S. (9 Wheat.) 1 (1824).

35. Ibid., p. 203.

36. 76 U.S. (9 Wall.) 41 (1869).

37. 156 U.S. 1 (1895).

38. Ibid., p. 12.

39. Ibid., p. 13.

40. 301 U.S. 1 (1937).

41. Ibid., p. 37.

42. 317 U.S. 111 (1942).

43. Ibid., p. 128.

44. See, e.g., *Perez v. United States*, 402 U.S. 146 (1971) (upholding anti-loan-sharking provisions of the Consumer Credit Protection Act as a permissible use of the commerce power).

45. See, e.g., *Heart of Atlanta Motel, Inc. v. United States*, 379 U.S. 241 (1964) (upholding use of the commerce power to craft civil rights legislation).

46. See Pub. L. No. 106–346, 114 Stat. 1356.

47. 483 U.S. 203 (1987).

48. Ibid., p. 207 (internal quotation marks omitted).

49. "Mr. Madison's Report" to the Virginia Assembly, in 4 *Elliot's Debates* p. 551.

50. U.S. Const. amend. XIV, § 1.

51. See Henry J. Abraham, *Freedom and the Court: Civil Rights and Liberties in the United States* (New York: Oxford University Press, 1988) p. 42; Raoul Berger, *Federalism: The Founders' Design* (Norman, Okla.: University of Oklahoma Press, 1987) pp. 160–1; Jeffrey Rogers Hummel, *Emancipating the Slaves, Enslaving Free Men: A History of the American Civil War* (Chicago, Ill.: Open Court, 1996) pp. 297–302; *Civil Rights Cases*, 109 U.S. 3, 22 (1883).

52. "No freeman shall be taken, imprisoned, or disseized, or outlawed, or exiled, or in any way harmed . . . save by lawful judgement of his peers or by the *law of the land*." Magna Carta, chapter 39 (emphasis added).

53. See Antonin Scalia, *A Matter of Interpretation: Federal Courts and the Law* (Princeton, N.J.: Princeton University Press, 1997) pp. 24–5; see also Paul Craig Roberts and Lawrence M. Stratton, *The Tyranny of Good Intentions* (Roseville, Cal.: Forum, 2000) p. 13; *In re Winship*, 397 U.S. 358, 382 (1970) (Black, J., dissenting) ("For me the only correct meaning of that phrase is that our government must proceed according to the 'law of the land'—that is, according to written constitutional and statutory provisions as interpreted by court decisions.").

54. AH, Remarks on an Act for Regulating Elections, February 6, 1787, *PAH* 4:35.

55. See *Allgeyer v. Louisiana*, 165 U.S. 578 (1897) (first major Supreme Court decision to use substantive due process to strike down a state law). For a general discussion of the development of substantive due process, see 2 Ronald D. Rotunda and John E. Nowak, *Treatise on Constitutional Law: Substance and Procedure* (St. Paul, Minn.: West Group, 1999) pp. 569–95.

56. 198 U.S. 45 (1905).

57. Ibid., p. 57.

58. See *West Coast Hotel Co. v. Parrish*, 300 U.S. 379 (1937) (upholding state minimum wage requirements and signaling an end to the *Lochner* era).

59. For a discussion of the doctrine of incorporation, see Abraham, supra note 51, pp. 38–117.

60. Stephen B. Presser, *Recapturing the Constitution: Race, Religion, and Abortion Reconsidered* (Washington, D.C.: Regnery Publishing, Inc., 1994) p. 161.

61. 32 U.S. (7 Pet.) 243 (1833) ("These amendments demanded security against the apprehended encroachments of the general government—not against those of the local governments.").

62. Ibid., p. 250.

63. 381 U.S. 479 (1965).

64. Ibid., p. 484.

65. A penumbra is defined as "the partial or imperfect shadow outside the complete shadow of an opaque body, as a planet, where the light from the source of illumination is only partly cut off." *The Random House Dictionary of the English Language* 1068 (1973).

66. *Griswold*, 381 U.S. p. 527 (Stewart, J., dissenting).

67. Ibid.

68. See *Clark v. Jeter*, 486 U.S. 456, 461 (1988) (explaining the level of judicial scrutiny used for classifications); see also 3 Rotunda and Nowak, supra note 55, pp. 205–94 (explaining the Court's treatment of classifications).

69. 518 U.S. 515 (1996).

70. Ibid., p. 520.

71. Ibid., p. 567 (Scalia, J., dissenting).

72. See John Hart Ely, "The Apparent Inevitability of Mixed Government," 16 *Constitutional Commentary* 283 (1999) (observing that the message of

substantive due process "is clear: government by the people may be an ennobling myth, but sometimes the people get it wrong, and as the reflective elite element in our lawmaking system, the justices must keep them within the bounds of what is acceptable to the reasoning class"); Larry Cata Backer, "Disciplining Judicial Interpretation of Fundamental Rights: First Amendment Decadence in Southworth and Boy Scouts of America and European Alternatives," 36 *Tulsa Law Journal* 117 (2000) (arguing for a return to constitutional black letter law). But see Laurence Tribe and Michael C. Dorf, *On Reading the Constitution* (Cambridge, Mass.: Harvard University Press, 1991) p. 66 (arguing that judges must make substantive value choices).

73. Taylor, supra note 11, p. 57.

6 Lessons for Today

1. See John Taylor, *Construction Construed, Constitutions Vindicated* (New York: Da Capo Press, 1970) (1820) p. 58.
2. David R. Beam, Forecasting the Future of Federalism: Task and Challenge, in ACIR, *The Future of Federalism in the 1980s* (1980) p. 7.
3. See The Personal Responsibility and Work Opportunity Reconciliation Act of 1996, *codified as amended at* 8 U.S.C.A. §§ 1601–66 (West 1999 & Supp. 2000).
4. Edward L. Rubin, Puppy Federalism and the Blessings of America, in Frank Goodman, ed., *Annals of the American Academy of Political and Social Science*, March 2001, p. 38.
5. But see George P. Fletcher, *Our Secret Constitution: How Lincoln Redefined American Democracy* (New York: Oxford University Press, 2001) p. 10 (arguing that our nation was supposed to resemble European nations more than we realize).
6. See Daniel J. Elazar, *Covenant and Polity in Biblical Israel* (New Brunswick, N.J.: Transaction Press, 1994).
7. Johannes Althusius, *Politica*, Frederick S. Carney, ed. (Indianapolis, Ind.: Liberty Fund, 1995) (1603).
8. See, e.g., James T Patterson, *The New Deal and the States: Federalism in Transition* (Princeton, N.J.: Princeton University Press, 1969) p. 207 (observing that dual federalism died "because the states alone, for good or ill, have lacked the potential to solve the problems of urban, mid-twentieth century America"); Jane Perry Clark, *The Rise of a New Federalism: Federal-State Cooperation in the United States* (New York: Russell & Russell, 1965) p. 293 ("[A] federal system of government proves to be a ineffectual pill for curing the economic and social earthquakes of today.").
9. For an excellent paper offering practical reasons for federalism, see Alexander Tabarrok, Arguments for Federalism (2001) (http://independent.org/ tii/Presentations/Federalism.html).
10. In 1973 Congress decreed that as a precondition to the receipt of federal highway funds states had to change their maximum speed limits to 55 miles

per hour. This legislation was enacted in response to the energy crisis of the 1970s, but lingered until 1995 when Congress finally realized that such a measure was inappropriate for a nation with such diverse driving conditions. See *Nevada v. Skinner*, 884 F.2d 445 (9th Cir. 1989) (recounting the history of the mandatory speed limit and examining a state challenge to the law).

11. For a refutation of the view that higher speed limits lead to more traffic fatalities, see Stephen Moore, *Speed Doesn't Kill: The Repeal of the 55-MPH Speed Limit* (Washington, D.C.: The Cato Institute, 1999) (observing that the fatality rate fell after 1995 in states adopting higher speed limits).

12. See *New State Ice Co. v. Liebmann*, 285 U.S. 262, 311 (1932) (Brandeis, J., dissenting).

13. *Federalist* No. 47, p. 244 (James Madison) (Bantam Books, ed., 1982).

14. See, e.g., Herman Schwartz, *The Supreme Court's Federalism: Fig Leaf for Conservatives*, in Goodman, supra note 4, pp. 119–31 (arguing that states' rights have always been used to oppress and that modern calls for federalism are nothing more than continued efforts by certain majorities to oppress minorities); Paul E. Peterson, *The Price of Federalism* (Washington, D.C.: Brookings Institution, 1995) p. 9 ("[T]he powers of state and local governments have been used too often by a tyrannical majority to trample the rights of religious, racial, and political minorities."). But see Marci Hamilton, Are Federalism, and the States Really Anti-Civil Rights, as Liberals Often Claim? (2003) (http://writ.news.findlaw.com/hamilton/20030102.html) (arguing that "[t]he anti-civil-rights states the liberals are decrying, however, don't really exist anymore—as evidenced by the fact that the problems liberals point to are decades old.").

15. See, e.g., John C. Calhoun, Speech on the Reception of Abolition Petitions, in Ross M. Lence, ed., *Union and Liberty: The Political Philosophy of John C. Calhoun* (Indianapolis, Ind.: Liberty Fund, 1992) pp. 463–76; Southern Manifesto on Integration, in 2 Melvin I. Urofsky, ed., *Documents of American Constitutional and Legal History* (New York: Alfred A. Knopf, 1989) p. 261.

16. See Forrest McDonald, *States' Rights and the Union: Imperium in Imperio 1776–876* (Lawrence, Kan.: University Press of Kansas, 2000) (chronicling the use of states' rights by both Northern and Southern states when clashing with the national government); James Jackson Kilpatrick, *The Sovereign States: Notes of a Citizen of Virginia* (Chicago, Ill.: Henry Regnery Company, 1957) (same).

17. See 3 *Elliot's Debates* pp. 73 and 192.

18. *Debates in the House of Delegates of Virginia, on Certain Resolutions Before the House* (Richmond, Va.: Thomas Nicolson, 1798) p. 22.

19. See Douglas Ambrose, ed., *Henry Hughes and Proslavery Thought in the Old South* (Baton Rouge, La.: Louisiana State University Press, 1996) pp. 118–38.

20. Garrison quoted in John L. Thomas, *The Liberator: William Lloyd Garrison* (Boston, Mass.: Little, Brown and Company, 1983) p. 329; for a general discussion of Garrison's theory of secession, see Thomas, supra, pp. 305–37;

John Jay Chapman, *William Lloyd Garrison* (New York: Beekman Publishers, Inc., 1974) pp. 155–7.

21. U.S. Const. art. IV, § 2, cl. 2 & 3.

22. 1 Stat. 302 (1793).

23. Garrison quoted in Jeffrey Rogers Hummel, *Emancipating the Slaves, Enslaving Free Men* (Chicago, Ill.: Open Court, 1996) p. 21.

24. For a discussion of Garrison's hopes for secession, see Paul Finkelman, "The Founders and Slavery: Little Ventured, Little Gained," 13 *Yale Journal of Law and the Humanities* 413, 445–7; see also Hummel, supra note 21, pp. 55–60.

25. Thomas J. DiLorenzo, "The Great Centralizer: Abraham Lincoln and the War Between the States," 3 *The Independent Review* 243, 252 (1998); see also Hummel, supra note 23, pp. 21–2.

26. DiLorenzo, supra note 25, p. 253.

27. See Hummel, supra note 23, p. 352.

28. Ibid., pp. 354–5; see also Robert Brent Toplin, *The Abolition of Slavery in Brazil* (New York: Atheneum, 1972) pp. 96–9.

29. For an account of the graft and waste that went with the building of the transcontinental railroad, see Burton W. Folsom, Jr., *The Myth of the Robber Barons* (Herndon: Va.: Young America's Foundation, 1991) pp. 17–39. Folsom also chronicles the building of successful railroads without the use of government funds.

30. See ibid.

31. U.S. Const. art. I, § 8, cl. 12. For a discussion of the constitutionality of Lincoln's summoning of troops, see Webb Garrison, *The Lincoln Know One Knows* (Nashville, Tenn.: Rutledge Hill Press, 1993) pp. 83–9.

32. See ibid., pp. 95–100.

33. See ibid., pp. 101–6.

34. U.S. Const. art. I, § 9, cl. 2.

35. For a discussion on the Merryman affair, see J.G. Randall, *Constitutional Problems Under Lincoln* (Gloucester, Mass.: Peter Smith, 1963) pp. 161–3.

36. *Ex Parte Merryman*, 17 F. Cas. 144, 152 (D. Md. 1861).

37. Robert S. Harper, *Lincoln and the Press* (New York: McGraw-Hill Book Co., 1951) pp. 257–64 (discussing suppression of newspapers under Lincoln).

38. Michael Kent Curtis, "Lincoln, Vallandigham, and Anti-War Speech in the Civil War," 7 *William & Mary Bill of Rights Journal* 105, 119–20 (1998).

39. Ibid., pp. 121, 122.

40. Ibid., p. 133.

41. Ibid., p. 125.

42. The banishment of newspapermen became a common tool used by the Lincoln administration. See Garrison, supra note 31, pp. 201–2.

43. Clinton Rossiter, *Constitutional Dictatorship: Crisis Government in the Modern Democracies* (New Brunswick, N.J.: Transaction Publishers, 2002) p. 223. Lincoln's reign was indeed a dictatorship. As David Donald has noted:

Nobody knows how many Northern civilians were imprisoned without due process of law; estimates range from fifteen thousand to thirty-eight thousand. It required but a line from the President to close down a censorious newspaper, to banish a Democratic politician, or to arrest suspected members of a state legislature.

David Donald, *Lincoln Reconsidered* (New York: Alfred A. Knopf, 1966) p. 189.

The powers which the executive assumed and the prerogatives which he claimed were far reaching. They seemed, if applied to great excess, to offer the opportunity for a dictatorship. All this was out of keeping with the normal tenor of American law.

Randall, supra note 35, p. 183.

44. For the text of the act, see *Prigg v. Pennsylvania*, 41 U.S. (16 Pet.) 539 (1842).
45. Ibid.
46. Ibid., p. 612.
47. Ibid., p. 622.
48. 60 U.S. (19 How) 393 (1857).
49. Ibid., p. 450.
50. The Vermont Resolution is quoted in Kilpatrick, supra note 16, p. 212.
51. Ibid., p. 213.
52. 62 U.S. (21 How.) 506 (1859).
53. The Wisconsin Resolution is quoted in Kilpatrick, supra note 16, pp. 214–15.
54. 514 U.S. 549 (1995).
55. Ibid., p. 564.
56. Ibid., p. 584 (Thomas, J., concurring). For an in-depth critique of the substantial effects test, see Arthur B. Mark, III, United States v. Morrison, "The Commerce Clause and the Substantial Effects Test: No Substantial Limit on Federal Power," 34 *Creighton Law Review* 675 (2001).
57. 529 U.S. 598 (2000).
58. Ibid., p. 615.
59. 117 S. Ct. 2365 (1997).
60. Ibid., pp. 2376–7.
61. 517 U.S. 44 (1996).
62. "'Standing to sue' means that party has a sufficient stake in an otherwise justiciable controversy to obtain judicial resolution of that controversy." *Blacks Law Dictionary* 978 (6th ed. 1991).
63. An actual case or controversy exists when "there is a substantial controversy, between parties having adverse legal interests, of sufficient immediacy and reality to warrant the issuance of declaratory judgment." *Blacks Law Dictionary* 923 (6th ed. 1991).
64. TJ to Spencer Roane, September 6, 1819, *WTJ* 12:136.
65. John Taylor to Wilson Cary Nicholas, October 26, 1807, in David N. Mayer, ed., "Of Principles and Men: The Correspondence of John Taylor of Caroline with Wilson Cary Nicholas, 1806–1808," 96 *Virginia Magazine of History and Biography* 345, 367–8 (1988).

66. James Madison, *Notes of the Debates in the Federal Convention of 1787* (New York: W.W. Norton & Company, 1987) p. 626; see also William J. Quirk and Robert M. Wilcox, "Judicial Tyranny and Constitutional Change," *Chronicles: A Magazine of American Culture*, February 1998, pp. 18–21.

67. TJ to Thomas Lomax, March 12, 1799, *WTJ* 9:63.

68. USA Patriot Act, Pub. L. No. 107–56, 115 Stat. 272 (2001).

69. Ashcroft quoted in John W. Whitehead and Steven H. Aden, "Forfeiting 'Enduring Freedom' for 'Homeland Security': A Constitutional Analysis of the USA PATRIOT Act and the Justice Department's Anti-Terrorism Initiatives," 51 *American University Law Review* 1081, 1100 (2002).

70. 115 Stat. p. 376.

71. 50 U.S.C.A. § 1805(a).

72. Pub. L. No. 107–56 § 218.

73. 66 Fed. Reg. 55062, 55064.

74. Detention, Treatment, and Trial of Certain Non-citizens in the War Against Terrorism, 66 Fed. Reg. 57833 (Nov. 13, 2001).

75. Ibid. at § 2(a).

76. See *In re Hamdi*, No. 02-7338, 2003 U.S. App. Lexis 198 (4th Cir. January 8, 2003).

77. *Ex Parte Quirin*, 317 U.S. 1, 25 (1942).

78. See Robert F. Nagel, "*Nationalized Political Discourse*," 69 *Fordham Law Review* 2057 (2001).

79. 121 S. Ct. 1711 (2001).

80. Ibid., p. 1719. Marijuana litigation continues to occupy many federal courts. In October 2002, for example, the Ninth Circuit Court of Appeals affirmed on First Amendment grounds a permanent injunction prohibiting the federal government from either revoking a physician's license to prescribe controlled substances or conducting an investigation of a physician that might lead to a license revocation when the basis of the government's action is solely the physician's recommendation of the use of medical marijuana. See *Conant v. Walters*, 309 F.3d 629 (9th Cir. 2002).

81. Nevada Assembly Bill No. 453 (2001). In the November 2002 elections, the citizens of Nevada rejected a proposed constitutional amendment that would have permitted individuals 21 and older to possess up to three ounces of marijuana.

82. See, e.g., Felix Morely, *Freedom and Federalism* (Indianapolis, Ind.: Liberty Press, 1981) p. 5 (arguing that federalism "serves admirably to foster freedom without the sacrifice of order"); Samuel H. Beer, *To Make a Nation: The Rediscovery of American Federalism* (Cambridge, Mass.: The Belknap Press of Harvard University Press, 1993) p. 387 ("The argument which was foremost in the minds of the framers and which still holds greatest promise as a rationale for states is the argument from liberty.").

83. Edward S. Corwin, The Passing of Dual Federalism, in Alpheus T. Mason and Gerald Garvey, eds., *Essays by Edward S. Corwin* (Gloucester, Mass.: Peter Smith, 1970) p. 146.

Appendices

1. *VCCG* pp. 143–51.
2. *VCCG* pp. 152–4.
3. *VCCG* pp. 155–6.
4. 2 The Republic of Letters pp. 1080–4.

INDEX

Locators in **bold** face indicate images.

About the Author

William J. Watkins, Jr. is a Research Fellow at The Independent Institute and a legal scholar specializing in constitutional law and health law. He received his J.D. cum laude from the University of South Carolina School of Law and is a former law clerk to Judge William B. Traxler, Jr. of the U.S. Court of Appeals for the Fourth Circuit. Mr. Watkins's articles have appeared in *The Independent Review, South Carolina Law Review, Chronicles, Social Critic, America's Civil War,* and other publications. His popular articles have appeared in the *Washington Times* and *Ideas on Liberty.* He is the recipient of the CALI Award and R. Glen Ayers Award for Historical Writing.

INDEPENDENT STUDIES IN POLITICAL ECONOMY

For further information and a catalog of publications, please contact:

THE INDEPENDENT INSTITUTE

100 Swan Way, Oakland, California 94621-1428, U.S.A.

510-632-1366 • Fax 510-568-6040 • info@independent.org • www.independent.org